TO END WAR

An Introduction: Ideas,
Books, Organizations, Work
that can help

Revised Edition

prepared for those
who wish to aid in work
to end war

Robert Pickus
and Robert Woito

World Without War Council

PERENNIAL LIBRARY
Harper & Row, Publishers
New York, Evanston, and London

For: Rambam, Noah, Katrina, Andrea, and Brian

This book was originally published by the World Without War Council. It is here reprinted by arrangement.

TO END WAR (*Revised Edition*)

CONTENTS

Our Intention: A Note to the Reader

This book is the product of eleven years of work for a world without war undertaken from a two-story gray frame house at 1730 Grove Street in Berkeley, California. Its intended audience is the person most likely to initiate the action that can end war.

We've met him many times in those years. We've encountered him in church basements and television studios, in union halls and on campuses, at Chamber of Commerce meetings, and at conventions of engineers and mental health professionals. We've sold books to him, organized petitions and demonstrations with him, raised money from him. We've argued Just War theory, Marxist politics, Christian ethics, American society, Vietnam, the Middle East, and the ABM. We've visited him in jail and on army posts and in his home. We've been praised and cursed by him.

In all these places, we've encountered every sort and condition of mankind; men and women different in a thousand ways but distinguished by a single common characteristic: they will be American citizens in the eighth decade of the twentieth century.

We believe they can initiate the action needed to end war.

It is, at present, most unlikely that they will do so.

WHERE WE ARE

Our country is now part of the problem of war, even a major part. Few American citizens take the goal of ending war seriously. At this writing, even major segments of the American peace movement evince little

interest in that goal. There, the currently dominant
ideas call for a single-minded focus on opposing
American military policy, on achieving American withdrawal from world politics, and on refocusing American energies and resources on the problems of our
cities and our domestic environment. In much current
peace activity there is no program or policy that ties
the movement to the central political problem of the
twentieth century: controlling the threat of war. There
is only opposition to American military power. Such
opposition can be part of a thoughtful peace position;
it is not, in itself, such a position.

There were a few brief years after World War II
and the shock of Hiroshima when a different spirit
moved in our country. The goal of ending war was
then taken seriously. *The New Yorker* magazine could
at that time devote an entire issue to a moving statement on the first use of nuclear weapons on human
beings; the Tennessee State legislature passed resolutions favoring world federalism; physicists throughout
the country, in response to their crucial role in the
development of nuclear weapons, were almost uni-
versally contributing to one peace organization or
another and finally set up their own. Though most of
these efforts were unsophisticated or ill conceived,
there was no doubt about the *will* to pursue the goal.

A very different situation prevails today. Dr.
Strangelove's subtitle has come true. We have learned
to stop worrying and, if not love, at least accept the
Bomb. In the mainstream of America, where most
accept a dominantly military national policy, a military-industrial grouping commands ever larger appro-
priations. Among those challenging that situation, a
dangerous combination of passion and ignorance has
increasing influence. The discussion of the root questions of ethics and war is desultory and shallow even

in our seminaries. New Just War theories supporting the use of mass violence in the interest of justice dominate the discussion there and even in important sections of the anti-war movement. Political leaders surveying the Vietnam tragedy turn away not simply from a military foreign policy but from *any* attempt by America to shape the course of world politics.

There is a new liberal-radical form of isolationist thought moving in America today. It is focused not on preserving the *status quo* as was the conservative isolationism of the thirties, but on changing America. It rejects engagement in world politics not because of other nations' shortcomings, as was common in the thirties, but because America itself is seen as inadequate. Whatever the difference in political coloration, there is again a turning away of America from the central task of world politics. A more realistic assessment of America's capabilities and problems is part of the explanation as is the currently fashionable rejection of America and all its works in many circles that consider themselves progressive. A loss of confidence in even the possibility of achieving the goal is another part of the explanation. Whatever the cause, the result is clear: we are no longer, even in advanced sectors of our society, a nation working to end war.

For those few in this country who are committed to work for a world without war it is, then, a bad time. Despite the peace movement headlines, there is no vision of the whole task, no commitment to pursuing it, no confidence in a body of thought capable of achieving it. Even given such a body of thought we still lack, in a field now hopelessly fragmented, the organizational vehicle capable of making the interconnections necessary for successful national influence. All this in a country still dominated by reliance on national military power for security, still caught in a futile oscillation between military attempts to impose our will on world politics and temporary, futile withdrawals from the attempt to shape international reality.

THE INDIVIDUAL'S RESPONSIBILITY

Given these realities, why look to the American *citizen* for the new initiatives needed? Can laymen lead in the construction of international or supranational institutions that can interdict the use of mass violence? Why turn to American citizens instead of to government for action that can develop a sense of world community strong enough to allow such institutions to resolve conflict without violence? Why regard America, of all nations, as likely to help certain and needed change come in the new nations with minimal violence?

For three reasons: because present governmental leaders won't undertake these tasks; because citizens can; because the fulfillment of the best in our tradition requires that they do.

We live in a world dominated by war. Any present American administration takes office with a spoken or unspoken commitment to the people of the United States to organize national military power for the security of this nation. *We cannot count on present governmental figures to lead us to peace because their primary commitment is dictated by military contingencies. The domain of that commitment is set not by their choice but by the degree of threat posed by other nations' military programs.* For entering a war or an arms race prepared to come in second is the worst possible course of action. So governments talk peace and do as they have always done: prepare for and wage war.

Only the American people can authorize a fundamental change of direction. Without the burden of immediate governmental responsibility they can initiate currents of thought and policy that break with traditional conceptions of security and deal more adequately with a world of nuclear weapons. The means for citizen action are at hand. Despite currently popular attacks on the political process in this country, entry into the public policy arena is wide open. American government *does* reflect public belief and concern. But there is not yet in this country agreement on policies that can control the threat of war, nor is there the will to take the risks involved in pursuing them. When there is, Washington will reflect public understanding and America will lead in work for a world without war.

There is a third reason for addressing American citizens and the non-governmental organizations through which they affect public policy. Much that is central to our religious and political tradition requires action to end war. The fulfillment of the promise America has represented in world history can come only if we control the threat of war. Just as our political tradition, reflecting our belief in man's innate dignity and worth, turns us to this goal, so our immense power gives promise of a significant contribution to its fulfillment.

WHY WE DON'T ACT

Given, then, the crucial role of the American citizen in work for a world without war, the openness of our political process as a mechanism for turning such ideas into public policy and the fact that key elements in our tradition turn us to this goal, why have we not pursued it?

It is in part a matter of will. Ending war is the primary political task of our time. A formed public purpose is the essential requisite to the pursuit of great ends in our society; and we have lost that public purpose. Modern anthropology and fundamentalist Christianity can be read as arguing the futility of the goal. Surely contemporary reality teaches us that lesson. Even pacifists are embarrassed by the flat statement of it. It is easier to attack the military-industrial complex.

This failure of will is at root a matter of faith, but it also derives from a sense of individual powerlessness, which in turn relates to the lack of a believable perspective on *how* to pursue the goal of ending war. Few encounter a coherent body of thought capable of sustaining such a goal. Very different currents would move in American politics, were there widely shared ideas on *how* to achieve a world order rooted in belief in the dignity and worth of individual men and capable of bringing about needed change without violence. Without a realistic perspective adequate to the whole task, the citizen stands bewildered and immobilized, or limited to dramatic and sometimes counter-productive protest.

To End War

Those convinced that all we have to do is establish supranational legal institutions, or teach Gandhian philosophy, or achieve disarmament or weapons parity, or destroy communism or private property will find this book stimulating but not reassuring. For *To End War* is hostile to single answers. But it is also hostile to that thought which posits war as "in the nature of things" and therefore ineradicable. A curious and prevalent form of this argument sees war as a consequence of social injustice or personal tension. Ending war then becomes contingent on achieving a world of perfect justice and harmony or fundamentally altering human souls or psyches on a mass basis. Since achieving these ends is unlikely, we can, so the argument goes, expect war to continue to dominate life on earth.

To End War rests on other assumptions, specified in Part II. One of them asserts that, though no single answer suffices, there *is* a body of thought on what we must do to make our nation a leader in ending war. *To End War* seeks to organize that thought, argue for its practicability and acquaint the non-expert citizen with it.

To End War was originally published as a selective, annotated bibliography. The first editions established twelve categories within which the essential ideas, issues and alternatives to war could be surveyed. Those categories constituted a definition of the war/peace field. They listed the seminal books in each part of the field, identified those which offer the best introduction and those which make a significant contribution to a body of thought that can end war.

Schools, libraries and organizations across the country ordered the various editions of this bibliography, produced originally for use in regional peace education work. But many people have complained that the bibliography was making an implicit argument in its categorization, in its annotations and emphasis. "Why not make it explicit?" the critics said.

In this 1970 edition of *To End War* we have tried to do so. We have introduced each bibliographic section with an essay defining that part of the war/peace field and introducing the layman to its primary contending schools of thought. Arguments expanded to book length in the bibliographic section are brought in summary fashion into a coherent relationship to opposing perspectives. But *To End War* is not a neutral or scholarly survey. We do not suggest that there are many different, equally valid ways of viewing each problem. The judgment that differing views are equally valid is, after all, just as difficult to make as the judgment that one view is superior to another.

The organization of this book, the introductions to each section, the annotations and end pieces are written on the assumption that ending war is a meaningful and attainable goal. The main body of the book is a linked argument, an answer to the question: what policies could achieve that end? Parts II and III put the argument together. By offering a clear moral and political context for the work needed, we hope to counter the pervasive sense of inadequacy that prevents so many concerned men and women from playing their crucial role in work to end war.

CONTEXT

Most citizens confronting war/peace issues—the ABM, Vietnam, nuclear proliferation—are confused by a welter of contradictory and often highly technical arguments. How, they ask, can they responsibly enter into arguments requiring expert knowledge of the past thirty years of South Asian history or the technical feasibility of weapons systems still on the drawing board? Do not the President and his experts know best? Perhaps they do on these expert matters; but not, we assert, on the primary choices which the citizen of this country must make or, in any case, accept the responsibility for making.

To End War asserts that the citizen can enter the war/peace public policy argument with confidence. He can do so when he understands the difference between the citizen's responsibility and that of the expert. He can fulfill the citizen's responsibility by thinking clearly about the values and by choosing the goals which set the framework in which the expert performs his function.

This book seeks to help readers clarify their goals, define the objectives essential to the achievement of those goals, identify the obstacles to such objectives, and consciously affirm the fundamental value position which undergirds their framework of thought and belief.

For it is that framework that determines most people's stand on war/peace issues. Thus, it is not difficult, in most cases, to know where a man stands on the ABM if you know that he regards the American military-industrial complex (or alternatively, Communist Russia or China) as *the* threat to world peace. Such a person finds the expert argument he needs to support his fundamental approach to war/peace issues. It is these political and value choices, not the technical or situational arguments, that usually determine one's approach to war/peace problems.

By consciously constructing his own political and moral context for decisions on war/peace issues, a citizen fulfills his fundamental responsibility. He is, then, no longer a victim of the technical facts. He has more than an opinion on the issue. By so doing, he chooses a direction for national policy. He determines which problems the experts will try to solve. He establishes meaningful standards for judgment in specific controversies like the ABM or Vietnam decision.

Some of the contextual choices the individual can

make relate to fundamental assumptions about the nature of man. When biblical fundamentalists and interpreters of contemporary anthropology assert that there will always be wars and rumors of war, one can agree with that judgment or challenge it.

Some contextual choices involve analyses of contemporary world conflict. Does political context X identify "the Communist" (or the "American military-industrial complex") as the single villain on the world scene? Does recognition of the inevitability of conflict condemn us to *war*? Are the only choices, therefore, acquiescence to an enemy's will or preparation for war?

Some are fundamental value choices. Is it romantic nonsense or is it right and reasonable to extend the moral impulse beyond your family, your nation, to your enemy? Should our country consciously seek to influence the course of events in other countries? Under what circumstances, if any, is it right to bomb cities?

Whether one is aware of them or not, these contextual choices are substantial to most decisions on specific war/peace issues.

In Part II we summarize a frame of thought that is the result of making such choices. It is a context we believe adequate to the problems of a world dominated by war and undergoing radical and, in many respects, hopeful change. We state its assumptions. We examine the alternative political and moral contexts which we believe are inadequate. All of this is offered in embarrassingly compressed fashion, but the bibliography spells out the argument and the counter arguments.

To End War establishes ground for intelligent choice on specific issues. It suggests *standards* for determining which choices move us toward controlling the threat of war.

In Part III we suggest ways in which a citizen can relate his new understanding to effective political action. One section provides means by which a layman can determine whether he understands a subject well enough to make a substantive contribution to policy discussion in that particular field. Another section provides an introduction to organizations working in this field and a checklist for evaluating their positions and programs. Still another section introduces readers to the primary periodical sources of information in the field; the *Reading Man's Filter* enables the reader to choose his sources of information deliberately.

Our goal is to end organized, mass violence as a means of achieving security or promoting justice. Most people deny by their actions, if not intellectually, that ending war is a meaningful goal. The structure of our argument against that denial is to examine the major causes of war and then to develop alternative ways of resolving or processing the conflicts which arise from such causes.

Men in this century *can* commit themselves to developing and testing in the world political arena available alternatives to war. But we will most likely, judging by past experience, continue to prefer organized killing and follow that route to the end of human history. Ideas, arguments and confidence that there is a way to make sense of it all will help. But it is in the end a matter requiring more than reasonable discussion. It is, as we have said, a matter of will, a problem of faith: not alone the commitment of the few who join organizations, but a formed public will to heed Ecclesiastes' vision.

You could help form that will.

In the hour when the holy one, blessed be He, created the first man,

He took him and let him pass before all the trees of the Garden of Eden,

And said to him:

See my works—how fine and excellent they are!

Now all that I have created for you have I created.

Think upon this and do not corrupt and desolate my world.

For if you corrupt it, there is no one to set it right after you.

Midrash   Rabbah 7
Ecclesiastes VII, 12

December 1969
Berkeley, California

Robert Pickus

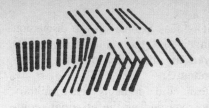

UNDERSTANDING THE STRATEGIES OF WAR:
A FIRST STRATEGY OF PEACE

Changing people's minds about war is the central educational task of our time. It can best be performed by those aware of the hard facts of military power which are, for so many, the central realities. Therefore, we begin with the facts of war: the strategies by which men organize themselves for mass violence, the weapons they use, the contemporary consequences of these weapons and strategies.

Those working for peace sometimes ignore discussions of weapons and military strategies. Our task, they say, is controlling the threat of war, not learning how to wage it. In so doing, they choose the right goal. But progress toward it is unlikely without understanding the arguments of those who do rely on national military power for security.

The 1969 ABM discussion is a case in point. During much of 1969, this controversy dominated the headlines. For the first time in twenty years the military strategy of maintaining peace by developing our ability to destroy entire societies was challenged by a shift in military thinking. Improving our ability to defend ourselves was offered to replace an overwhelming reliance on our offensive capabilities for security. Many saw that the ABM involved another massive military expenditure and argued in effect for the old balance of terror. Those who believed security requires an alternative to *any* dominantly military approach, brought their ideas to bear on the discussion best when they understood the military arguments involved, but entered the discussion offering a non-military security strategy.[1]

For many Americans and for many years, military deterrence has been regarded as the essential requisite for the maintenance of peace. Deterrence strategists contended that so long as an adversary believed the consequences of his resort to military violence would be prohibitively high to himself, there would be no nuclear war. Those challenging deterrence theory rejected the morality of a nuclear threat, pointed to the fact that deterrence had not prevented over thirty post–World War II wars and argued that deterrence does not help achieve peaceful settlement of international conflict but engenders suspicion and fear which are obstacles to peaceful settlement. In good part it appears that deterrence strategists have won the argument. Even at the height of anti-Vietnam war feeling few challenge reliance on nuclear deterrence.

Those committed to developing alternatives to reliance on national military power for security are necessarily drawn into discussions of military strategy.

Ignoring the contemporary military discussion is one error. Focusing entirely on the weapons and the consequences of their use is another. Many contemporary peace organizations concentrate on opposing the development of American military power or on explaining the consequences of nuclear war. Given the dangerously enlarged role of the military in American

[1] See for example the two most widely publicized books on the ABM controversy: *ABM, An Evaluation of the Decision to Deploy an Antiballistic Missile System* (anti-ABM # 352) and *Why ABM? Policy Issues in the Missile Defense Controversy* (pro-ABM # 349) and compare them to *The ABM and a World Without War* (# 348).

life, and the realities of nuclear warfare, such an emphasis is not wholly awry. Anti-militarism makes the most sense, however, when those rejecting military deterrence offer alternative proposals for meeting legitimate American security and value concerns. Those teaching the horror of nuclear war are most persuasive when they recognize and deal with the threat of military power in the hands of other nations' political leaders. They are more likely to gain a hearing if their strategy for peace suggests action that will move other nations, as well as our own, away from reliance on national military power.

Here, then, is a peace bibliography that begins with a focus on the weapons of war. That is where most men and nations are. Understanding the military facts of the contemporary world is an important part of preparing yourself to work for a world without war.

The books chosen for this section discuss nuclear, biological and chemical warfare. They examine strategies of guerilla war, of limited war and of nuclear deterrence. They detail world military expenditures, the consequences of some thirty post–World War II wars and the probable consequences of a future nuclear war.

UNDERSTANDING THE CAUSES OF WAR: A SECOND STRATEGY OF PEACE

Those concerned with ending war must also consider why most men believe such a goal is unattainable and consequently continue to rely on national military power for security. Changing their minds requires understanding what it is that leads them to accept warfare. Primary interest therefore turns not to the means of fighting but to the question of what causes war.

Albert Einstein posed this question in an important exchange with Sigmund Freud:

> *The quest for international security involves the unconditional surrender by every nation, in a certain measure, of its liberty of action. . . . The ill-success . . . of all the efforts . . . to reach this goal leaves us no room to doubt that strong psychological factors are at work, which paralyze these efforts.*

Einstein and Freud explored a psychological answer to the question of what causes war. *Readings in World Politics* (# 3)[2] brings together their correspondence and nine other statements each representing a very different view of the cause of war.

These alternative views of what causes war have served as one of the organizing principles of *To End War*. Most sections of this book focus on a cause of war and on alternative approaches to handling that causal factor.

Surely the weapons themselves are one cause. Therefore we first consider the facts of military power and then a variety of approaches to arms control and disarmament. But our understanding of the problem of war posits multiple causes, not a single one. Subsequent chapters therefore discuss other causes of war. Our approach requires an understanding of these causes (not a final resolution of the theoretical argument over them) before attempting to devise a strategy capable of controlling the fact and threat of war. A careful consideration of alternative views of the causes of war is recommended as one of the most useful entries to serious thought about war/peace problems.

[2] The numbers in the text refer the reader to a numbered bibliographic entry.

MULTIPLE CAUSES

Implicit in *To End War's* approach to this discussion is a rejection of two frequently encountered views. The first posits a single cause of war, such as communism or capitalism. Proponents of such monocausal explanations are, in a curious sense, optimists. They believe that war will end when the cause of war which they have singled out is destroyed. Consequently they often argue that war itself is the means that will end war. At the other end of the argument are the pessimists, those that survey history, discern the multiplicity of forces leading to war and conclude that this very multiplicity of causes demonstrates the inevitability of war. They find something in the nature of man, social organization or international relations that assures the continuation of war. If war *is* "in the nature of things" there is no way to eliminate it. But is it? Conflict certainly is, perhaps even violence. But there is a difference between personal or small group violence and the mass indiscriminate violence of war. It may be possible to end war without the profound alterations of human souls or psyches that would be required to end *all* violence. Most stable national societies have done just that: ended war within their boundaries though conflict and even small group violence continue. While rejecting their conclusion, *To End War* does join the pessimists in their recognition of the many situations that increase the likelihood of war occurring. But these causal conditions are not infinite. They can be delimited and we can act to avoid or alter such conditions.

The optimists referred to above try, on the other hand, to resolve a complex problem with a single answer. There is, nevertheless, much to learn from each of their formulations. Thus the pacifist assertion "war will cease when men refuse to fight" misses the fact that most men prefer to fight—if not fighting means accepting injustice. Still, the pacifists' emphasis on the crucial role of individual choices in producing warfare leads us to an important question: what view of justice would lead men to reject war as a means of securing justice?

Another optimistic slogan, "World Peace through World Law" purports to identify *the* requisite for peace. Such an assertion often ignores the absence of a sense of world community capable of sustaining world law. Further, it rarely answers those who rightly reject a world of law and stability, if that choice means no change in conditions of life which deny basic human needs. But again, those arguing the absence of law as a primary cause of war do advance an important understanding. Ending war does not require easing all the tensions that lead to conflict. It requires agreement on some method other than mass violence for processing or resolving conflict.

We can learn something from each single-cause explanation. One can construct, from those very different perspectives, a body of thought more adequate to the problem of ending war than any single approach. In subsequent sections of *To End War* we consider the other primary causes of war and alternative understandings of what must be done to meet their challenge. Only *after* such an examination can one decide if ending war is a viable goal.

To End War, then, sees contemporary military facts and current military thinking as a part of the war/peace field worthy of the peace seeker's attention. Similarly, a careful review of the argument over the causes of war is essential. The causes of war argument offers one useful construct with which to test the adequacy of a variety of strategies for peace.

The Causes and Nature of War

1 MAN, THE STATE AND WAR, A Theoretical Analysis *by Kenneth N. Waltz, 263pp, 1965, Columbia University Press, $1.95.* Distinguishes between causes of war originating in the nature of man (weakness, instincts, desire for power, boredom), the nature of political communities (the tendency to substitute foreign enemies for domestic ones) and the nature of international relations (sovereign states in conflict without supranational means for resolving conflicts and assuring compliance). An extremely useful categorization and introduction to the problem.

°INF   2 A STUDY OF WAR *by Quincy Wright, 451pp, 1964, abridged edition, University of Chicago Press, $2.95.* A basic study which argues that all of the causes of war can be subsumed under "politico-technological, juro-rational, socio-ideological, and psycho-economic" causes. Contends that world interdependence and a developing sense of world community makes possible world law which could eliminate war.

°TEW   3 READINGS IN WORLD POLITICS, *Robert Goldwin (ed.), revised by Tony Pearce. 644pp, 1970, Oxford University Press, $3.95.* Best single introduction to the concepts that are central to any discussion of world politics. Classical and modern selections illustrate alternative perspectives. The section on the causes of war is especially useful.

4 WORLD POLITICS, The Writings of Theorists and Practitioners, Classical and Modern, *Arend Lijphart (ed.),*

°INF means an influential book whose creative, scholarly or political impact makes it a landmark in the field. INT means a book that is particularly useful to those just entering the field, offering a concise summary statement or a useful introductory survey. TEW means the book is especially recommended as contributing ideas that can help move us toward ending war.

448pp, 1966, Allyn and Bacon, Inc., $5.25. An introduction to the basic concepts and persistent issues of world politics that underlie the fact of war. This anthology includes classical political theorists and political practitioners from Theodore Roosevelt to U Thant. These are brief, introductory readings of a very high quality.

INF   5   WAR, POLITICS AND POWER *by Karl Von Clausewitz, 304pp, 1962, Henry Regnery Co., $1.95.* One classic definition of the nature of war which explains war's tendency to escalate as a function of war's duration and the significance of the issues involved.

6   WAR AND PEACE: A Theory of International Relations *by Raymond Aron, 810pp, 1967, Praeger, $4.95.* A French sociologist defines wars' social functions while pointing to the irrationality of nuclear war, and the tendency of other types to lead to that extreme. He offers little hope that nonviolent ways of conducting international conflict will be found.

7   THE STATE OF WAR *by Stanley Hoffman, 276pp, 1965, Praeger, $2.25.* A study of the functioning of a major institution and its role in Western political life.

8   THE ABOLITION OF WAR *by Walter Millis and James Real, 217pp, 1963, Macmillan, $1.95.* An analysis of the "war system" which maintains that the development of weapons of mass destruction and the unification of the globe presages war's end.

(see also 137, 199, 386, 579, 581, 583, 607, 612, 622 and 626)

Multiple Causes

INT   9   THE THREAT OF NUCLEAR WEAPONS, Questions and Answers on the Effects of Their Possible Use *by the United Nations, 19pp, 1968, United Nations, $.10.* A panel of scientists from both communist and noncommunist countries conclude that "civilization as we know it would inevitably come to an end" if nuclear weapons were used in large numbers, yet the "risk of nuclear war remains as long as there are nuclear weapons."

10 GUERRILLAS IN THE 1960'S *by Peter Paret and John Shy, 98pp, 1962, Praeger, $1.50.* A study of guerilla warfare.

11 CBW, Chemical and Biological Warfare, *Steven Ross (ed.), 209pp, 1969, Beacon Press, $1.95.* Essays on current CBW weapons (chemicals, psychedelics, napalm, defoliants), CBW research policies in the U.S., the U.S.S.R. and Great Britain and the ethical questions involved.

12 CHEMICAL AND BIOLOGICAL WARFARE, America's Hidden Arsenal *by Seymour M. Hersh, 307pp, 1969, Doubleday, $1.45.* A comprehensive and well-documented description of the development of such weapons in the U.S. and elsewhere. The author argues that the secrecy surrounding these weapons prevents appropriate concern about their control or use, thus the lack of pressure for international disarmament agreements.

TEW   **13 UNLESS PEACE COMES,** A Scientific Forecast of New Weapons, *Nigel Calder (ed.), 243pp, 1968, Viking Press, $1.95.* An international group of scientists study likely weapon developments: infectious dust clouds, orbital bombs, computerization of conventional war, new techniques of guerilla warfare, nerve, skin and blood gases, submersile vehicles, robots, and cobalt bombs. A dispassionate, chilling study.

14 HOW CAN THE UNITED STATES BEST MAINTAIN MANPOWER FOR AN EFFECTIVE DEFENSE SYSTEM?, *132pp, 1968, Library of Congress, $.45.* A collection of excerpts and a bibliography relating to the National High School Debate Topic, 1968–69, from the Legislative Reference Service, Library of Congress. This pamphlet includes articles on Selective Service, Lottery, Universal Service and a Volunteer Army.

(see also 348-354)

Military Strategy

15 ON ESCALATION *by Herman Kahn, 308pp, 1965, Penguin Books, $1.65.* A detailed study of the relationship between levels of violence and types of disagreement which attempts to apportion the level of violence to the end sought.

16 ON THE USES OF MILITARY POWER IN THE NUCLEAR ERA *by Klaus Knorr, 185pp, 1966, Princeton University Press, hardcover, $5.00.* Argues that while stopping territorial conquest, nuclear weapons have reduced national security.

17 THE DEBATE OVER THERMONUCLEAR STRATEGY, *Arthur Waskow (ed.), 114pp, 1964, D.C. Heath Co., $2.25.* Selections by Herman Kahn, Robert McNamara, John F. Kennedy, Barry Goldwater, Robert Osgood, Walter Millis, James Real and others. Annotated bibliography.

TEW   18 AMERICA ARMED: Essays on U.S. Military Policy, *Robert A. Goldwin (ed.), 144pp, 1965, Rand McNally, $1.50.* Includes essays favoring American peace initiatives, unilateral disarmament, defenses of present policy, and advocates of the full use of American military power.

19 PROBLEMS OF NATIONAL STRATEGY, *Henry Kissinger (ed.), 477pp, 1965, Praeger, $4.95.* An anthology of writings largely confined to the question of what type of deterrence is most likely to achieve national security.

20 STRATEGY AND CONSCIENCE *by Anatol Rapoport, 323pp, 1964, Schocken, $2.95.* A careful study of games theory as it relates to strategic decision making. Argues that games involve presuppositions which need to be examined or else strategy will consider only the vectors of force involved while the game itself affects all aspects of social life. Concludes with a call for ideological disarmament designed to encourage liberalizing tendencies within the Soviet Union.

Deterrence

INF   21 ON THERMONUCLEAR WAR *by Herman Kahn, 668pp, 1969, (second edition), Macmillan, $3.95.* A pioneer work in establishing strategic reasoning as a province of rational thought. Sets forth the available alternatives opened by a variety of military strategies and examines the consequences of each. Blasts open the realities of military thought by facing the possibility of 50 million or 150 million corpses and nevertheless arguing (in addition to having a deterrent capability) that we might want "an ability to actually fight and survive a war."

22 **ARMS AND INFLUENCE** *by Thomas Schelling, 293pp, 1966, Yale University Press, $1.95.* An investigation of some of the principles by which nations use military power as a bargaining agent in achieving influence over other nations. The most incisive book on the international politics of threat, i.e. deterrence.

23 **PEACE AND STRATEGY CONFLICT** *by William Kinter, 264pp, 1967, Praeger, hardcover, $6.95.* An advocate of arms superiority at all levels (from nuclear weapons to guerilla warfare) argues that a preponderance of military power is most likely to achieve peace by maximizing the chances for forcing diplomatic concessions from the Soviet Union and other Communist powers.

24 **THE DEADLY LOGIC:** The Theory of Nuclear Deterrence *by Philip Green, 361pp, 1967, Schocken, $2.45.* A logical critique of the theory of deterrence.

(see also 208)

Consequences

INT 25 **THE CENTURY OF TOTAL WAR** *by Raymond Aron, 368pp, 1966, Beacon Press, $2.25.* Penetrating study of the new characteristics of modern war, e.g., the total mobilization of the population, the inseparability of civilian and military targets and the use of weapons of mass destruction.

26 **COMMUNITY OF FEAR** *by Harrison Brown and James Real, 40pp, 1960, Center for the Study of Democratic Institutions, $.25.* Surveys the developments in modern weaponry and dramatically portrays the consequences of their use.

27   **MEN IN ARMS, A History of Warfare and Its Inter-relationships with Western Society** *by Richard A. Preston and others, 402pp, 1964, Praeger, $2.95.* A study of the development of warfare from ancient times to the present.

27A   **THE WARRIORS, Reflections on Men in Battle** *by J. Glenn Gray, 242pp, 1967, Harper & Row, $1.95.* Drawn from personal experiences of the author in World War II, the reflections in this singular book explore the appeals of battle, the images of the enemy and the effects of war on those who participate in it.

28   **A HISTORY OF MILITARISM, Civilian and Military** *by Alfred Vagts, 542pp, 1959, rev. ed., Macmillan, $2.95.* Distinguishes between militarism and military organization while seeking to demonstrate that armies have traditionally begun a war with the weapons and strategy of the last war. A useful analysis of the relationship between military and diplomatic pursuits.

29   **HIROSHIMA** *by John Hershey, 116pp, 1966, Bantam Books, $.60.* Powerful description of the atomic attack and its aftermath. Hershey visited Hiroshima after the attack and reconstructed the day from accounts of survivors.

30   **THE FALLEN SKY: Medical Consequences of Thermonuclear Attack,** *Physicians for Social Responsibility (ed.), 134pp, 1963, Hill & Wang, $1.50.* Includes sections on the human and ecological effects, and on biological and psychiatric damage, as well as blast destruction.

31   **NUCLEAR DISASTER** *by Tom Stonier, 225pp, 1963, World Publishing, $2.25.* A scientific analysis of the effects of nuclear war on a society. Studies the projected affect of a 20 megaton explosion over New York City.

32   **WORLD REFUGEE REPORT** *by U.S. Committee for Refugees, 31pp, 1968, $1.00.* A report on the world's sixteen million war refugees—humans made homeless by war in the twentieth century.

33   **THE VIOLENT PEACE, A Report on Wars in the Postwar World** *by Carl and Shelley Mydans, 479pp, 1968,*

Atheneum, hardcover illustrated, $12.50. A survey of thirty post–World War II wars. The text reflects the authors' disappointment in the failure of the U.N. to remove "the scourge of war forever," while the pictures and descriptive material suggest some of the consequences.

34   **WORLD MILITARY EXPENDITURES, 1966–67** *by U.S. Arms Control and Disarmament Agency, 24pp, 1968, U.S. Govt. Printing Office, $.35.* A study of worldwide spending on arms which finds that 159 billion dollars was spent on arms in 1966, compared to 8 billion for economic development. Also gives trends from 1962–66, and compares military expenditures country by country.

(see also 301-354)

II DISARMAMENT: PROBLEMS AND APPROACHES

The facts of war are surveyed here from a different point of view. Our focus is not on competing military strategies and weapons development, but on the attempt to control or end systematic organization for mass violence in war.

Today all policies are defended as peace policies. Military deterrence theory, for example, argues that peace is secured when the general level of armament makes attack obviously unprofitable. Deterrence theorists cite the fact that nuclear war has not occurred despite twenty-four years of intense competition in nuclear weaponry. They argue, further, that disarmament can itself cause war, recalling in support of their view the events leading to the Munich Agreement (1939) and the subsequent German invasion of Czechoslovakia. One cannot, they would argue, distinguish advocates of peace from advocates of war simply by determining attitudes toward arming or disarming. Contemporary military deterrence theory thus presents itself as a policy for peace. Books on deterrence theory are, however, not listed in this section of *To End War*. Our primary focus here is on thought aimed at curtailing or reversing the arms race, not on proposals for conducting it in a way that prevents war.

In Chapter I we considered the full spectrum of military policies from preventive war to deterrence. Advocates of disarmament reject primary reliance on such policies. They see the arms race itself as a cause of war. They support this assertion by citing historical examples from the Peloponnesian War (Thucydides, # 644) to World War I (Palmer, # 123), and also by showing that the psychological effect of preparing for war militates against the peaceful resolution of conflict (Seed, # 62).

Advocates of disarmament offer four alternative approaches to the avoidance of war: arms control (a policy closely allied to deterrence theory), multilateral disarmament by negotiated agreement, unilateral disarmament, and multilateral disarmament through unilateral initiatives. Books covering this full spectrum are annotated in this chapter.

ARMS CONTROL

The school of thought which is probably most influential in America today argues that disarmament, while desirable, is not achievable. Instead, it urges a focus on arms control (Bull, # 43) as an achievable goal which would enhance the balance of power among nations and thereby help maintain peace. Hedley Bull succinctly summarizes the position:

> *A balance of power between opposed nations or alliances—the possession on both sides of such forces and weapons that neither is able to impose its will on the other—is an important though precarious source of international security; precarious, because while it persists, it provides no guarantee against war and defeat, and because it is not bound to persist but is inherently unstable; important, because in a world that is armed and divided—armed because it is divided and likely to remain divided—no less precarious source of international security is available.*

He then recommends a number of ways to set *limits*

to the deployment of arms and to render the balance of power more stable. Bull's recommendation of arms control, rather than disarmament, follows from his analysis of what is possible, given the state of international relations today. Advocates of *disarmament* (e.g., Noel-Baker, # 52) share his premise that armaments are dangerous; they contest his argument that, under present conditions, only arms control can be achieved.

MULTILATERAL DISARMAMENT
BY NEGOTIATED AGREEMENT

Advocates of disarmament argue that there is something fundamentally wrong with a world in which men mass into armies that threaten to destroy whole societies, if not civilized life itself. They argue not only from such moral judgments but also from specific achievements on the way to an agreement on general, complete, universal and enforceable disarmament. They list as steps toward a disarmed world the test ban treaty and agreements to ban weapons from outer space and to keep Antarctica disarmed and open to inspection. Disarmers argue that the democratic values which they share with advocates of deterrence and arms control are incompatible with an arms race. Advocates of disarmament also note that armaments are costly (over $168 billion world wide in 1967) and that these funds are desperately needed to combat man's perennial enemies—disease, poverty and ignorance.

Proponents of arms control and deterrence agree with much of the above but point to the persistent reality of power relations among men. One must, they say, choose surrender to a conqueror's will, or prepare to meet an opponent's threat or use of military power *with* military power.

Advocates of disarmament reply that there are many forms of power other than the threat or use of military violence. They assert further that the utility of violence is greatly exaggerated, for "violence can only subdue, it cannot reconcile antagonists" (Burke). In a world with thermonuclear weapons we *must* find ways, short of war or the threat of war, to resolve conflict. They see agreement on universal, enforceable, inspected disarmament as essential to the growth of world law: an alternative and nonviolent way of resolving conflict. Disarmers deny the armers' primary assumption. They deny that reliance on national military power for security is any longer a rational policy.

But how are we to move toward disarmament?

Most disarmament proposals call for negotiated agreements among all nations which establish a timetable for moving steadily toward a disarmed world, kept so by agreement on inspection procedures (cf. *Current Disarmament Proposals,* # 49). Such proposals are usually closely related to proposals for world political and legal development.

UNILATERAL DISARMAMENT

Some (e.g., Sibley, # 58, Carter, # 59), surveying the failure of past disarmament conferences, see little hope for such negotiated agreement; but they regard disarmament as the prerequisite for continuation of human life on this earth. Some nation, they say, must therefore lead the way. A variety of practical and moral arguments are offered in defense of a policy of unilateral disarmament by the United States or England. Some unilateralists rest their case entirely on religious grounds and the injunction "thou shall not kill." Others argue the practicality of unilateral disarmament as the best way to survive in the nuclear age, or the best way to get others to disarm, too.

Critics point out that one side's refusal to arm is just that. It is no guarantee that the other side will not wage war. No, say the unilateralists, whatever else it is, unilateral disarmament *is* a defense against war. Aggressors may occupy our nation, they say, (and some unilateralists advocate some form of organized nonviolent defense [# 512–516] as a viable way to defend their communities) but we would rather deal with that evil than with nuclear war. The armers respond by pointing again to the reality of power. Your refusal to deal with that reality, say the armers, is just yours. By withdrawing from the power struggle, you do not end war, you leave the chances of war and the world's future to others, accepting a conquered people's role for yourself.

Multilateral Disarmament Through Unilateral Initiatives

A synthesis which seeks to combine the sound elements in all the above views is a policy of American initiative action designed to achieve agreement on universal, inspected disarmament. Its distinguishing characteristic is action taken *prior* to agreement which maximizes chances for agreement in situations where agreement could not previously be achieved.

Such a policy aims at the multilateralists' goal of universal agreement, but it shares the unilateralists' recognition that disarmament negotiations have not in fact resulted in disarmament. Given no agreement on disarmament and a refusal either to surrender or to reenter the arms race, there is yet one hopeful policy: unilateral action designed to produce pressure for multilateral agreement.

The idea is to choose moves toward disarmament which are likely to be reciprocated in kind by an opponent. Such a move would have the following characteristics: 1) clearly reducing the threat to the opponent while weakening the initiator's defense only slightly; 2) making clear that reciprocal action by the enemy is required if further progress toward disarmament is to be achieved; 3) not demanding commitment to reciprocation by the enemy as a precondition for the initial move.

Such an initiative policy assumes that it is in the interest of all men to move toward freedom from the threat of war. It assumes further that there are elements within all nations and in the world community that can bring effective pressure to bear on recalcitrant national leaders. It is this last assumption that critics of unilateral initiatives deny.

Advocates of an initiative strategy argue that such a series of acts could in the end achieve the unilateralist's goal of a world disarmed. To succeed the policy would have to make clear a nation's intent to disarm *while* strengthening international peace-keeping machinery. It would have to gradually reduce the level of real and perceived military threats to opponents *while* bringing pressure to bear on them for reciprocal action. Such a policy would have to satisfy the arms control adherents by facing up to the realities of power. Disarmament initiatives make the most sense as a part of an overall peace initiatives strategy designed to help develop a sense of world community capable of sustaining world law and to move us ahead on the other roads to a world without war considered in this book. See (# 348) *The ABM and a World Without War* (pages 13 to 45) and (# 301) *Viet-*

nam Peace Proposals (pages 39 to 42) for examples of how a policy of American initiatives can be applied to crisis issues in a way which advances long term *To End War* goals (*see also Chapter 14*).

The books in this section, then, survey the full spectrum of approaches to arms control and disarmament as well as specific problems such as the economics of disarmament, the policing of disarmament agreements and the relationship of disarmament to the achievement of world law. They offer the best in thinking about an American initiatives strategy.

We can ill afford the naivité and sentimentality that have characterized so many past approaches to the disarmament problem. But we cannot achieve a world without war without solving the problem of how we are to get agreement on universal, enforceable, inspected disarmament.

Surveys of the Field

INT   35 **DISARMAMENT AND ARMS CONTROL** *by Lincoln Bloomfield, 73pp, 1968, Foreign Policy Association, $.85.* An able historical outline, reporting on the current status of and future prospects for disarmament agreements. Special focus on the problem of achieving universal participation, particularly by Communist China, in such agreements.

TEW   36 **THE FUTURE OF THE STRATEGIC ARMS RACE: Options for the 1970's** *by George W. Rathjens, 64pp, 1969, Carnegie Endowment, $.60.* Clarifies many of the complex issues by examining the basic premises on which strategic decisions are made.

37 **ARMS CONTROL AND NATIONAL SECURITY,** *U.S. Arms Control and Disarmament Agency, 24pp, 1968, U.S. Govt. Printing Office, $.50.* A useful summary of disarmament and arms control negotiations since World War II. Argues that national security cannot be equated with

superiority in nuclear weaponry, but fails to draw significant implications for U.S. defense policy.

38 **DOCUMENTS ON DISARMAMENT,** U.S. *Arms Control and Disarmament Agency, 820pp, 1967, U.S. Govt. Printing Office, $2.50.* A useful compilation of official statements from more than thirty countries, including the United States and China.

39 **U.S. ARMS CONTROL AND DISARMAMENT AGENCY'S NINTH ANNUAL REPORT, January 1, 1969 —December 31, 1969,** *55pp, 1969, U.S. Govt. Printing Office, $.35.* Summary of the agency's efforts and the statutes of various arms control and disarmament agreements.

40 **THE DEMILITARIZED WORLD AND HOW TO GET THERE** *by Walter Millis, 61pp, 1964, Center for the Study of Democratic Institutions, $.50.* A discussion of various routes to disarmament.

40A **ARMAMENT OR DISARMAMENT** *by Frank Zeidler, 64pp, 1970, Lutheran Church in America, $.75.* One of four pamphlets published by the Lutheran Churches' Board of Social Ministry, this one relates Christian theology to the arms race and suggests guidelines for those seeking arms control and disarmament.

(see also 172A, 113A, 98A)

41 **DOCUMENTS ON DISARMAMENT 1968,** *893pp, 1969, U.S. Arms Control and Disarmament Agency, $3.75.* Includes documents from the U.N. Eighteen-Nation Disarmament Committee hearings, comments on and signatories of the Non-Proliferation Treaty, statements by U.S. Government officials and a bibliography of U.N. and other disarmament documents.

INF 42 **THE UNITED NATIONS AND DISARMAMENT, 1945–1965** *by the Office of Information, United Nations, 338pp, 1967, United Nations, hardcover, $4.50.* Depicts the United Nations' efforts in the field of disarmament over a 20-year period; particularly the work of the Atomic Energy Commission, proposals for arms control, general and complete disarmament, the ban on nuclear weapons tests, and the prevention of the spread of nuclear weapons.

(see also 134 and 140)

Arms Control

INF   43 **THE CONTROL OF THE ARMS RACE** *by Hedley Bull, 235pp, 1965, Praeger, $1.95.* Examines the theory and practice of arms control which the author believes is achievable, while disarmament is not.

44 **THE PROSPECTS FOR ARMS CONTROL,** *James Dougherty (ed.), 370pp, 1965, McFadden Books, $.95.* An anthology by authors more committed to the reliance on national military power than arms control (which makes their sensitivity to the obstacles of disarmament most useful). Selections by Herman Kahn, Sidney Hook, Robert Levine, Thomas Schelling and many others.

45 **COMMUNIST CHINA AND ARMS CONTROL, A** Contingency Study, *1967–1976, Yuan-li Wu (ed.), 181pp, 1968, Hoover Institution Publications, $5.00.* A study prepared for the U.S. Arms Control and Disarmament Agency which attempts to forecast China's foreign and domestic attitudes and policy goals as they relate to arms control.

46 **THE ARMS RACE AND SINO-SOVIET RELATIONS** *by Walter Clemens, Jr., 176pp, 1967, Columbia University Press, hardcover, $6.95.* The author views an arms race between China and the Soviet Union as the central issue of the 1970's. He argues that the balance of power and economic factors will determine both the military potential of each power and their attitudes towards arms control.

47 **ARMS CONTROL AGREEMENTS** *by David Wainhouse and others, 179pp, 1968, Johns Hopkins Press, hardcover, $6.95.* Focuses on inspection and verification problems. Concludes by recommending a single international verification organization.

47A TOWARDS A STRATEGIC ARMS LIMITATION AGREEMENT *by Herbert Scoville, Jr., 47pp, 1970, Carnegie Endowment, $1.00.* A study of the need for arms limitation agreements in the face of new weapon system developments. Examines the obstacles and alternatives to such agreements.

48 STRATEGIC PERSUASION: Arms Limitation Through Dialogue *by Jeremy Stone, 176pp, 1967, Columbia University Press, hardcover, $6.95.* The author focuses on the problem of credibility in arms control negotiations and argues that the direct exchange of information through both official and unofficial sources can help achieve agreement.

(see also 349, 350, 386 and 554)

Multilateral Disarmament Through Negotiations

49 CURRENT DISARMAMENT PROPOSALS, World Law Fund, *195pp, 1964, World Law Fund, $2.00.* The texts.

50 A COMPARISON AND EVALUATION OF CURRENT DISARMAMENT PROPOSALS *by Marion McVitty, 43pp, 1964, World Law Fund, $.50.* Discusses problems of verification, inspection, control and other issues of international disarmament negotiations.

51 WHO WANTS DISARMAMENT? *by Richard Barnet, 141pp, 1960, Beacon Press, $1.45.* Studies of possibilities of disarmament in the light of Soviet and American goals.

INF **52 THE ARMS RACE** *by Philip Noel-Baker,*
TEW *603pp, 1958, Oceana, $3.00.* A careful historical analysis with specific recommendations. A classic on disarmament.

(see also 119 and 236)

Multilateral Disarmament Through Initiatives

53 DISENGAGEMENT, A Plan For Area Disarmament, *Turn Toward Peace (now World Without War Council),*

6pp, 1964, $.10. A regional approach to disarmament through international arms control agreements and enforcement procedures.

54 **PEACE BY FINESSE** *by Joseph Still, 74pp, 1967, Promoting Enduring Peace, free.* Argues for a disarmed peace zone as one way to develop the sense of world community essential to world law.

INT   55 **A STRATEGY OF PEACE** *by John F. Kennedy, 8pp, 1963, $.10.* American University speech of June 11, 1963 which announced the Nuclear Test-Ban Treaty as the first step in a strategy designed to seek out those areas in which cooperation with Communist nations is fruitful, despite the many issues which divide us.

56 **TOWARD A STRATEGY OF PEACE,** *Walter Clemens, Jr. (ed.), 264pp, 1965, Rand McNally, $3.95.* An anthology which develops the themes of Kennedy's 1963 speech, including selections of a Soviet spokesman, Adlai Stevenson, Pope John XXIII and others dealing with problems of human rights, arms control and disarmament, revolution, hunger and international organization.

TEW   57 **AN ALTERNATIVE TO WAR OR SURRENDER** *by Charles Osgood, 151pp, 1963, University of Illinois Press, $1.45.* When nations cannot agree, what should a nation that rejects surrender or a continuation of the arms race do? A former president of the American Psychological Association argues for a strategy of graduated unilateral acts designed to reduce tension and establish a climate in which agreement becomes more likely.

(see also 131, 218, 221, 237, 238, 239, 298, 301 and 348)

Unilateral Disarmament

58 **UNILATERAL INITIATIVES AND DISARMAMENT** *by Mulford Sibley, 64pp, 1964, American Friends Service Committee, $.35.* A variant on the initiatives approach which argues that the initiatives should be continued, regardless of whether they are reciprocated.

Includes an appeal for Civilian Defense (nonviolent resistance) as an alternate means of national defense.

59 UNILATERAL DISARMAMENT, Its Theory and Policy from Different International Perspectives, *April Carter (ed.), 68pp, 1965, Housmans, $.50.* Ten essays on unilateral disarmament as a policy for the U.S. and Great Britain; the implications of such policies for other countries are also considered.

(see also 508, 512, 513, 514, 515, 516 and 518)

Safeguarding Agreements

60 INDIVIDUAL RESPONSIBILITY UNDER A DISARMAMENT AGREEMENT IN AMERICAN LAW *by Daniel Partan, 66pp, 1965, Duke Rule of Law Research Center, $.25.* Argues for an individual's responsibility to report national violations of international disarmament agreements. Advocates the adoption of a U.S. Constitutional amendment to establish such a responsibility, combined with a challenge to other world powers to reciprocate.

61 SECURITY IN DISARMAMENT, *Richard Barnet and Richard Falk (eds.), 441pp, 1965, Princeton University Press, $2.65.* An anthology which deals with inspection problems, impartiality of international police and issues surrounding unilateral intervention vs. supranational authority.

62 THE PSYCHOLOGICAL PROBLEM OF DISARMAMENT *by Philip Seed, 72pp, 1966, Housmans, $1.00.* The effect of political identification with a nation-state on the possibility of achieving international agreements on disarmament.

63 THE UNITED STATES IN A DISARMED WORLD *by Arnold Wolfers and others, 236pp, 1966, Johns Hopkins Press, $2.25.* A critique by a group of scholars of the ACDA plan for general and complete multilateral disarmament. Concludes that the government plan is idealistic and that the plan does not consider let alone meet all of the possible dangers involved in its implementation. Reprints the ACDA plan.

The Economics of Disarmament

64   **REPORT FROM IRON MOUNTAIN ON THE POSSIBILITY AND DESIRABILITY OF PEACE** *introduction by Leonard Lewin, 109pp, 1967, Delta Books, $1.95.* Ostensibly an official government report, this satirical exploration of the consequences of peace for American society and the economy is, among other things, a merely clever presentation of some contemporary Marxist views of the causes of war; but it is also a useful highlighting of problem areas that block a more wholehearted American effort to achieve a disarmed world.

65   **ECONOMIC IMPACT OF DISARMAMENT,** *U.S. Arms Control and Disarmament Agency, 28pp, 1962, U.S. Govt. Printing Office, $.25.* An assessment of the problem which would face the U.S. if a disarmament agreement or arms control measure were adopted. The impact on jobs and defense contractors, as well as on other industries is assessed.

66   **ECONOMIC AND SOCIAL CONSEQUENCES OF DISARMAMENT** *by the United Nations, 66pp, 1962, United Nations, $.75.* Studies the effect of disarmament on the international economy, the structural problems of transition, the social consequences of disarmament and possible increased welfare for many people.

67   **ECONOMIC AND SOCIAL CONSEQUENCES OF DISARMAMENT, Replies of Governments and Communications from International Organizations** *by the United Nations, 304pp, 1962, United Nations, $3.00.* National governments consider the possible impacts as described by selection # 66.

68   **DEFENSE AND DISARMAMENT: The Economics of Transition,** *Roger Bolton (ed.), 180pp, 1966, Prentice-Hall, $1.95.* Includes a statement by a major defense con-

tractor, by Norman Cousins (editor of *Saturday Review*) and by others concerning the problems of transition from a wartime to a peacetime economy.

Note: All of the publications listed in this book may be ordered by simply listing the numbers of the publications desired and mailing with your check to the World Without War Council, 1730 Grove Street, Berkeley, California 94709. Please indicate the numbers are from the 1970 edition of *To End War*. Please anticipate from three to eight weeks for delivery of hardcover books. Complete ordering information available on request.

Without world development and a strengthened sense of world community, disarmament is a chimera, at best an interregnum. A disarmed world in which millions of human beings live lives in terrible deprivation will not long remain disarmed. As their awareness of their deprivation grows, so will the appeal of violence to correct the injustice of their lives. Nor can world legal processes be established as an alternative to violent conflict without a strengthened sense of world community. Once law could be imposed by imperial power; no longer. Today a disarmed world requires consent, keeping it disarmed requires a developed sense of unity and mutual responsibility among men.

Those working for a world without war must therefore understand alternative approaches to achieving world development and world community. How are the developing nations to meet the human needs of their people, now aware that "it doesn't have to be like this"? In a world ruled by nationalist and ideological passions, but made ever more interdependent by modern technological, communications and economic realities, how are we to achieve that recognition of interdependence that would make law possible? *Can* such a sense of world community make it possible for law to arise from consent instead of being imposed by violence?

Ending war requires answering such questions. But there is another compelling reason why we must understand these problems and choose the paths most likely to lead to their resolution. Most of the world's people are hungry. One hundred thousand starve to death each year in Calcutta alone. World per capita income per year averages only $136.00. Most of the world's children do not go to school. Life expectancy is scarcely forty years. Basic medical needs are unmet. Opportunities for useful employment and for education are severely limited (U Thant, # 97). Life for most is, indeed, "nasty, brutish, and short." Because we are shamed and disgraced by such conditions we should try to change them.

Such circumstances provide one of the most powerful contemporary justifications for violence. We cannot expect men to turn away from war and violence if doing so means acquiescing to such conditions.

Many in the West (e.g., Heilbroner, # 296) argue as follows. The pitiful circumstances of two billion or more persons, half of whom are under twenty-one, justifies mass violence if it will produce needed change. Only mass violence *will* produce change, for economically powerful groups profit from existing conditions and wish to retain them. Only an elite committed to ruthless action, backed by a people set in motion and organized by an ideological commitment, is capable of ending such exploitation. The acts of such a revolutionary elite, though bloody and hateful, are necessary if the human potential of most people on this earth is to be fulfilled.

Heilbroner's argument is familiar, whether justified in Marxist or economic development terms. One urgently committed to changing such conditions may still reject mass violence as the best route to needed change in the developing nations. War and violence do not feed, clothe, educate or build. They kill. Mass violence is, itself, a major obstacle to the conditions necessary for rapid economic growth.

The problems of modernization are complex. Marx argued that in the industrialization process the "accumulation of wealth at one pole is, at the same time, accumulation of agony, toil . . . slavery and misery at the opposite pole" (Marx, # 244). He argued from the empirical evidence available to him about the industrial revolution in England. But it is possible, as the subsequent development of England demonstrates, that industrial growth can benefit all who participate in the economy by increasing the amount of wealth, and that by political processes a more equitable—though not equal—distribution can be achieved. It is possible today, for example, for a privately owned corporation to invest in another country, to make a profit and at the same time improve the economic circumstances of the people who are employed, and in turn through their increased wages and taxation, improve the general economic condition of the country. It is also possible that a privately owned enterprise will use its influence within a country to prevent workers from achieving a significant share of the profits, to deny the country itself a fair revenue through taxation, and to block its economic and political development.

A careful examination of the development of a modern industrial base in Puerto Rico, Japan, Yugoslavia, the Soviet Union, Israel, and India does not lead to agreement with Heilbroner's stark judgment.

C. E. Black, # 77, charts seven paths which nations have followed. All the nations above as well as the United States, West Germany, and Spain are following different courses. Neither socialism nor capitalism assures economic development, much less anything approaching equitable distribution of newly-created wealth. Communist China's widely publicized progress is now subject to many questions. Population growth has, for example, eroded the gains many nations have made (Heer, # 105).

There are, however, areas of agreement about the requisites of and the obstacles to economic development. Clearly national rivalries have prevented coordinated efforts to develop continental and regional resources and markets. The relationship between economic development and cultural and political change has been carefully surveyed (# 83). Many proponents of world economic development see the attempt to produce change through violent revolution as a major obstacle to the development process and therefore mark the urgency of opening *non*violent routes to needed change. They call on the rich nations of North America, Europe and Japan to fulfill their moral and practical obligation to help most of the rest of the world achieve self-sustained economic growth (Ward, # 129). They agree that past efforts have been shamefully inadequate in scope, in planning and in execution.

The United Nations' goal of 1 per cent of the rich nations' gross national product per year for development has not been met. The U.S. lags behind seven other nations in its contribution, which is less than .5 per cent per year of our gross national product. Since 1961 the amounts available for aid on a world basis have leveled off, while the ability to contribute has increased (# 102). This is a consequence of the failure of many aid programs in the past to produce desired growth; it also results from a continuing failure on the part of most of the world's rich to accept responsibility for changing the conditions of life of the world's poor. Today therefore, despite the fact that there is economic growth in both the rich nations and the poor, the disparity between their economic circumstances is increasing.

BILATERAL OR MULTILATERAL AID

In the last twenty-five years, 90 per cent of available economic assistance has been administered on a bilateral basis involving only a granting and a receiving nation. The remaining 10 per cent has been multilateral assistance—many nations planning and administering aid programs together (# 102). Most individuals who recognize national rivalries as a cause of war, and who believe that a world economy has emerged, prefer the multilateral approach to governmental bilateral arrangements, though almost any form of capital input is helpful. Multilateral aid programs—governmental or private—reduce the chances of a powerful nation misusing an assistance program and can also help strengthen international institutions and promote cooperation on a regional basis. There has been an increasing recognition of the value of multilateral assistance, although clearly there are appropriate tasks for national as well as international efforts.

In the last twenty-five years international governmental organizations have developed at a rapid rate. As international needs have been recognized, international organizations have been built. Operating in the development field are the International Monetary Fund, the International Bank for Reconstruction and Development, the United Nations Food and Agriculture Organization, the United Nations Educational, Scientific and Cultural Organization, the World Health Organization, the International Labor Organization (# 150) and the United Nations Conference on Trade and Development. In addition there have been significant programs organized and financed by voluntary organizations (# 101).

WORLD COMMUNITY

Concern with world economic and social development has stimulated the explosive expansion of international institutions since 1940. Scientists from many nations forced to deal with ecological and technical problems on a world scale have, problem by problem, added to a sense of world community that eclipses national and ideological boundaries. This chapter's bibliography begins with problems of economic development but then turns to books focused on the problem of world community. Coffin (# 102), for example, emphasizes the need for motivation on the part of the rich nations. Concern for human need should surely be the prime motivation. But another reason to act could be the recognition that the problem of ending war requires a massive increase in the amounts made available to aid the developing nations. A major change in the quality of mind and spirit that separates us from the community of man is needed before we act on these recognitions.

It is because a common focus on problems of world development can aid in *creating* a sense of world community that we list in this chapter books on problems of world community. Space exploration, world ecology and population problems all provide occasions for strengthening a sense of unity essential to sustaining a world legal and political authority. Such an authority, legitimized by freely given consent, is perhaps the central requisite for lasting peace.

In Chapter 4 of *To End War* we consider the political and legal opportunities for controlling the threat of war that will open as we do achieve a sense of world community. The obstacles posed by present attitudes in the Communist world and our own coun-

try are considered in Chapters 5 and 6. The moral
and religious ground for sustaining such an acceptance
of responsibility is considered in Chapter 8. Here and
in Chapter 7 we focus on the problems posed by attitudes in the new nations and by ethnocentric attitudes in all men. We examine attempts to define common standards (e.g., the U.N. Declaration of Human
Rights, # 108) and to deal with such common problems as population and pollution.

Problems of world development and world community are thoroughly intermixed. Together they provide the motivation for, and the growing possibility
of, world institutions capable of containing the threat
of war.

Conditions

69   WHAT IS IT LIKE TO LIVE ON $100 PER YEAR?
*by Committee for World Disarmament and World Eco-
nomic Development, 2pp, 1967, $.02.* A description of the
life circumstances of the majority of human beings now
living.

INT   70   REPORT ON THE WORLD SOCIAL SIT-
UATION *by the United Nations, 208pp, 1969, United
Nations, $3.00.* How most of the world lives.

71   OVERCOMING WORLD HUNGER, *Clifford M.
Hardin (ed.), 177pp, 1968, Prentice-Hall, $1.95.* An an-
thology examining population growth and control, the need
for better nutritional use of existent food supplies and the
methods and organizations involved in expanding the
world's food supply.

72   WORLD DISARMAMENT AND WORLD ECO-
NOMIC DEVELOPMENT KIT *by Committee for World
Disarmament and World Economic Development, 99pp,
1967, $1.00.* A kit of magazine reprints and essays de-
scribing the need for rapid economic development which
suggests that much of the capital needed is now being
wasted on armaments.

73 THE STRUGGLE AGAINST WORLD HUNGER *by D. Gale Johnson, 60pp, 1968, Foreign Policy Association, $.85.* Moderately optimistic assessment of the chances of overcoming world hunger. Compares world population growth and world food production abilities. Argues for a major U.S. contribution to world food and nutritional programs through the UN Food and Agriculture Organization.

74 MEN AGAINST POVERTY: WORLD WAR III, *Arthur Blaustein and Robert Woock (eds.), 456pp, 1968, Random House, $2.45.* Forty widely different views of how men can eliminate poverty. Included are essays which argue alternately that international organizations, revolution, bilateral aid, socialism, capitalism, managerial stability and/or technological development can end poverty.

INF   75 THE ECONOMIC HISTORY OF WORLD POPULATION *by Carlo M. Cipella, 128pp, 1962, Penguin Books, $.95.* For nine-tenths of his existence, man has been a predatory hunter. Cipella explains how the agricultural revolution and the industrial revolution have made possible a better life for a much larger population.

75A PEASANT WARS OF THE TWENTIETH CENTURY *by Eric Wolf, 364pp, 1970, Harper & Row, $4.95.* An anthropolitical study of peasants and their roles in five revolutions: the Mexican, Russian, Chinese, Vietnamese and Cuban.

Paths Toward Modernization

INF   76 THE STAGES OF ECONOMIC GROWTH *by W. W. Rostow, 178pp, 1960, Cambridge University Press, $1.65.* Overview of the pre-conditions needed for take-off into sustained economic growth. Argues for capital accumulation as the crucial factor.

77 THE DYNAMICS OF MODERNIZATION, A Study of Comparative History *by C. E. Black, 253pp, 1966, Harper & Row, $1.60.* Black outlines seven different paths which nations have followed in achieving a modernized economy. He demonstrates that violence is not essential and that instead, violence may retard the accumulation of capital, the emergence of a centralized bureaucracy, modern educational facilities and the sense of common purpose needed for development.

78   SOCIAL ORIGINS OF DEMOCRACY AND DICTATORSHIP *by Barrington Moore, 559pp, 1967, Beacon Press, $2.95.* A comparative study of England, the U.S., India, Russia and Japan which concludes that democratic institutions develop within a social context in which rural elements are either missing or violently eliminated. Moore prefers violence and tyranny (in situations requiring rapid social change) to democratic governments which fail to make needed changes and thus cause greater suffering.

78A   SOCIALISM AND THE FUTURE *by Robert Heilbroner, 11pp, 1969, Commentary, $.50.* Argues that totalitarian socialism is the most humane way to rapidly industrialize a country.

79   THE SPRINGTIME OF FREEDOM *by William McCord, 301pp, 1965, Oxford University Press, $2.25.* The author recognizes the appeal of authoritarian solutions while demonstrating the desirability of rapid economic growth in political freedom. Argues that economic growth and political freedom go best together.

80   ASIAN DRAMA: An Inquiry into the Poverty of Nations *by Gunnar Myrdal, 2,500pp, 1968, Pantheon (three volumes), $10.00.* Critical of Marxist and Keynesian economics, Myrdal offers an in-depth analysis of South Asia's struggle toward modern economic and democratic political institutions. Rejecting a single model as well as many economic concepts derived from Western experience, Myrdal portrays the complexity and the drama of the world's most populous area's attempts to achieve self-sustained economic growth.

81   ECONOMIC BACKWARDNESS AND ECONOMIC GROWTH *by Harvey Leiberstein, 295pp, 1957, John Wiley & Sons, $2.25.* A detailed, often mathematical study, of why economic backwardness exists and how it can be overcome.

82 NATIONALISM IN ASIA AND AFRICA, *Elie Kedourie (ed.), 576pp, 1964, Meridian, $3.95.* Selections by Tom Mboya, Sun Yat-Sen, Damodar Hari Chapekar and others combining nationalism with revolutionary fervor. Illustrates the importance of nationalism in countries to whom nationhood is a new, if not an alien, concept.

83 THE POLITICS OF MODERNIZATION *by David E. Apter, 481pp, 1965, University of Chicago Press, $2.95.* An important study of the modernization process focusing on the formation of political values, professionalism, innovation and ideology.

84 THE IDEOLOGIES OF THE DEVELOPING NATIONS, *Paul Sigmund (ed.), 427pp, 1967, Praeger, $3.95.* An anthology including selections by Nkrumah, Gandhi, Castro and others.

INF 85 THE FUTURE OF THE UNDERDEVELOPED COUNTRIES: Political Implications of Economic Development *by Eugene Staley, 483pp, 1966, Praeger, $3.95.* An important work which relates economic development to political development if growth is to take place in a democratic political context.

86 POLITICS OF THE DEVELOPING NATIONS *by Fred von der Mehden, 140pp, 1969, Prentice-Hall, $1.95.* Treats the effect of nationalistic/tribal, generational, ethnic, religious and economic conflict as it affects political development.

87 ISSUES OF POLITICAL DEVELOPMENT *by Charles W. Anderson, Fred von der Mehdern and Crawood Young, 240pp, 1967, Prentice-Hall, $4.50.* A useful introduction to the difficulties of political development.

88 BLOSSOMS IN THE DUST, The Human Factor in Indian Development *by Kusum Nair, 201pp, 1965, Prae-*

ger, *$2.25*. A study of resistance to change at the village level in India.

89 **THE STRATEGY OF ECONOMIC DEVELOPMENT** *by Albert Hirschman, 217pp, 1966, Yale University Press, $1.45*. Advocates concentrated efforts in one sector of the economy to maximize the speed of over-all economic development. The author served as an economic advisor in Latin America.

90 **DEVELOPMENT PROJECTS OBSERVED** *by Albert Hirschman, 197pp, 1967, Brookings Institute, $2.25*. A study of economic development projects financed by the World Bank which assesses the causes of success or failure in eleven specific projects.

(see also 140, 185, 252, 296, 401 and 518)

U.S. Efforts—Bilateral Aid

91 **THE CASE FOR DEVELOPMENT** *by Charlotte Roe, 8pp, 1967, Committee for World Economic Development and World Disarmament, $.10*. A concise answer to a number of criticisms of the idea that rich nations can and should contribute to the economic development of other nations.

92 **A NEW CONCEPT OF FOREIGN AID** *by Senator J. W. Fulbright, 8pp, 1966, $.10*. The Chairman of the Senate Foreign Relations Committee advocates multi-national consortiums, regional planning conferences and international development programs instead of nation-to-nation programs.

93 **FOREIGN AID AT THE CROSSROADS** *by League of Women Voters, 78pp, 1967, $.75*. An examination of the pro's and con's of foreign aid.

94 **CULTURAL FRONTIERS OF THE PEACE CORPS,** *Robert Textor (ed.), 363pp, 1966, MIT Press, $3.45*. Sixteen essays by social scientists on the Peace Corps in seven countries; the problems and the accomplishments. The concluding essay by the editor is especially valuable.

(see also 210, 211)

International Efforts—Multilateral Aid

95 **THE ABC'S OF INTERNATIONAL DEVELOP-MENT** *by the League of Women Voters, 6pp, 1969, $.30.* A concise but comprehensive guide to international development programs. Identifies different types of aid programs, their successes and limits and assesses the prospect for the Second U.N. Development Decade in the seventies.

96 **THE UNITED NATIONS DEVELOPMENT PRO-GRAM: A Note on the Range and Results of the Activities** *by the United Nations, 16pp, 1968, $.10.*

TEW   97 **U.N. DECADE OF DEVELOPMENT AT MID-POINT** *by U Thant, 44pp, 1966, United Nations, $.30.* An evaluation by the Secretary General of the failures of this international effort.

98 **WORLD DEVELOPMENT, The Challenge to the Churches** *by World Council of Churches, 65pp, 1968, $1.00.* The official report of the Conference on World Cooperation for Development which is offered to the churches by a conference of specialists.

98A **INTERNATIONAL DEVELOPMENT: Challenge to Christians** *by Brian Hull, 93pp, 1970, Lutheran Church in America, $.75.* Arguing against the view that development is just economic growth, the author demonstrates the desirability of multinational intermediaries between the rich nations and the poor.

(One of a series. See also 113A, 172A, 40A)

99 **ACTION TIMES TEN, The United Nations Development Programme** *by Paul Hoffman, 50pp, 1969, United Nations Illustrated, $1.75.* A survey, by its director, of the U.N. Development Decade's accomplishments and limitations.

100 **ADDRESS TO THE BOARD OF GOVERNORS** *by Robert McNamara, 15pp, 1968, free.* The President of the World Bank outlines an enlarged development role for the World Bank.

TEW   101   **THE RECORD AND THE VISION** *by the United Nations Association, 77pp, 1966, United Nations Association, $1.00.* A description of the activities of American voluntary organizations in international development projects.

TEW   102   **THE GLOBAL PARTNERSHIP, International Agencies and Economic Development,** *Richard Gardner and Max Millikan (eds.), 498pp, 1968, Praeger, $3.95.* An anthology which describes both the need for and the growth of international organizations in the field of economic development.

103   **INTERNATIONAL ACTION TO AVERT THE IMPENDING PROTEIN CRISIS,** *a report submitted to the United Nations Economic and Social Council, 106pp, 1968, United Nations, $1.50.* This report describes the growing gap between food production and population growth and offers fourteen specific proposals for international action to overcome the problem.

103A   **PARTNERS IN DEVELOPMENT—Report of the Commission on International Development,** *Lester Pearson, chairman, 402pp, 1969, Praeger, $2.95.* A former Canadian Prime Minister, Pearson argues that the fate of the world community depends upon reversing the world-wide trend toward declining foreign aid appropriations. Advocates increased utilization of international organizations to foster development.

104   **UNITED NATIONS COMMITTEE ON TRADE AND DEVELOPMENT: North-South Encounter** *by Bronislav Gosavic, 80pp, 1968, Carnegie Endowment, $.60.* Describes the efforts since 1964 of UNCTAD, a committee set up by predominantly underdeveloped countries to help international trade and enhance development programs.

(see also 144, 145, 153, 219, 225 and 391)

Population

105   **READINGS ON POPULATION,** *David Heer (ed.), 234pp, 1968, Prentice-Hall, $3.95.* An excellent anthology

which discusses the origins of the current dramatic population growth, theories about its causes and alternative ways of limiting it.

106 POPULATION, The Vital Revolution, *Ronald Friedman (ed.), 274pp, 1964, Doubleday, $1.25.* An anthology of articles which examine the effect of population growth on economic development.

106A WHO SHALL LIVE?, Man's Control Over Birth and Death *144pp, 1970, Hill & Wang, $1.75.* An American Friends Service Committee working party examines the full range of ethical issues involved: abortion, contraception, euthanasia, population policy, acclimating traditional Quaker testimonies to contemporary liberal thought.

107 THE POPULATION BOMB *by Paul Ehrlich, 222pp, 1968, Ballantine Books, $.95.* Ehrlich argues that the population explosion will lead to global famines, wars, starvation and 500 million deaths in the 1970's. The author concedes he may have overstated the case for population control.

107A SEEDS OF CHANGE, The Green Revolution and Development in the 1970's *by Lester Brown, 224pp, 1970, Praeger, $2.50.* The author argues that new strains of wheat and "miracle rice," provide the essential weapons to win the world war on hunger in the 1970's. He considers the political problems in doing so, and speculates whether new discoveries will widen or close the gap between the rich nations and the poor.

(see also 389-391)

Human Rights

TEW 108 UNIVERSAL DECLARATION OF HUMAN RIGHTS *by the United Nations, 6pp, $.02.* Text of the convention adopted in 1948.

109 HUMAN RIGHTS AND THE INTERNATIONAL COMMUNITY, The Roots and Growth of the Universal Declaration of Human Rights, 1948–1963 *by Egon Schwolb, 96pp, 1964, Anti-Defamation League, $1.45.* A study of the human rights which all United Nations members are committed to and which they ought to respect.

110   **THE KEY TO HUMAN RIGHTS: Implementation** *by William Korey, 70pp, 1969, Carnegie Endowment, $.60.* Asserting that "international law on human rights" as elaborated by the (U.N.) Charter, the Declaration of Human Rights and now the Covenants, has been clearly defined, the author "looks forward to the development of international institutions which can implement them."

111   **HUMAN RIGHTS AND FUNDAMENTAL FREEDOMS IN YOUR COMMUNITY** *by Stanley Stuber, 128pp, 1968, Association Press, $.95.* An attempt to state concretely what individuals in local communities can do to implement the provisions of the Universal Declaration of Human Rights.

TEW   112   **WORLD HABEAS CORPUS** *by Luis Kutner, 295pp, 1962, Oceana, hardcover, $7.50.* Argues the need for making *habeas corpus* guarantees world-wide. The author advocates setting up supranational courts to which any individual might appeal to force a government to show due cause for his imprisonment.

(see also 56, 171 and 178)

Toward a World Community

113   **THE FAMILY OF MAN**, *Edward Steichen, 192pp, 1955, New American Library, $2.25.* A remarkable photographic portrayal of things which all men, despite every diversity, share: birth, childhood, love, growing old, death, fear of war, hope, wonder, joy.

113A   **WORLD COMMUNITY: Challenge and Opportunity** *by Richard Niebanck, 74pp, 1970, Lutheran Church in America, $.75.* An extremely well thought-out and ably presented analysis of the necessary components of a developing world community: economic and social development, disarmament, confronting global environmental problems, achieving some form of world law, including enforcement of human rights . . . and peace. (One of a series. See also 172A, 40A, 98A)

114 LANDMARKS IN INTERNATIONAL CO-OPER-ATION, *Office of Public Information, 133pp, 1965, United Nations, hardcover, $3.00.* Describes the functioning of various United Nations organizations in achieving international cooperation. Covered are the fields of world health programs, economic development programs, communication, education and international law.

115 PROPAGANDA, Toward Disarmament in the War of Words *by John B. Whitten and Arthur Larson, 304pp, 1964, Oceana, hardcover, $8.50.* Arguing that propaganda is a threat to peace, the authors argue for bilateral or multilateral treaties to secure the right to reply and freedom of information. Also advocates a United Nations Broadcasting Service.

116 INTERDEPENDENCE ON A SMALL PLANET *by Emile Benoit, 18pp, 1966, Columbia Journal of World Business, $.15.* An examination of the emergent world economy and the consequences posed for national economic policies.

117 PROBLEMS OF THE WORLD ECONOMY *by Richard Bailey, 201pp, 1968, Penguin Books, $.95.* A study of the economic interdependence of nations which emphasizes the impact of technology.

118 RESHAPING THE WORLD ECONOMY, Rich Countries and Poor, *John A. Pincus (ed.), 176pp, 1968, Prentice-Hall, $1.95.* An excellent anthology of writing on population, development, foreign aid, interdependence and trade. Essays by Barbara Ward, Gunnar Myrdal, Milton Friedman and others.

119 DISARMAMENT AND WORLD ECONOMIC IN-TERDEPENDENCE, *Emile Benoit (ed.), 260pp, 1967, Columbia University Press, hardcover, $8.00.* A study relating disarmament and world economic interdependence which argues that closing the gap between the rich nations and the poor is essential if a sense of world community is to be achieved.

120   WAR AND PEACE IN THE GLOBAL VILLAGE *by Marshall McLuhan, 196pp, 1968, Bantam Books, $1.45.* McLuhan argues that communication media have turned the world's nation states into a global village by forcing them to interact intimately every day.

121   ALLIANCES AND THE THIRD WORLD *by George Liska, 61pp, 1968, Johns Hopkins Press, $1.75.* A study of the less-developed nations in world affairs and the role of regional and sub-regional alliance between small powers. The author concludes that such alliances have functioned usefully as institutional stabilizers of political behavior.

121A   A FAMILY OF NATIONS, *James Rausch (ed.), 144pp, 1970, Ohio State University Press, $1.25.* Prepared by the U.S. Catholic Conference, Division of World Justice and Peace; an anthology, examining the culture of nation-states which now make up the world community.

122   INTERNATIONAL POLITICAL COMMUNITIES, *512pp, 1966, Doubleday, $1.95.* An anthology of essays on the problems and prospects of existing regional and world organizations which are made up of sovereign nation-states yet designed to regulate relations between them.

INF   **123   THE MAKING OF THE MODERN WORLD** *by Joel Colton and R. R. Palmer, 996pp, 1965, Knopf, hardcover, $12.95.* A standard history text which argues that we are now witnessing the Europeanization of the globe, although the process of global unification is a reciprocal one.

124   THE MOST PROBABLE WORLD *by Stuart Chase, 239pp, 1968, Penguin Books, $1.45.* Extends the trend lines of technological development, urbanization, energy storage and utilization, and world interdependence into a forecast of a likely world government by . . . ?

125 **PAST AND FUTURE** *by William H. McNeil, 217pp, 1954, University of Chicago Press, $1.75.* A study of the effect of war upon human history and an analysis of the current world situation.

126 **THE RISE OF THE WEST, A History of the Human Community** *by William McNeil, 896pp, 1963, Mentor Books, $1.65.* A history of the world drawing on the contribution of all of the world's cultures to the world community.

127 **HISTORY OF MANKIND, CULTURAL AND SCIENTIFIC DEVELOPMENT** by UNESCO Vol. 1, part 1, **PREHISTORY** *by Jacquetta Hawkes, 873pp, 1965, Mentor Books, $1.25.* Vol. 1, part 2, **THE BEGINNINGS OF CIVILIZATION** *by Leonard Woolley, 636pp, 1965, Mentor Books, $1.25.* The first two volumes of UNESCO's history of mankind, pointing out man's antiquity, the rarity that is civilized life, and the common heritage of today's world population.

128 **NATIONALISM AND IDEOLOGY** *by Barbara Ward, 124pp, 1966, Norton, $1.25.* The last fifty years have witnessed the change of every major institution save one—the nation-state. The author considers nationalism in an era of international ideologies and argues for a belief in man as the basis of a world society.

129 **THE LOPSIDED WORLD** *by Barbara Ward, 126pp, 1968, Norton, $1.25.* Ward describes the growing disparity between the rich nations of the world and the poor and calls for an energetic program of foreign aid designed to meet the problem of economic deprivation. She sees such a program as a just response to an economically, religiously and socially interdependent world.

TEW 130 **DYNAMICS OF WORLD POLITICS, Studies in the Resolution of Conflict** *by Linda Miller, 294pp, 1968, Prentice-Hall, $3.95.* A study of the relationship of conflict resolution to the development of a sense of world community.

TEW   131   **BLUEPRINT FOR PEACE**, *Richard Gardner (ed.), 404pp, 1966, McGraw-Hill, $2.95.* Reports of the White House Conference on International Cooperation in twenty subject areas. The proposals for initiative acts the U.S. could take make this a particularly valuable anthology for those who wish the U.S. to lead in building a sense of world community.

(see also 26, 378, 381, 399, 425, 504, 533 and 557)

IV INTERNATIONAL ORGANIZATION AND WORLD LAW

Wars between groups of men forming social units always take place when these units—tribes, dynasties, churches, cities, nations—exercise unrestricted sovereign power.

Wars between these social units cease the moment sovereign power is transferred from them to a larger or higher unit.

These statements by Emery Reves succinctly capture one view of the cause of war and point to one way of eliminating it. His belief that an overarching authority is essential to keep sovereign social units from warring has a long history. Pierre Dubois (1307), Dante Alighieri (1309), Erasmus (1517), Sully (1595), Emeric Crucé (1623), William Penn (1693), Hugo Grotius (1625), Abbe de Saint-Pierre (1716), Jean-Jacques Rousseau (1761) and Immanuel Kant (1795) each developed in their own way the idea of international law, binding arbitration between nation-states, supranational authority or world government. Studying the fate of their early plans for peace is a sobering experience. The history of the Hague Conference agreements, the League of Nations and our current experience with the International Court of Justice and the United Nations are not much more encouraging.

Given this history of international organizations many conclude that achieving world peace through world law is no more than an enduring illusion. Advocates of world law respond by pointing out that while the U.N. had failed to resolve conflicts between the superpowers, it was not given the power to do so. In lesser conflicts, such as Iran (1946), Indonesia (1947), Suez (1956) and Cyprus (1968) the U.N. aided significantly in the nonviolent resolution of conflict. In addition, the U.N. has served as a forum for clarification of objectives and goals and its functional agencies have a long list of impressive achievements. Accepting the need for strengthening international institutions into instruments of world law, advocates chart at least five different ways of doing so: 1) by developing regional and functional international institutions; 2) by nation-states changing their approach to the present United Nations; 3) through United Nations Charter revision; 4) by creating under treaty a new world organization in cooperation with the U.N. and 5) through a world constitutional convention.

Those supporting these views base their case on more than peace plans and the urgent world need for supranational authority. They see in thermonuclear weapons and today's increasingly interdependent world the previously missing requisites for world organization. As evidence that the world is becoming increasingly interrelated, they point to the emergence of an international or world economy (# 118), to the creation of common bureaucratic forms of organization (# 117, to the increase in world travel and communications (# 114), to the formation of international military alliances and to world health and environmental needs. One indication of this interrelatedness is the system of rules, precedents and obligations now being enlarged through cases carried to the International Court of Justice and other tribunals. The slow development of international law and of widespread support for its operation, say some, is the best way to achieve legal and political structures capable of resolving international conflict without violence. Another indication of interrelatedness is the many functional and regional organizations which have been organized to meet common problems. The development of these international organizations in the past thirty years is unprecedented in the number of people and units involved and in the variety of functions performed. Among the regional organizations are the European Economic Community, the Organization of American States and the Latin American Free Trade Association. Among the functional organizations are The World Meteorological Organization, World Health Organization, the International Bank for Reconstruction and Development and the United Nations Development Program.

Skeptics reply by pointing out that the world's interrelatedness makes world wars as well as world law possible. Meeting functional needs, changing administrative arrangements, developing regional organizations—none of these directly confront the problem of war.

REGIONAL AND FUNCTIONAL INTERNATIONAL ORGANIZATIONS

Advocates of strengthening international institutions and world law differ in their response to the skeptics' doubts. Some reply by pointing to the practical needs of the world which offer the most likely ground on which to form new international and in some cases supranational communities. Others point to the danger of war, which, they argue, necessitates world law and world government.

For those advocating a focus on common needs, the problem is not obtaining structural changes in legal and political organizations like the United Nations or the International Court of Justice, but developing a sense of world community that is the essential prerequisite to any such change. By *sense of community* they mean the expectation across national and ideological barriers that common problems will be resolved by peaceful processes. The best way to encourage the development of a sense of community is, in their view, to focus on functional needs (e.g., the coordination of air transportation) not war/peace questions.

Others place their hopes on organization among nations in geographical proximity. Sometimes regional ties are sufficiently strong because of historical experiences, common cultures or common needs to make regional organization feasible. For example, a number of European international institutions have been organized in the last twenty-five years and a little progress has been made toward uniting Western Europe under one supranational authority (# 233).

Thus, the way to achieve world law, those now advocating regional or functional approaches say, is to demonstrate the effectiveness of international organizations in areas where there are recognized, practical needs and/or already existing political communities.

Many who reject the view that world peace through world law is possible agree that functional and regional international organizations can operate effectively if they are consistent with national self-interest. But the core reality of modern political life, such skeptics argue, is psychological loyalty to the nation-state. That fact, plus today's deep ideological divisions and conflicts of interest, make any voluntary yielding of sovereignty to a body capable of enforcing world law extremely unlikely. They go on to argue that nationalism, a growing force in Asia, Africa and Latin America, is stronger than ideological commitments or economic interests. The skeptics conclude that world law and world government, although a logical way to avoid nuclear war, remain under present conditions what they have always been: a dream. The pre-condition for avoiding war today is a realistic assessment of national interest, not the creation of external controls. Some form of balance of power between nation-states, they say, is our best hope for peace (# 143).

Still, even those advocating national-interest diplomacy support international organizations of some kind. The point of division with those committed to world law comes in differing estimates of how interrelated the world now is and in disagreement over what level of community is necessary before world organization becomes possible.

WORLD LAW: THE U.N., CHARTER REVISION AND CONSTITUTIONAL CONVENTION APPROACHES

The slow process of creating a sense of world community through functional or regional international organizations elicits only moderate excitement from those who see the potential destruction of mankind as the overriding issue. However little we may be interrelated in some ways, however different men, creeds and loyalties may be today, proponents of world law argue, mankind acquired a common enemy August 6, 1945. They nevertheless disagree about what new kinds of institutions are necessitated by the threat of nuclear war.

Proponents of achieving world law within the presently constituted United Nations argue that the key to effective international institutions is great power agreement. When the great powers agree, the United Nations is effective; when they do not, any international organization powerful enough to stand in their way would probably do more harm than good. They would thus prefer to work within the existing U.N. framework, seeking to obtain public support in all countries for voluntary cooperation through the United Nations.

Advocates of a World Constitutional Convention argue that the world is interrelated enough now to sustain a world government and that it is national governments, not people, that hinder the expression of an existent sense of world community. They do not favor working through the United Nations because it is composed of national governments and because they agree with the skeptics' central charge: no nation-state can be expected to yield voluntarily the necessary portion of its sovereignty or voluntarily accept international decisions when they violate national self-interest. Constitutionalists point to the failure to implement the U.N. Charter's provisions for reorganization, to the adoption by the United States of the Connally Reservation which limits the jurisdiction of the International Court of Justice and to the refusal of the U.S.S.R. and other powers to grant any degree of compulsory jurisdiction to the World International Court of Justice (# 141). These proponents of world law conclude that what is needed is not strengthened international institutions but new world institutions. They would achieve world law through a world constitutional convention which would draft a constitution for the world (e.g., # 188) and then present it to people within various nation-states. While national governments would be called upon to send delegates to the convention, the World Constitutionalists are prepared to operate independently of national governments if necessary. In this way, they hope to achieve a world government representing people, not nation-states. They find a precedent in the convention that drafted the U.S. Constitution which begins "We the people. . ." not "We the states. . . ."

Advocates of world law who reject this approach point out the difficulty of securing ratification of such a constitution, particularly since there are many different types of government, most non-democratic, and each would have to approve of a political process which could end in a decrease in their powers. They argue that the world cannot wait until every nation-state permits its citizens to choose a form of government. Instead, they advocate some form of world federalism which they hold is possible today. For World Federalists, the problem of achieving world law is one of persuading national governments that it is in their self-interest to yield a portion of this sovereignty to supranational institutions. They argue that the problem is not to challenge people's national identity but to persuade them to add a new political identity— world citizen. Grenville Clark and Louis Sohn's *World Peace through World Law* (# 184) has been a basic text of this movement. Clark and Sohn advocate achieving world law either by revising the United Nations Charter or by creating, in cooperation with the United Nations, a World Disarmament and World Economic Development Organization which would be capable of binding arbitration in international disputes involving the use of violence.

Although it is true that the history of past peace plans has been one of failure and although it is true that there are enormous problems in achieving world law, we nevertheless recognize today that the absence of effective international institutions is a prime cause of war. Such institutions are now coming into existence. The possible rewards for those who solve the problems in achieving world law are eloquently stated as the goals of the United Nations:

1) To save succeeding generations from the scourge of war.

2) To reaffirm faith in fundamental human rights.

3) To establish conditions under which justice and respect for the obligations arising from treaties and other sources of international law can be maintained.

4) To promote social progress and better standards of life in larger freedom.

The books in this chapter examine the many existing international organizations, their functions and operating experience and their limitations. An extensive list of works on international intervention and mediation is included, as are books on regional organization and world law. Books describing the alternative paths to the World Federalists' and World Constitutionalists' goal conclude this chapter's bibliography.

General Surveys of the Field

132 WORLD WAR OR WORLD LAW? *16pp, 1966, $.15*. A variety of approaches to achieving world law presented pictographically.

133 PEACEFUL SETTLEMENT AND THE COLD WAR *by Daniel Partan, 46pp, 1965, Duke Rule of Law Research Center, $.25*. Outlines the capabilities of present international institutions and the need for new structures capable of responding to different types of conflict.

INT   134 PEACE, the Control of National Power *by Phillip Van Slyck, 186pp, 1963, Beacon Press, $1.75*. A carefully ordered seminar on the fundamental problems of achieving world order. Reading assignments are from Clark and Sohn, *World Peace through World Law* (# 184) and *Legal and Political Problems of World Order* (# 135). An excellent introduction to problems of world law and world government.

135 LEGAL AND POLITICAL PROBLEMS OF WORLD ORDER, *Saul Mendlovitz (ed.), 822pp, 1962, World Law Fund, $2.25.* An anthology of articles on the basic problems.

TEW **136 THE STRATEGY OF WORLD ORDER,** *Richard Falk and Saul Mendlovitz (eds.), 2,298pp, 1966, World Law Fund, (Volumes I–IV), $10.00.* A projected six-volume set which attempts to develop an academic discipline oriented toward the principal policy question of our times: achieving world order. Each volume is an anthology of carefully selected material, with connecting notes and discussion questions appended to each article. Volume I presents the plan of this systematic study and gathers articles on the various theoretical problems involved in the prevention of war. The subject matter and some of the authors of each volume are given below. The first four volumes comprise a set.

137 Volume I, **TOWARD A THEORY OF WAR PRE-VENTION** *394pp, 1966, World Law Fund, $2.50.* Selections by Kenneth Boulding, Herman Kahn, Quincy Wright, Harold Lasswell and others. Notes, discussion questions and suggested readings follow each article. The editors' strong guiding hand makes each of these volumes a college course in itself, not just an anthology.

138 Volume II, **INTERNATIONAL LAW** *382pp, 1966, World Law Fund, $2.50.* Selections by Falk and Mendlovitz, Louis Henkin, Inis Claude, Stanley Hoffman and others.

139 Volume III, **THE UNITED NATIONS** *848pp, 1966, World Law Fund, $3.50.* Selections on the League of Nations, the International Court of Justice, peace-keeping, financing and proposals for a world police force.

140 Volume IV, **DISARMAMENT AND ECONOMIC DEVELOPMENT** *672pp, 1966, World Law Fund, $3.50.*

Articles by Jerome Wesner, Thomas Schelling, Charles Osgood, Richard Barnet, Emile Benoit, U Thant and others.

141 **WHEN NATIONS DISAGREE** *by Arthur Larson, 251pp, 1961, University of Louisiana Press, hardcover, $5.00.* A useful introduction to the argument for building world peace through world law.

142 **THE INSECURITY OF NATIONS** *by Charles Yost, 272pp, 1968, Praeger, $2.75.* Nixon's Ambassador to the U.N. argues the same case as Larson: "There will never be security for nations and peoples until there exists some impartial and effective international authority."

INF 143 **POLITICS AMONG NATIONS, The Struggle for Power and Peace** *by Hans J. Morgenthau, 615pp, 1967, (fourth edition), Knopf, $11.25.* The basic text in the field which states the case for a realistic assessment of the national interest (as opposed to moralistic or legalistic concerns) as the best guide to formulation of foreign policy. Morgenthau considers the development of supranational authorities consistent with the national interest.

144 **THE QUEST FOR PEACE,** *Andrew Cordier and Wilbur Foote (eds.), 390pp, 1965, Columbia University Press, $2.95.* Twenty-four lectures in memory of Dag Hammarskjold by Adlai Stevenson, Dean Rusk, Lester Pearson, Barbara Ward and others. The lectures consider the role of the United Nations in peace-keeping and in addressing the economic and human problems of new and developing nations.

145 **PATHS TO WORLD ORDER,** *Andrew Cordier and Kenneth Maxwell (eds.), 161pp, 1967, Columbia University Press, $1.75.* Another anthology with an especially useful essay on Dag Hammarskjold's development of the office of U.N. Secretary-General.

146 **QUESTIONS AND ANSWERS ABOUT THE WORLD COURT** *by Arthur Larson, 60pp, 1965, Duke Rule of Law Research Center, $.25.* The Chairman of Duke University's Rule of Law Research Center relieves many

fears by succinct, knowledgeable answers to questions raised about the role and powers of the world court.

146A THE FUTURE OF THE INTERNATIONAL LEGAL ORDER, Volume I, **Trends and Patterns**, *Richard Falk and C. E. Black (eds.), 618pp, 1969, Princeton University Press, hardcover, $15.00.* A multi-volume enterprise, this initial volume assesses the state of international law today.

147 THE MAZE OF PEACE, Conflict and Reconciliation Among Nations, *Alan Geyer (ed.), 128pp, 1968, Friendship Press, $1.45.* Geyer, editor of *The Christian Century*, and three others provide guidelines for Christians as they think through their obligations concerning war, violence and reconciliation, as set in the framework of achieving world law.

(see also 130, 131, 206, 314, 364, 494, 590, 592, 593 and 595)

Regional International Institutions

148 REGIONAL ENFORCEMENT MEASURES AND THE UNITED NATIONS *by John Halderman, 29pp, 1963, Duke Rule of Law Research Center, $.25.* Outlines the reciprocal relationship between regional and United Nations means of arbitrating disputes.

149 THE DEVELOPMENT OF INTERNATIONAL LAW BY THE INTERNATIONAL LABOR ORGANIZATION *by Daniel Partan, 29pp, 1965, Duke Rule of Law Research Center, $.25.* A study of the impact over the last fifty years of one international organization.

150 BEYOND THE NATION STATE, Functionalism and International Organization *by Ernst Haas, 586pp, 1968, Stanford University Press, $3.85.* An argument for a functional approach to strengthened international organization; includes a case study of the International Labor Organization.

151 THE EVOLUTION OF INTERNATIONAL ORGANIZATIONS, *Evan Luard (ed.), 334pp, 1967, Praeger,*

$2.95. Examines the development of the United Nations, the European Economic Community, the International Monetary Fund and other international organizations.

151A SEARCH FOR PEACE: Readings in International Relations, *David Brook (ed.), 425pp, 1970, Dodd-Mead, $4.95.* Surveys the possibilities of a world order; discusses the basic concepts and problem areas.

152 A WORKING PEACE SYSTEM *by David Miltrany, 221pp, 1966, Quadrangle, $2.25.* A functional analysis of regional international institutions. Introduced by Hans Morgenthau.

153 INTERNATIONAL REGIONALISM, *Joseph Nye, Jr. (ed.), 432pp, 1968, Little, Brown, $4.50.* An anthology discussing regional international organizations and internal conflict, economic development and world order. Selections by David Miltrany, Henry Kissinger, Linda Miller, Ernst Haas, Stanley Hoffmann and others.

(see also 122, 230-233, 243 and 587)

International Intervention and Mediation

INT   154   **TO KEEP THE PEACE, The United Nations Peace Force** *by Geoffrey Carnall, 20pp, 1965, Housmans, $.25.* A critical analysis of past operations by an individual who advocates a permanent United Nations peace force.

TEW   155   **A UNITED NATIONS PEACE FORCE** *by William Fyre, 227pp, 1960, Oceana, hardcover, $5.00.* The best introduction to the need for and difficulties in achieving and maintaining a United Nations peace force.

INF   156   **CONTROLLING CONFLICTS IN THE 1970'S,** *United Nations Association, 59pp, 1969, United Nations Association, $1.00.* A prestigious panel of U.S. experts recommends the establishment of a permanent U.N. peace-keeping force, and also discusses financing, control, maintenance and training of such a force.

157   **PEACEKEEPING: 1969, A Survey and Evaluation Prepared for Friends Peace Committee (Quakers)** *by*

Charles Walker, 28pp, 1969, Friends Peace Committee, *$.30.* Surveys the renewed interest in U.N. peace-keeping machinery and describes proposals for a World University to train an international civil service. Advocates steps toward the formation of an alliance of disarmed nations, "willing on invitation to undertake peace-keeping assignments" of a nonmilitary nature and the revitalization of the World Peace Brigade, an international team trained in nonviolence, specializing in nonviolent conflict resolution.

158 **THE UNITED NATIONS AND THE USE OF FORCE** *by Claude Inis, Jr., 59pp, 1961, Carnegie Endowment, $.60.* A careful, concise analysis of the issues involved in U.N.'s use of military force.

159 **THE DOCTRINE OF THE OUTLAWRY OF WAR** *by N. K. Nawaz, 33pp, 1964, Duke Rule of Law Research Center, $.25.* A historical overview which includes modern cases of national intervention (Hungary, Cuba), concluding with an examination of the role of international law in outlawing war.

160 **SYNOPSES OF UNITED NATIONS CASES IN THE FIELD OF PEACE AND SECURITY,** *Catherine Teng (ed.), 294pp, 1969 Carnegie Endowment, $1.50.* Concisely outlines each U.N. involvement in world crises: covers duration, issues, U.N. objectives and results.

161 **THE UNITED NATIONS EMERGENCY FORCE** *by Gabriella Rosner, 294pp, 1963, Columbia University Press, hardcover, $7.50.* A comprehensive analysis of the United Nations Suez Operation: political background, the legal basis for the peace-keeping force, and organizational problems in mounting the operation.

162 **TO KATANGA AND BACK** *by Conor Cruise O'Brien, 352pp, 1966, Universal, $2.45.* A condemnation of the United Nation's operation in the Congo by a participant observer.

163 **THE INTERMEDIARIES, Third Parties in International Crisis** *by Oran Young, 427pp, 1967, Princeton University Press, hardcover, $10.00.* Analysis of the forces

which influence the chances of success when third parties attempt to end or prevent violent international conflict.

164   WORLD ORDER AND LOCAL DISORDER *by Linda Miller, 235pp, 1967, Princeton University Press, hardcover, $6.50.* Analysis of the role the United Nations has played and failed to play in internal wars.

165   THE U.N. SECRETARY-GENERAL AND THE MAINTENANCE OF PEACE *by Leon Gordenker, 380pp, 1967, Columbia University Press, hardcover, $8.50.* A study of the U.N. Secretariat showing how Trygve Lie, Dag Hammarskjold and U Thant have conceived the role of the Secretary-General.

166   INTERNATIONAL MILITARY FORCES *by Lincoln Bloomfield, 296pp, 1964, Little, Brown, $2.50.* A study of past and present international military forces which draws lessons from the Congo and Suez operations. Bloomfield proposes the establishment of a permanent U.N. peace-keeping force and discusses the problems of maintaining such a force.

166A   CONTROLLING SMALL WARS: A Strategy for the 1970's *by Lincoln Bloomfield and Amelia Leiss, 421pp, 1969, Knopf, hardcover, $8.95.* An assessment of the possibilities and limitation of international intervention to end civil or regional wars. A valuable study.

167   BIBLIOGRAPHY ON PEACE-KEEPING *by Albert Legault, 302pp, 1967, $5.00.* An excellent bibliography with detailed annotations.

(see also 61)

The United Nations

INT   168   BASIC FACTS ABOUT THE UNITED NATIONS *by the United Nations, 52pp, 1968, $.35.* A description of the U.N. structure, membership, committees and activities.

INT   169   QUESTIONS AND ANSWERS ABOUT THE UNITED NATIONS *by Arthur Larson, 61pp, 1969,*

Duke Rule of Law Research Center, $.25. Written, as was # 146, to meet the attacks that are so often based on misinformation or misunderstanding. Valuable in itself for its succinct presentation of the nature, organization, operation, utility and limits of the U.N.

170 CHARTER OF THE UNITED NATIONS AND STATUTE OF THE INTERNATIONAL COURT OF JUSTICE *by the United Nations, 85pp, 1968, United Nations, $.50.* The preamble of the charter outlines the purposes of the U.N., among them to "rid mankind from the scourge of war forever."

171 BASIC DOCUMENTS OF THE UNITED NATIONS, *Louis Sohn (ed.), 329pp, 1968, Foundation Press, $5.00.* A compilation of basic United Nations documents, including the texts of the covenants on human rights.

172 THIRD CONFERENCE ON THE UNITED NATIONS OF THE NEXT DECADE, A Report, *26pp, 1968, Stanley Foundation, $.10.* Sponsored by the Stanley Foundation, this conference included representatives from Yugoslavia, Pakistan, Iraq, U.S., U.S.S.R. and other countries. The joint statement issued at the end of the conference calls for strengthening the U.N.

172A INTERNATIONAL LAW AND INSTITUTIONS: Some Current Problems by Christopher Herman, *63pp, 1970, Lutheran Church in America, $.75.* Focusing on the U.N., the author points to the success of its functional agencies as demonstrating a feasible approach to the development of world institutions.

(see also 113A, 40A, 98A)

173 INTRODUCTION TO THE ANNUAL REPORT OF THE SECRETARY GENERAL, 15 June 1967 *by U Thant, 48pp, 1968, United Nations, $.50.* A cogent and realistic assessment by the Secretary-General of the current international situation and the relevance of the U.N. to a world in crisis.

174 THE UNITED NATIONS IN THE BALANCE, A Critical Evaluation of the First 20 years, *Leland Goodrich* *and Norman Padelford (eds.), 481pp, 1965, Praeger, $2.45.* An anthology of views, some sharply critical, some favorable, of the operations of the U.N.

175 EVERYMAN'S UNITED NATIONS, A Complete Handbook of the Activities and Evolution of the United Nations During Its First Twenty Years *by the United Nations, 634pp, 1968, United Nations, $2.50.* An excellent source.

176 THE UNITED NATIONS, A Short Political Guide *by Sidney Bailey, 141pp, 1965, Praeger, $1.75.* An introduction to the politics of the world body.

177 THE UNITED NATIONS AND THE RULE OF LAW *by John Halderman, 248pp, 1966, Oceana, hardcover, $7.50.* An analysis of how the rule of law in world affairs can be developed through the United Nations with particular reference to the handling of specific past controversies such as the Suez and Congo crises.

178 ISSUES BEFORE THE 25TH GENERAL ASSEMBLY, *Anne Winslow (ed.), 199pp, 1970, Carnegie Endowment, $1.25.* Annual survey of the vital issues facing the current General Assembly: peace-keeping activities, seating of Communist China, Decade of Development, and U.N. work to improve health, education and the achievement of human rights.

179 THE UNITED NATIONS AND THE SUPERPOWERS *by John Stoessinger, 210pp, 1970, Random House, $1.95.* Discusses the interaction of the U.S. and the U.S.S.R. in the United Nations and the effect of the superpowers on the organization, its peace, security, economic and social operations.

180 VETO IN THE SECURITY COUNCIL *by Sidney Bailey, 66pp, 1969, Carnegie Endowment, $.60.* This issue of *International Conciliation,* one of a series of highly expert studies in building international peace, examines the use and abuse of the veto by the superpowers.

181 THE UN AT TWENTY-FIVE, A Handbook for the Anniversary Year 1970, *Virginia Saurwein (ed.), 68pp,*

1969, Center for War/Peace Studies, $1.50. Includes a basic introduction to the United Nations, the role of the superpowers and the developing nations, provisions for charter revision, initiative acts by the U.S., the function of supporting voluntary organizations in U.N. work and resources.

(see also 42, 73, 95-97, 99, 102-104, 108, 115, 241, 266, 267, 295, 305, 320 and 638)

Charter Revision—World Federalism

182 **THE FEDERALIST PAPERS** *by Alexander Hamilton, James Madison and John Jay, 559pp, 1961, New American Library, $.75.* In another setting, three experts on government consider the problems of federalism: How to resolve conflicting, often hostile interest, without violence? What is the relationship between the size of a territory and the type of government? How can the consent of the governed be achieved and once achieved, continually reassessed? How can liberty be defended and territorial integrity preserved?

TEW   183 **INTRODUCTION TO WORLD PEACE THROUGH WORLD LAW** *by Grenville Clark and Louis Sohn, 52pp, 1966, World Law Fund, $.50.* This introduction to the text details how U.N. charter revision could make the U.N. an agency capable of making and enforcing world law in carefully limited areas.

TEW   184 **WORLD PEACE THROUGH WORLD LAW** *by Grenville Clark and Louis Sohn, 535pp, 1966, Harvard University Press, hardcover, $8.50; paper, $2.50.* This is the most thorough and detailed attempt to make the case for world law and to specify with great care the alternative roads to achieving world law. Considers systematically the spectrum of political, military, economic and legal problems involved. Argues for two possible routes: U.N. charter revision or a treaty on world disarmament and world development growing out of the United Nations.

185 TOWARDS A GLOBAL FEDERALISM *by William O. Douglas, 177pp, 1968, New York University Press, hardcover, $7.95.* A Supreme Court Justice makes the case for a supranational authority capable of making the arbitration of disputes between nation-states binding. Douglas considers world federalism an indispensable part of safeguarding and extending human rights, not a detriment to them. The advantages of world federalism for economic development are carefully considered.

World Constitutional Convention

186 OUTLINES OF A WORLD CONSTITUTION AND HUMAN RIGHTS IN A WORLD FEDERATION *by Thomas Breitner, 8pp, 1967, $.10.* Concise attempt to outline a constitution for a world federation capable of replacing war by laws which guarantee the rights of the individual, as articulated in the Bill of Rights and the Universal Declaration of Human Rights.

187 WORRIED WOMAN'S GUIDE TO WORLD PEACE THROUGH WORLD LAW, *Lucile Green and Esther Yudell (eds.), 100pp, 1966, $1.00.* Five different approaches to achieving world law: U.N. Charter revision, a new U.N. charter, agreement among nation-states, imposition of a new charter by a superpower or a world constitutional convention. The editors favor the last method.

TEW   **188 A CONSTITUTION FOR THE WORLD,** *Elizabeth Mann Borgese (ed.), 112pp, 1965, Center for the Study of Democratic Institutions, $1.00.* An attempt to accomplish the difficult task of formulating a constitution which would eliminate war, and establish the preconditions of justice. Originally drafted in 1948 by a committee headed by Robert Hutchins and including Rexford Tugwell, Stringfellow Barr, Mortimer Adler and others, this constitution is still a model to be improved upon.

This essay is written as we enter the 1970's. Just ten years ago the Senate Committee on Foreign Relations commissioned thirteen major reports on U.S. Foreign Policy. No more systematic or far-reaching foreign policy research effort had ever been undertaken by the Congress. All the reports on the basic aims of U.S. foreign policy—and their application to Asia, Africa, Europe, weapons technology, international organizations, etc.—agreed that the United States "can exert a major influence on the events of the next decade." By 1963 the United States was formally committed to these goals:

1) Universal and complete disarmament under international controls;

2) Strengthening the United Nations and its agencies into instruments of world law;

3) Economic and other assistance for Africa, Asia and Latin American countries in their revolution of modernization;

4) Communication, exchange and peaceful settlement with the Communist world so that those countries will join us in pursuing these goals.

These statements in the 1963 State Department Citizens' Report reflected, eighteen years later, the priority of purpose Hiroshima and Nagasaki taught the American people.

A very different situation now prevails. Popular books on foreign policy problems bear titles like *The Limits of Intervention,* and *Power and Impotence, the failure of U.S. Foreign Policy* (# 119). The chairman of the Senate Foreign Relations Committee himself titled his book on U.S. foreign policy *The Arrogance of Power* (# 225). These books teach what may be alternatively described as a general lowering of goals, or a more modest and realistic approach to world affairs. The term "national priorities" is encountered everywhere today even in the titles of peace organizations. The priorities envisioned are usually domestic, not those requisite to ending war.

In this climate the first problem in the argument over U.S. foreign policy involves alternate goal conceptions and therefore differing views of the proper level of American engagement in world affairs. It is an old argument running from George Washington's "Farewell Address" to Stringfellow Barr's *Let's Join the Human Race*. Stillman and Pfaff (# 229) argue that the tradition of an American mission in the world is messianic and "a disguise for our insecurity and violence." They point to American "flawed national realities" which "cannot be mended by an increasingly intense and uncompromising political mission to the world and to history." They decry quasi-theological missions and call for a straight national interest approach to foreign policy decision making. Its primary end, in their view, should be this nation's security and well-being.

Others who may equally deplore dominantly military attempts to impose our will on the world offer other standards. They continue to call for American leadership in achieving world disarmament and world law (# 242), for a major American engagement with the problems of developing nations (# 241), for a deliberate attempt to encourage forces within the Communist world that will join us in pursuing such goals (# 237). They reject a single-minded focus on opposition to *American* militarism. That is seen as *part* of the problem but not an adequate rallying point for those concerned to end war.

Whatever the reader's judgment regarding the proper goals of U.S. foreign policy, they must be pursued in a radically different international environment in the 1970's. Little remains of the bi-polar world of the fifties and sixties. There is now an open break between the two major Communist powers (# 280); there is a growing feeling in Europe and America that the Cold War is over and there is a consequent weakening of the North Atlantic Alliance; there is now a painful, erratic but nevertheless persistent movement of Eastern European Communist states toward greater autonomy; in sum, there is a much more complex international environment with a larger number of independent actors.

It is, however, no more encouraging a scene for those committed to work to end war. Nationalism remains the dominant force, stronger than ideological ties and in the world of new nations as fierce an obstacle to world organization as ever in the old. There is the terrible reality of the growing gap between the rich nations (Communist and non-Communist) of the north and the poor nations of the south and the demonstrated inability of the United Nations to keep the peace, resulting in its present low esteem. There is finally the fact of war itself; the multiple fact at this writing of war in Vietnam, war in the Middle East, war in Nigeria/Biafra, war in the Sudan. It is no wonder so many in the forefront of social thought in America today choose other "priorities."

But it is also a period of some hope. The last chapter of *To End War* summarized the emergence of an entire new family of international functional agencies. There has clearly been an intensified recognition throughout the world that the whole world community should accept responsibility for the welfare of all its parts. Before World War II, say Richard Gardner and Max Millikan (# 102), few lists of the primary problems of the world community would have included the economic and social development of the less developed countries. One need only compare the proportion of the world's population aware of League of Nations activity with those actually touched by the United Nations to demonstrate the increased significance of today's world organization. Another plus is today's more realistic assessment of the obstacles to the achievement of the goals of world development and world organization.

In America the harsh rigidities of the Cold War have been broken and those committed to a "forward strategy," the military defeat of Communism, find themselves isolated from the main currents of American life. Even the more moderate commitment to the military containment of Communism is subject to severe criticism. Documents like Andrei Sakharov's (# 257A) and the Soviet Union's peace initiative at Tashkent (serving the interest of the world community by aiding a peaceful resolution of the Pakistani/Indian conflict), are signs of similar movement in the world of European Communism.

There is also a growing sophistication among American peace adherents. Many recognize that the rejection of reliance on national military power can help produce a war instead of prevent one. They are therefore seeking both American and other great power agreement on the essential conditions for a disarmed world under law. One now encounters voices marking the moving and widespread demand for peace as futile if it produces no more than a return to a focus on domestic problems and to the narrow calculation of national interests that preceded America's intensified engagement in world affairs thirty years ago.

Although critics of U.S. foreign policy of the 1960's are agreed that a dominantly military U.S. foreign policy blocked the pursuit of the goals stated above, there is as yet no agreement on what new foreign policy approach should be adopted. Widely differing assumptions underlie the rejection of a dominantly military U.S. foreign policy. For example, the books annotated in this chapter of *To End War* criticize U.S. policy in the 1960's because:

a) it was, as always, a product of an exploitive American imperialism. (*Critics: New Left and Old*, # 213 to 217)

b) it was a primarily military response to a more than military threat. Caught in the requirements of a military stance it became an obstacle instead of an aid to progressive change and the achievement of a world without war. (*Critics: Democratic Socialist and Pacifist*, # 218 to 221)

c) it was over-committed in Asia and pursued objectives we were incapable of fulfilling. (*Critics: A New Engagement: Europe* and *A New Engagement: Asia*, # 230–235)

d) it was committed primarily to national military programs and national diplomacy, thereby undermining or at least not strengthening international institutions. (*Critics: A Changed Engagement: International Organizations*, # 236–243).

Some critics of U.S. policy justify a focus on domestic problems and politics because they see these realities as decisive influences on the formation of foreign policy. Theirs, they would say, is not a turning away from work to end war but a more effective strategy of change.

A mistaken strategy, say those in disagreement. The fundamental shaping influence, they say, is the international reality the President must confront. Clearly both domestic and international realities shape the U.S. response, but, domestic change, say the internationally oriented, cannot alter the harsh realities of world politics. Whatever the current state of race relations in this country, or the form of our economy, and whatever the influence of domestic military structures on political decision-making, U.S. foreign policy will be primarily shaped by military and diplomatic moves in the world political arena. It is therefore mistaken, they say, to believe that a focus on domestic problems is the most effective way to change the character of world politics.

Whether approached directly or through a focus on changing the character and structure of American life, those concerned to end war will have to confront an agenda of foreign policy issues not very different from that of the 1960's although in a changed international environment. What, for example, should this country do regarding the proportion of its gross national product that it gives to international economic development and the instrumentalities (national, international or private) which will be used for such aid; what should it do regarding the new weapons systems that could be built and deployed or the arms control and disarmament measures which could be negotiated; what, regarding the need for intelligence information for a wise formulation of foreign policy versus the dangers of covert intelligence agencies to a democracy? What, regarding the continued attempt to isolate, as against initiatives to open relations with, Communist China?; what, regarding the relationship of the U.S. to the United Nations and other international institutions?

Whatever values or goals those making foreign policy decisions may have, they will have to face such issues in the 1970's. Chapter 7 discusses a foreign policy issues agenda and Part II the contexts within which people will make their decisions about these issues. *To End War* has emphasized the primary importance of these contextual choices. Roger Fisher's recent book (# 587) develops one distinctive context, suggesting a foreign policy approach that seeks its goals through compromise and adjustment, "fractionating" conflict and offering "yessable propositions" instead of threat manipulation and the tactics of terror.

One emphasis, already noted, which sets a context for discussion of war/peace issues is the current call for limits, or for domestic priorities. While the call for limits in U.S. foreign policy is well-conceived in a context based on the premise that the U.S. must either impose its will by violence or withdraw from world politics, it is ill-conceived if America is either capable without mass violence of leading in work for a world without war or cannot in fact withdraw from world politics.

Another context in which Americans may approach foreign policy questions emphasizes a changed and intensified engagement in international organizations (# 236–243. Advocates of American peace initiative acts (World Without War Council and Etzioni, # 237 and Osgood, #239) offer another distinctive foreign policy stance. They believe an initiative strategy gives most promise of creating the climate and the pressures that could lead to agreements with the Communist world on basic measures of arms control and disarmament.

We have yet to gather in our country agreement on an American approach to the world, which offers hope of American leadership in controlling the threat of war. The condition of war or peace in the world is a function of national not world decisions today. And no nation's decisions as to its goals are of greater importance than ours. Conflict today is not simply a matter of opposition across national boundaries. It is frequently a matter of winning allegiances within national societies. Simply avoiding nuclear war has been a primary concern of foreign policy decision makers. It is not enough. Many now see, in a world to be shaped and reshaped by the explosive currents of change moving at the end of the twentieth century, a dynamic approach to the nonviolent resolution of inevitable conflict is a better definition of the task.

To End War's perspective on U.S. foreign policy gives highest priority to winning the allegiance of men in all nations to the successful completion of that task.

The United States and the Cold War

INF   189   **AMERICAN DIPLOMACY, 1900–1950** *by George F. Kennan, 127pp, 1963, Mentor Books, $.60.* Kennan covers U.S. foreign policy during several crises from the Spanish-American War to the Berlin Blockade. Included is Kennan's famous "Mr. X" article outlining the justification for the containment strategy adopted in 1948.

190   **ATOMIC DIPLOMACY** *by Gar Alperovitz, 317pp, 1965, Random House, $2.45.* Argues that the cold war began in 1945 as a result of Truman's attempt to reverse Roosevelt's policies toward the Soviet Union.

191   **RISE AND DECLINE OF THE COLD WAR** *by Paul Seabury, 171pp, 1966, Basic Books, $4.95.* Maintains that the cold war began in 1947 after Stalin's refusal to abide by the Potsdam and other agreements. Concludes that the cold war, in its classic sense, ended in 1963 and that a new phase of international politics has begun.

192   **A NEW HISTORY OF THE COLD WAR** *by John Lukas, 348pp, 1966, Doubleday, $1.45.* A diplomatic his-

torian presents a comparative history of Russia and America since 1763 emphasizing the division of Europe into Soviet and U.S. spheres of influence. The work concludes with an analysis of the probable outcome of the current deadlock.

193 **THE COLD WAR AS HISTORY** by *Louis Halle, 434pp, 1967, Harper & Row, hardcover, $6.95.* An attempt to do for the cold war "what Thucydides did for the Peloponnesian War" by a former State Department policy advisor.

194 **AFTER 20 YEARS: Alternatives to the Cold War in Europe** by *Richard Barnet and Marcus Raskin, 243pp, 1966, Vintage Books, $1.95.* Argues that the cold war in Europe is dead and that the present U.S. commitment to NATO is anachronistic.

195 **BEYOND THE COLD WAR** by *Marshall Shulman, 111pp, 1966, Yale University Press, $1.25.* Outlines changes in U.S.-Soviet relations since 1945 which have altered the rationale and weapons of the cold war. Shulman argues that the West must shift toward greater concern for the underlying causes of conflict and away from the old slogans of the cold war.

196 **IMPERIAL AMERICA, The International Politics of Primacy** by *George Liska, 115pp, 1967, Johns Hopkins Press, $2.25.* A reasoned argument for American use of its military power throughout the world as a means of maintaining world peace.

INF 197 **A THOUSAND DAYS** by *Arthur M. Schlesinger Jr., 967pp, 1965, Fawcett, $1.65.* A sympathetic description of the Kennedy administration, particularly of interest for the description of Kennedy's peace initiative strategy begun with the nuclear test-ban prior to the signing of the treaty.

198 **AMERICAN FOREIGN POLICY SINCE WORLD WAR II** by *John Spanier, 289pp, 1965, Praeger, $2.25.* The author identifies liberalism with a failure to recognize the importance of power in world affairs and believes this

failure has resulted in the lack of direction and failures of American foreign policy since World War II.

American Foreign Policy: Some Overviews

INT   199 **READINGS IN AMERICAN FOREIGN POLICY,** *Robert Goldwin (ed.), 709pp, 1959, Oxford University Press, $2.20.* Probably the best anthology on the crucial concepts and persistent tendencies of American foreign policy. Presents classic and contemporary readings from a variety of perspectives on American expansionism, the relationship between democracy and foreign policy, U.S. and international organizations and on the principles which should guide American foreign policy.

200 **FOREIGN POLICY AND DEMOCRATIC POLICIES: The American and British Experience** *by Kenneth Waltz, 352pp, 1967, Little, Brown, $3.95.* A study of the interrelation between democratic domestic experiences and foreign policy.

201 **DOMESTIC SOURCES OF FOREIGN POLICY,** *James Rosenau (ed.), 354pp, 1967, Macmillan, hardcover, $8.50.* An anthology of differing views on the relationship between internal social structure, political attitudes and institutions and foreign policy. Selections by the editor of the *Journal of Peace Research*, Johan Galtung and by Herbert McClosky, Kenneth Waltz and others.

202 **IDEALS AND SELF-INTEREST IN AMERICA'S FOREIGN RELATIONS** *by Robert Osgood, 491pp, 1963, University of Chicago Press, $2.95.* Osgood argues that neither national self-interest nor utopian idealism offer an intelligent context for foreign policy decision making. The trick is to relate ideals to political realities.

203 **THE ISOLATIONIST IMPULSE** *by Selig Adler, 507pp, 1961, Macmillan, $2.95.* Examines the roots and different expressions of isolationist sentiment in the U.S. since World War I. Argues that both a withdrawal from foreign affairs and a militant crusading spirit spring from a single root: a self-conscious fear of differences.

204 REALITIES OF AMERICAN FOREIGN POLICY by George F. Kennan, 120pp, 1966, Norton, $1.25. A discussion of the principles which Kennan believes should underlie U.S. foreign policy. He criticizes the U.S. for too frequently applying moral and legalistic categories to problems to which they do not apply.

205 POWER, FREEDOM AND DIPLOMACY by Paul Seabury, 424pp, 1963, Random House, $2.45. A study of the intricate relationship among these three concepts.

206 LAW, POWER AND THE PURSUIT OF PEACE by Eugene V. Rostow, 133pp, 1968, Harper & Row, $1.60. A former Undersecretary of State provides an historical view of the U.S. commitment to international institutions and argues for distinguishing between unjust and just wars. He concludes that the great powers must be the world's policemen until international authority is sufficiently strong to take up the burden.

207 AGENDA FOR THE NATION, Kermit Gordon (ed.), 620pp, 1968, Doubleday, $3.95. A look at the problems facing the Nixon administration, particularly in international relations. Sections on the U.S. and low-income countries, the dollar and the world economy and an essay by Henry Kissinger are particularly important.

208 THE ESSENCE OF SECURITY by Robert McNamara, 176pp, 1968, Harper & Row, $1.65. The former Secretary of Defense outlines his view that security is best maintained, not just by a threat of massive retaliation, but by having available a variety of military options. Includes McNamara's description of why he believes economic development in the third world may be as important as military strategies in avoiding war.

208A U.S. FOREIGN POLICY: Perspectives and Proposals for the 1970's, Paul Seabury and Aaron Wildavsky (eds.), 215pp, 1969, McGraw-Hill, $3.50. An examination of the post–Lyndon Johnson U.S. foreign policy options. The essays consider long-range policy proposals in the light of U.S. national interest, question the justification for intervention in the third world, seek to establish criteria for recognition or nonrecognition and deal with U.S. policy toward all areas except Europe. Paul Seabury's essay "The Revolt Against Obligation" provides a useful framework for the subsequent articles.

(see also 380, 523, 587, 608, 615 and 616)

U.S. Government Policy Statements

209   A POCKET GUIDE TO FOREIGN POLICY IN-FORMATION MATERIALS AND SERVICES, *U.S. Department of State, 14pp, 1969, U.S. Govt. Printing Office, $.10.* Lists the publications, periodicals, historical documents and newsletters which give official State Department and Presidential views. Includes Speakers Bureau information and available audio-visual materials.

210   DEPARTMENT OF STATE BULLETIN, *40pp, weekly, U.S. Govt. Printing Office, $.30, ($10.00 per year).* The official record of U.S. foreign policy, including key policy statements, transcripts and special articles by experts.

211   FOREIGN POLICY BRIEFS, *2pp, bi-weekly, U.S. Govt. Printing Office, $2.25 (per year).* Summary of important foreign policy developments and background information.

212   U.S. FOREIGN POLICY FOR THE 1970'S, A NEW STRATEGY FOR PEACE, *by Richard Nixon, 160pp, 1970, U.S. Govt. Printing Office, $.75.* Provides the main outlines of Nixon's foreign policy: military deterrence, reduced commitments, international alliances, and negotiations.

U.S. Foreign Policy Critics: New Left and Old

213   THE GREAT EVASION *by William Williams, 187pp, 1964, Quadrangle, $2.25.* An American Marxist historian argues that U.S. foreign policy is interventionist because the U.S. is capitalistic. He therefore argues that prior to changing U.S. foreign policy it is essential to change the economy from which it springs.

214 **CONTAINMENT AND CHANGE** *by Carl Oglesby and Richard Shaull, 248pp, 1967, Macmillan, $1.45.* A New Left analysis and rejection of the Western tradition. U.S. foreign policy is seen as part of the Westernization of the globe which is to be resisted, but peculiarly enough, the means of resistance is the Western idea of individual conscience.

215 **CONTAINMENT AND REVOLUTION,** *David Horowitz (ed.), 252pp, 1967, Beacon Press, $2.45.* An anthology of writers who oppose U.S. intervention in revolutions either from a justification of revolution per se or from isolationist views. Explains the origins of the cold war and subsequent U.S. foreign policy as a result of U.S. fear of Communist revolutions.

216 **IRONIES OF HISTORY** *by Isaac Deutcher, 278pp, 1966, Oxford University Press, hardcover, $5.75.* A Marxist analysis of American foreign policy by an un-reconstructed, pre-Stalinist, Marxist.

217 **AMERICAN POWER AND THE NEW MANDARINS** *by Noam Chomsky, 404pp, 1969, Random House, $2.45.* Taking Vietnam as his touchstone, Chomsky blames liberals in general and liberal intellectuals in particular for Vietnam and much else. He advocates joining resistance communes, calls for a "de-nazification" of American society, and considers the "revival of anarchist thinking in the New Left and the attempts to put it into practice the most promising development of the past years." Chomsky does not believe a change in U.S. foreign policy is likely without a change in U.S. economic and social structures. A change to what is not clear.

U.S. Foreign Policy Critics: Democratic Socialist and Pacifist

TEW 218 **SPEAK TRUTH TO POWER** *by Steve Cary, Robert Pickus et al, 68pp, 1958. American Friends Service Committee, $.35.* While affirming the Gandhian commitment to truth and political justice as a basic value

for pacifists, this study asserts that an exclusive concern
for a witness to love among men which does not face
political reality is neither more moral nor more likely to
end war than traditional justifications for war. Thus, this
book requires those who call themselves pacifists to accept
responsibility for finding alternative ways of defending
values and forcing needed change.

219   AMERICAN POWER IN THE 20th CENTURY *by
Michael Harrington, 55pp, 1967, League for Industrial
Democracy, $.50.* A democratic socialist and author of *The
Other America*, Harrington argues that the contradictions
in our foreign aid programs have widened the gap between the rich and poor nations. This trend can be re-
versed if the U.S. adopts a democratic foreign policy.

220   A DISSENTER'S GUIDE TO FOREIGN POLICY,
Irving Howe (ed.), 349pp, 1969, Doubleday, $1.75. A
collection of eighteen essays which focus on the problems
of democratic engagement in international affairs. Included
are criticisms of American action in Venezuela and Vietnam, a reassessment of the Cold War and U.S. interven-
tionism, and a useful debate over whether economic
development can be accomplished in a democratic framework.

221   SEATTLE CITIZEN'S REPORT, *Derek Mills (ed.),
50pp, 1969, World Without War Council, $.50.* A mimeo-
graphed discussion paper which offers guidelines for a
foreign policy based on democratic values and committed
to U.S. peace initiatives designed to foster progress toward a world without war.

U.S. Foreign Policy Critics: A Call for Limits

222   A NEW FOREIGN POLICY FOR THE U.S. *by
Hans Morgenthau, 256pp, 1969, Praeger, $2.75.* A leading
political scientist argues that, in 1969, the U.S. needs to
undergo a change in foreign policy comparable to the
change in 1948 when the U.S. first became committed to
collective military alliances, containment and economic

development programs as a means of halting the spread of Communism.

223 THE LIMITS OF POWER: America's Role in the World *by Eugene McCarthy, 363pp, 1968, Dell, $.75.* Urges a broader distribution of responsibilities among the world powers, and with international organizations. McCarthy argues that the Senate Foreign Relations Committee should help formulate standards to guide U.S. participation in world affairs.

224 ABUSE OF POWER *by Theodore Draper, 244pp, 1967, Viking Press, $1.95.* Draper offers a lucid rebuttal of the arguments supporting U.S. policy in the Dominican Republic and South Vietnam but does not here outline an alternative foreign policy.

225 THE ARROGANCE OF POWER *by J. W. Fulbright, 264pp, 1967, Vintage Books, $1.95.* Covers a broad range of foreign policy questions while advocating economic development assistance be dissociated from military assistance and channeled through international organizations.

226 A TIME OF WAR, A TIME OF PEACE *by George McGovern, 203pp, 1968, Vintage Books, $1.65.* A study of the problems of arms reduction, the draft, and the dangers of developing a crisis mentality. McGovern outlines a new foreign policy.

227 INTERVENTION AND REVOLUTION, America's Confrontation with Insurgent Movements Around the World *by Richard Barnet, 302pp, 1968, Meridian, $2.95.* An analysis of U.S. intervention in Greece, Lebanon, the Dominican Republic and Vietnam which concludes that the U.S. cannot and should not attempt to suppress revolutionary movements. Barnet recommends a multilateral (United Nations) approach to international conflict resolution.

228 PAX AMERICANA, The Cold War Empire—How It Grew and What It Means *by Ronald Steel, 371pp, 1967,*

Viking Press, $1.85. Steel believes the U.S. has acquired an empire in a "fit of absence of mind." He argues that intervention against Communism, rather than for democracy or economic development, has characterized American policy. He concludes with a plan for discrimination in intervening in a pluralistic world.

229   POWER AND IMPOTENCE, The Failure of America's Foreign Policy *by Edmund Stillman and William Pfaff, 244pp, 1967, Harper & Row, $1.95.* Concludes that the U.S. should seek to reduce its commitments in Europe, Japan and Latin America and serve as a reserve for other free world powers, rather than trying to impose American values on the world.

(see also 296)

U.S. Foreign Policy Critics: A Changed Engagement—Europe

230   THE ATLANTIC ALLIANCE: Problems and Prospects *by Harold van B. Cleveland and Jean B. Cleveland, 63pp, 1966, Foreign Policy Association, $.85.* Viewing the nations of the North Atlantic as forming a political community, the authors assess the common defense, economic, social and political problems of that entity. Trade liberalization, economic integration and common market problems are introduced.

231   QUEST FOR PEACE THROUGH DIPLOMACY *by Stephan Kertezy, 192pp, 1967, Prentice-Hall, $2.45.* Emphasizes the role a unified Atlantic community could play in strengthening international institutions.

232   A PEACE POLICY FOR EUROPE *by Willy Brandt, 225pp, 1969, Holt, Rinehart and Winston, hardcover, $5.95.* The former mayor of Berlin and now West Germany's chancellor, argues for his policy of détente.

232A   GERMANY: Illusions and Dilemmas *by Carl Landauer, 360pp, 1969, Harcourt, Brace and World, hardcover, $8.95.* A careful examination of the problems a divided Germany poses for world peace and a plea for realism in Western approaches to the problem.

INF   233   **THE DISCIPLINE OF POWER** *by George W. Ball,* 363pp, 168, Little, Brown, hardcover, $7.50. Rejecting America's universalism as quixotic, "world peace through world law" as illusory, Ball argues for a united Europe as a third great power, Japan as a fourth, which could reestablish a balance of power. This approach, Ball says, would be consistent with today's power realities and would assure the security of the humane, Westernized, industrialized powers.

U.S. Foreign Policy Critics: A Changed Engagement—Asia

234   **THE UNITED STATES AND CHINA IN WORLD AFFAIRS** *by Robert Blum, edited by A. Doak Barnett,* 287pp, 1966, McGraw-Hill, $2.95. A comprehensive review of U.S.-China relations since 1959 and their impact on international politics. The late Dr. Blum probes the attitudes and policies of both countries toward each other and makes numerous suggestions for a more constructive framework for U.S.-China policy.

235   **BEYOND VIETNAM: The United States and Asia** *by Edwin Reischauer,* 242pp, 1967, Vintage Books, $1.65. A former ambassador to Japan establishes a rule of thumb for U.S. assistance to other countries: "Any regime that is not strong enough to defend itself against its internal enemies probably could not be defended by us either and may not be worth defending anyway." Argues for U.S. support for regional and international institutions.

(see also 302)

U.S. Foreign Policy Critics: A Changed Commitment —To International Organizations

236   **PREVENTING W.W. III, Some Proposals,** *Quincy Wright, Morton Deutsch, & William Evans (eds.),* 460pp, 1962, Simon & Schuster, hardcover, $6.95. A series of

original proposals which outline steps the U.S. could take to stop the arms race, reduce international tensions and help build a world society.

237   **THE HARD WAY TO PEACE** *by Amitai Etzioni, 294pp, 1963, Macmillan, $.95.* Argues for peace through constructive unilateral initiative acts designed to build support for, and give power to, international institutions, i.e. the United Nations.

238   **WINNING WITHOUT WAR** *by Amitai Etzioni, 244pp, 1965, Doubleday, $1.25.* Argues for "winning" not as a victory for one power, but in the sense of building institutions for conducting without war the deep and real conflicts which divide the world.

239   **PERSPECTIVE IN FOREIGN POLICY** *by Charles E. Osgood, 94pp, 1967, Pacific Books, $1.50.* The author of the initiatives strategy outlines a perspective for viewing international relations based on the possibility of strengthening international institutions.

240   **TO MOVE A NATION: The Politics of Foreign Policy in the Administration of John F. Kennedy** *by Roger Hilsman, 702pp, 1967, Delta Books, $2.95.* A member of the Kennedy Administration argues that, with the exception of the Bay of Pigs disaster, President Kennedy made few serious errors while seeking to strengthen the Atlantic Community and the United Nations. Hilsman demonstrates the need for public participation in the decision-making process and discusses the limits which lack of public involvement brings.

241   **IN PURSUIT OF WORLD ORDER: U.S. Foreign Policy and International Organizations** *by Richard Gardner, 263pp, 1965 Praeger, $1.95.* A study of the brighter side of stated U.S. foreign policy goals and accomplishments. Argues for an increased commitment to international institutions.

TEW   242   **THE UNITED NATIONS AND U.S. FOREIGN POLICY** *by Lincoln Bloomfield, 268pp, 1967, Little, Brown, $3.50.* A study of the role of the U.N. in U.S.

foreign policy, particularly in the field of peace-keeping, but also in the areas of arms control and disarmament, peaceful uses of space and the sea bed, economic development, colonialism and human rights.

243   TANGLE OF HOPES: American Commitments and World Order *by Ernst Haas, 306pp, 1969, Prentice-Hall, hardcover, $7.95.* A study of American expectations and objectives in fostering and supporting many international organizations. Haas focuses on public opinion and interest groups as well as governmental policy in analyzing the overlapping authorities within international organizations, particularly the United Nations. He concludes that "current American policy toward international organizations (is) probably destructive of the chief values we cherish" and outlines an alternative policy designed to fulfill those values and improve the viability of international organizations.

(see also 35 and 301)

VI THE COMMUNIST NATIONS AND
INTERNATIONAL RELATIONS

It is difficult to examine objectively the problems posed by Communist ideology, political practice, and the foreign policy of Communist nations. Even those seeking an end to war are affected by pro- and anti-Communist currents sweeping the world since the Russian Revolution. Several points about Communism and war peace problems are, however, clear. There was war before any Communist state was established. It makes little sense to find *the* cause of war in "Communism." Similarly, the diversity of Communist countries today and intermittent warfare along the U.S.S.R. /China border suggest the possibility of wars between Communist powers. Both the opposition and the invaders in Czechoslovakia, and the several factions in the recent civil wars in mainland China describe themselves as Communist. It follows that neither world domination by Communist powers nor socialization of the means of production can be expected to end war.

Passionate reactions to Communism have nevertheless dominated the war/peace discussion in America for more than twenty years. For much of this period the American approach to world politics was fundamentally shaped by a perception of Communism as evil. Communism was seen as a monolithic, unchanging, totally evil force which posed the supreme moral and practical threat to American values and security. Resisting its spread was the primary objective of American policy. Staying ahead in the arms race was also believed to be the best way to prevent war. Anyone that challenged these ideas was regarded as a Communist or a fool. In this climate, thoughtful discussion of Communist policy and practice as it affected war/peace questions was difficult to sustain.

Thoughtful discussion was equally difficult to sustain within some sectors of the liberal and peace-oriented community. There, especially after Senator Joseph McCarthy's indiscriminate use of the label "Communist" to intimidate holders of a wide range of views divergent from his own, an anti-anti-Communist current grew in strength. This current posed increasingly serious obstacles to a balanced or even an open examination of Communist policy and practice. Many switched from a single-minded focus on the Communist threat to an equally unbalanced perception of America as the only villain in world affairs. Anti-Communism became identified with support for a dominantly military U.S. foreign policy (a position rejected by many opposed to war *and* to the expansion of totalitarian government). Any criticism of Communist policies became "McCarthyism," and pro-Communist politics masqueraded with ease, safe from critical examination, as "peace" politics.

Fed to some extent by various pro-Communist forces, this current drew its primary strength from elsewhere. Many individuals refrained from criticizing Communist policy and practice because, while they opposed Communism, they opposed a war against Communist countries even more, and feared that others would use publicly stated anti-Communist views to justify such a war. Others believed it was important to ignore ideological differences while seeking areas of accord that could help to reconcile divisions.

Whatever the motivation, this refusal to confront Communist reality has posed a serious obstacle to the development of genuine anti-war understandings. It has, sometimes, confused opposition to Washington's military policies with genuine opposition to war. The former can be part of a commitment to peace; but it can also be a part of a commitment to war against America. This peculiar blindness to Communist reality has led many people into a kind of dissent dominated by an automatic anti-anti-Communism that is as distorted in its view of Communist reality as the Communist devil theory it replaces. Such dissent matches in its vituperation, conspiracy theory and contempt for reason that of the Birch Society member it perceives in every opponent of Communist organizational goals.

Those concerned with how to end war should reject both a rigid and sometimes uninformed anti-Communism and a blind refusal to examine Communist policies and practices as they affect war/peace questions. Both approaches, whether they use the label "Communist" or "red-baiter" (the other side of the coin) block needed discussion and exploration and, as a consequence, are obstacles to rational decision. Clear thought requires an accurate description of a country's policies and practices. Prescription of a wise policy for dealing with those realities is another matter. Similarly, one can recognize the moral worth of individuals while opposing the evil they may do. These distinctions are crucial for those who wish to work for an end to war while retaining their opposition to political oppression. One can see the horror of a policy that in 1969 moved 25 million people from China's urban to rural areas for "political remolding"[1] while affirming a

---

[1] See *The New York Times*, April 6, 1969 and compare the curious hostility to any criticism of Communist regimes encountered in political groups supposedly devoted to peace and freedom.

common humanity with the people who are subject to that system. One can oppose such a system without derogating the importance of reaching political agreement with its leaders to end war.

Despite important differences among contemporary Communist movements and states, Communism is not a meaningless term. There are, for example, clear differences between Communist and democratic governments in attitudes toward violence, reconciliation of class hostilities, and the protection of minority views—differences in what is considered right as well as differences in practice.

Understanding these ideas, understanding the political systems and organizations of the Communist world and the way in which they affect American policy and political life, is essential to a sound approach to work in the war/peace field. Care is required in labeling any view, whether liberal, conservative, capitalist or Communist, but it is the worst kind of obfuscation to fail to recognize that there are distinctive Communist approaches to war/peace issues and to the problem of war itself. It is important to understand them.

Discussion of Communist countries and their policies has also suffered from a lack of objective information and a surfeit of propaganda. Limited independent information sources, restrictions on travel, the suppression of political opposition, the near total control of the media of communication in Communist countries make it difficult to validate the facts in discussions involving the Communist world.

The confusion, or at least the differences of opinion in such discussions, can also be traced to different criteria used in evaluating Communist regimes and policies. If the ability to industrialize a country rapidly is seen as the primary purpose of government, then one clear standard for judgment—the size of the gross national product—can be used. If, on the other hand, one considers other values, one may come to a very different view of the Communist world. For some the primary considerations are the freedom from arbitrary imprisonment, freedom to choose one's employment, the degree of academic freedom, participation in the government's decision-making process, the ability of a minority to organize politically and to be heard, and the degree to which the provisions of the Universal Declaration of Human Rights are observed.

No one who seriously desires to end war should underestimate the enormous technological, industrial and human resources which authoritarian and totalitarian governments can muster to gain foreign policy objectives (# 246). Neither should one underestimate the tremendous appeal and dynamic of Marxist-Leninist ideology, paticularly to an educated elite in an underdeveloped country. The assumption that such an intellectual elite can know the laws of history and thus justifiably impose needed change by violence is attractive to men living in circumstances that militate against any other approach to change. A government may thereby be legitimized as "the people's" without all the laborious and often frustrating apparatus of democratic decision-making. The seeming short-cut to economic development, the altruism combined with a religious sense of mission, the clear identification of "enemies," the acceptance of great tasks for the common good, all combine to make Communism appear to be an attractive, even a just, way to modernize a country.

One can recognize the appeal while rejecting the reality of Communism and still argue that ending war is a meaningful goal. The Communist world is diverse and changing. In 1969 Andrei Sakharov, a Soviet Nobel Prize winner, urgently stated the need for the development of a world government by the year 2000. The problem for those who take ending war as their goal is how to encourage a changing Communist world in the direction of agreement on the essential tasks: building institutions of world law, achieving universal and enforceable disarmament, sharing in a common commitment to world economic development, and enforcing the Universal Declaration of Human Rights.

The central question thus becomes one of determining what policies, what initiative acts by the U.S., would increase the likelihood of achieving such agreement and would produce concrete steps toward their fulfillment. The policies which appear most likely to hasten such trends are those which open channels of communication, which enhance understanding and build a sense of community across national and ideological boundaries, which seek out proponents of these goals and increase their influence in the Communist world. The peace seekers' central problem is to identify vectors of influence—external and internal—that could move leaders of the Communist world away from the arms race and toward disarmament, away from mass political violence and toward world institutions committed to human progress. Movement toward the resolution of our domestic problems is an important way to limit the power of Communist leaders. By so doing, we demonstrate viable alternatives to totalitarian means of achieving social goals.

Understanding the Communist world and understanding how to create allies there for work to end war is, then, one essential task for the peace seeker. This chapter of the *To End War* bibliography is devoted to aiding in that endeavor. The books in this chapter introduce the basic works of the Marxist tradition. They examine the diversity within and between different Communist countries. Included are the Sakharov manifesto on *Progress, Coexistence and Intellectual Freedom* (# 257A) and the Dubeck *Blueprint for Freedom* (# 283), examples of how Communist leaders are willing to challenge the system and pay the price for so doing. The bibliographical listings conclude with a number of works outlining nonviolent means of encouraging such trends and possibly producing a more hopeful outcome. Additional works may be found in the sections on *U.S. Foreign Policy* and on *Democratic Processes and the Peace Effort.*

The Foundations: Marxism and Its Revisions

INT   244 **BASIC WRITINGS OF MARX AND ENGELS,** *Lewis S. Feuer (ed.), 497pp, 1959, Doubleday, $1.95.* A selection of the major political writings of Marx and Engels.

INF   245 **TO THE FINLAND STATION** *by Edmund Wilson, 502pp, 1939, Doubleday, $1.95.* A study of the rise of modern socialist thought which is sympathetic to the idea that socialism is a logical outcome of Western European history. Critical of Stalinism.

246 **TOTALITARIANISM,** *Carl J. Friedrich (ed.), 386pp, 1954, Grosset and Dunlap, $2.25.* A collection of essays which analyze Communist and Fascist movements.

247 **MARXISM IN THE MODERN WORLD,** *Milorad M. Drachkevitch (ed.), 292pp, 1965, Stanford University Press, $2.95.* Raymond Aron examines Marxism as an argument for the dictatorship of a minority. Critical essays on Leninism, Stalinism, Titoism, Maoism and Castroism. Concludes with an essay on pluralistic Communism by Richard Lowenthal.

248 TERRORISM AND COMMUNISM *by Leon Trotsky, 191pp, 1961, University of Michigan Press, $1.95.* Trotsky defends terror in the Russian Revolution on the grounds that it was necessary to the defense of socialism. He argues that the party can permit no opposition and that terrorism is the only means to the highest moral ends of man: the socialist state. Trotsky himself became a victim of the police state he helped to create.

249 SELECTED WRITINGS OF MAO TSE-TUNG, *Anne Fremantle (ed.), 297pp, 1968, Bantam Books, $.75.* An anthology of key works on politics, economics and guerilla warfare.

250 THE THEORY AND PRACTICE OF COMMUNISM *by R. N. Carew Hunt, 315pp, 1968, Penguin Books, $1.45.* A study of Marxism, Lenin's contribution to Marxist theory and the effect of Stalin's policy of "socialism in one country" on the Soviet Union.

251 THE PERMANENT CRISIS *by Kurt London, 246pp, 1968, Johns Hopkins Press, $2.95.* Focuses on the U.S. confrontation with the Communist world in a time of rapid change within both blocs. London, an expert on Soviet politics, argues that Marxism-Leninism remains a key determinant of the international political behavior of Communist states, notwithstanding the divisions which have emerged.

252 COMMUNISM AND THE POLITICS OF DEVELOPMENT: Persistent Myths and Changing Behavior *by John Kautsky, 216pp, 1968, John Wiley & Sons, $3.95.* Analyzes Communism in the context of the politics of development, asserting that Communism is primarily a political and economic response of an elite committed to rapid modernization.

253 TOWARD A MARXIST HUMANISM *by Leszek Kolakowski, 220pp, 1968, Grove Press, $1.95.* A re-interpretation of Marxism by a Polish intellectual branded as a "revisionist" by the Soviet Union.

254   THE NEW MARXISM, Soviet and East European Marxism since 1956 *by Richard T. DeGeorge, 176pp, 1967, Pegasus, $1.95.* A study of Marxist-Leninist theory from Khrushchev's speech against Stalin until 1966. Emphasizes the changes which were taking place during the period.

(see also 365, 368, 400, 570, 600 and 601)

The Soviet Union

255   THE SOVIET UNION, A Half-Century of Communism, *Kurt London (ed.), 493pp, 1968, Johns Hopkins Press, $2.95.* An anthology assessing Soviet achievements and failures in political organization, industrial and agricultural production and foreign policy. Sober, careful, evaluation.

256   HALF A CENTURY OF SOCIALISM: Soviet Life in the Sixties *by William Pomeroy, 128pp, 1967, International Publishers, $.95.* An attempt to refute current criticism of the Soviet Union by pointing to economic reforms, the expansion of freedom of expression, foreign aid to North Vietnam and the Soviet Union's attitude toward China.

257   THE GOVERNMENT AND POLITICS OF THE SOVIET UNION *by Leonard Schapiro, 175pp, 1967, Random House, $1.65.* A careful description of the governmental channels: local and central government, courts, Communist party apparatus, Soviet bureaucracy. The author decries the absence of source material and the difficulty of obtaining reliable information.

TEW   257A   PROGRESS, COEXISTENCE AND INTELLECTUAL FREEDOM *by Andrei Sakharov, 99pp, 1969, Norton, $1.50.* A Soviet Nobel Prize winner argues the need for world community, denies that capitalism should be destroyed and demands intellectual freedom for Soviet intellectuals.

258   THE GREAT TERROR: Stalin's Purge of the Thirties *by Robert Conquest, 733pp, 1968, Macmillan, hard-*

cover, $9.95. A well-documented account of the purges of the thirties which emphasizes the immense scale (over 10 million perished) the methods, and the secrecy.

258A   IN QUEST OF JUSTICE, Protest and Dissent in the Soviet Union Today, *Abraham Brumberg (ed.)*, *480pp*, *1970*, *Praeger*, *hardcover*, $10.95. An extremely valuable book of documents of the growing dissent within the Soviet Union. Includes letters, petitions, selections from underground newspapers, stories and criticisms of trials and of the repression of a nonviolent opposition.

INT   259 REVOLUTIONARY RUSSIA: A Symposium, *Richard Pipes (ed.)*, *470pp*, *1969*, *Doubleday*, $1.95. Leading Western scholars evaluate the last 50 years of Russian history. Critical comments on each article make this anthology a useful introduction to the Soviet Union today. Articles by E. H. Carr, George Kennan, Hugh Seton-Watson, Adam Ulam, Bertram Wolfe and others.

260 THE FIRST CIRCLE *by Alexander Solzhenitsyn*, *580pp*, *1968*, *Bantam Books*, $1.25. Russia's famous novelist depicts Stalinist Russia as a concentration camp in which Stalin himself becomes a virtual prisoner in his own system. Although a timeless novel of the individual vs. the state, it is also a timely reminder. Solzhenitsyn caustically comments on "progressive Western journalists" taking the number of meat wagons in Moscow as indicative of abundance, while they are, in fact used to transport prisoners.

261   CANCER WARD *by Alexander Solzhenitsyn*, *559pp*, *1968*, *Bantam Books*, $1.25. Under what conditions do doctors or politicians have the right to lie or deceive their patients or subjects? A caustic reply to the Communist Party of the Soviet Union's answer to that question.

262   THE SOVIET BLOC, Unity and Conflict *by Zbigniew K. Brzezinski*, *599pp*, *1967*, *Praeger*, *hardcover*, $9.95. A history of conflicts and relations among Communist states since 1945. The author examines the role ideology plays in different Communist states and its interaction with specific institutions.

263 IDEOLOGY AND POWER IN SOVIET POLITICS *by Zbigniew K. Brzezinski, 180pp, 1965, Praeger, $1.95.* An analysis of the exercise of political power within a totalitarian political system.

264 SOVIET STRATEGY AT THE CROSSROAD *by Thomas W. Wolfe, 342pp, 1965, Harvard University Press, hardcover, $5.95.* Analysis of Soviet strategy, its problems and possible options since the Cuban crisis.

265 THE SOVIET ECONOMY: An Introduction, A. *Nove, 354pp, 1966, Praeger, $3.50.* An anthology on how decisions are made and on how the Soviet economy works.

266 THE SOVIET UNION AT THE UNITED NATIONS *by Alexander Dallin, 255pp, 1963, Praeger, $1.95.* Soviet diplomatic practice in an international organization.

267 THE SOVIETS IN INTERNATIONAL ORGANIZATIONS *by Alvin Rubinstein, 380pp, 1964, Princeton University Press, hardcover, $7.50.* Argues that the Soviet Union is becoming more interested in cooperation within the United Nations and other international organizations.

268 POLITICAL POWER: USA/USSR *by Zbigniew Brzezinski and Samuel P. Huntington, 461pp, 1964, Viking Press, $1.95.* A study of the similarities and differences between two different political systems concluding that both are gradually evolving but not converging.

China

269 AN ANNOTATED GUIDE TO MODERN CHINA, *National Committee on U.S.-China Relations, 27pp, 1967, $.25.* A useful bibliography of sources, and books covering Communist China and American-Chinese relations.

INF 270 THE UNITED STATES AND CHINA *by John K. Fairbank, 398pp, 1960, Viking Press, $1.85.* Basic background analysis of Chinese history and of the ascension to power of Mao Tse-tung.

271 THE BIRTH OF COMMUNIST CHINA *by C. P. Fitzgerald, 228pp, 1964, Penguin Books, $1.25.* Originally appearing in 1951, this work sees Communist China as an outgrowth of Chinese history in its denial of viable alternatives. Concludes with speculation about the future and the need for greater freedom for Chinese intellectuals.

272   **RED STAR OVER CHINA** *by Edgar Snow, 527pp, 1961, Grove Press, $.95.* Written in 1938, this partisan account offers insights into the origins of Chinese Communism. It is based on extensive conversations with Mao Tsetung and others.

273   **COMMUNIST CHINA AND ASIA** *by A. Doak Barnett, 574pp, 1960, Random House, $1.85.* Background on China and Communist China's foreign policy objectives by a leading expert on China.

274   **CHINA: How Communist China Negotiates** *by Arthur Lall, 301pp, 1968, Columbia University Press, $2.95.* The head of the Indian delegation to the Geneva Conference on Laos of 1961–62 argues that China's national interests, as well as ideological dogma, guide China's participation in international conferences. Lall also discusses North Vietnam's approach to international negotiations.

275   **THE AMERICAN PEOPLE AND CHINA** *by A. T. Steele, 321pp, 1966, McGraw-Hill, $2.45.* A study of American attitudes toward China which indicates that despite opposition to the Communist regime, a number of changes in U.S. policy toward China would receive public support, such as recognition, U.N. membership, cultural exchange, broadening trade relations and the like.

276   **CHINESE COMMUNISM** *by Robert C. North, 254pp, 1966, McGraw-Hill, $2.45.* A pictorial and narrative history of the rise of the Chinese Communist Party, its ascension to power and the results of the first fifteen years of rule.

277   **THE CHINESE VIEW OF THEIR PLACE IN THE WORLD** *by C. P. Fitzgerald, 72pp, 1960, Oxford University Press, $1.00.* A study of the continuity between

ancient and modern Chinese attitudes toward the "barbarian" external world.

278 LET'S TALK ABOUT CHINA TODAY, *American Friends Service Committee, 80pp, 1965, American Friends Service Committee, $.85.* An anthology of articles originally appearing in *The Political Quarterly* which examine the benefits of the Chinese Revolution.

INT   279 THE CHINA PUZZLE, *by the League of Women Voters, 50pp, 1967, League of Women Voters, $.75.* Studies the history of Communist China and recognition, trade, cultural exchange and other policy alternatives as issues in U.S. politics.

(see also 45, 46, 234 and 235)

Eastern Europe

280 WORLD COMMUNISM DIVIDED *by William E. Griffith, 58pp, 1966, Foreign Policy Association, $.75.* An examination of the many diverse, even antagonistic tendencies among Communist nations.

281 EASTERN EUROPE IN TRANSITION, *Kurt London (ed.), 361pp, 1966, Johns Hopkins Press, $3.45.* An anthology examining the new trends toward autonomy within the Soviet bloc.

282 THE COMMUNIST STATES AT THE CROSSROAD BETWEEN MOSCOW AND PEKING *by Adam Bromke, 272pp, 1965, Praeger, $3.45.* A survey of the problems facing different Communist states now that there is no longer a monolithic Communist movement.

283 CZECHOSLOVAKIA'S BLUEPRINT FOR FREEDOM: Alexander Dubcek's Statements, Original and Official Documents leading to the Soviet invasion of August 1968, *300pp, 1968, Aracon, $2.95.* Key documents which suggest the direction the suppressed attempts to liberalize the Czechoslovak government might have taken.

283A ON THE SITUATION IN THE CZECHOSLO-VAK SOCIALIST REPUBLIC, *155pp, 1969, (price and publisher not listed).* German Democratic Republic, Berlin, Germany. A justification of the Soviet and Warsaw bloc invasion of Czschoslovakia on the grounds that democratic trends threaten socialism. A variety of pro-invasion views are included.

284 THE CZECHOSLOVAK SOCIALIST REPUBLIC *by Zdenek Suda, 192pp, 1968, Johns Hopkins Press, $2.95.* Historical and analytical analysis of the movement for reforming the Communist system, the subsequent Russian occupation and the prospects for future Czechoslovak reforms.

285 THE NEW CLASS *by Milovan Djilas, 241pp, 1968, Praeger, $1.95.* Djilas argues that the Communist party has replaced the old ruling class. He advocates democratic socialism which protects civil liberties while allowing workers to participate in factory-level decisions.

Cuba

286 CUBA AND THE UNITED STATES: Long-range Perspectives, *John Plank (ed.), Brookings Institution, 265pp, 1967, hardcover, $6.75.* A collection of essays which attempt to provide a rationale for sounder U.S. policies.

287 CASTRO'S REVOLUTION *by Theodore Draper, 212pp, 1962, Praeger, $1.85.* Analysis of the factors leading to the success of Castro's revolution.

288 CASTROISM: Theory and Practice *by Theodore Draper, 250pp, 1959, Praeger, $1.95.* Argues from the perspective of one who recognizes the need for a democratic alternative to totalitarian Communist regimes and authoritarian military regimes.

289 CUBA UNDER CASTRO *by David D. Burke, 63pp, 1964, Foreign Policy Association, $1.00.* Argues that Castro has been far more successful in winning political control over Cuba than in achieving the economic goals set in 1960. Outlines policy choices for the U.S.

290 **THE ECONOMIC TRANSFORMATION OF CUBA** *by Edward Bernstein, 303pp, 1968, Monthly Review Press, $2.75.* An American economist who assisted in the socialization of Cuban industry from 1960–1963 comments on the successes.

291 **CUBA: Castroism and Communism, 1959–1966** *by Andres Suzrez, 266pp, 1967, MIT Press, $2.45.* A criticism of Castroism and its economic failings. Describes the distinctive form of Communism advocated by Castro while arguing that Castro's opposition to bureaucracy and the development of state institutions arises from his desire for personal power.

Policy Recommendations for Americans

292 **THERE IS A RIGHT WAY TO COUNTER COMMUNISM** *by George F. Kennan, 4pp, 1966, Fellowship, Publications, $.10.* Neither war nor hysteria is the right way, says Kennan, as he outlines a variety of political alternatives.

INF 293 **ON DEALING WITH THE COMMUNIST WORLD** *by George F. Kennan, 57pp, 1964, Harper & Row, $1.45.* Kennan, a noted Soviet scholar and American diplomat, cautions against stereotypic thinking about the Communist world. He suggests the poly-centrism among the various Communist countries should be welcomed by Americans and urges U.S. policy-makers to seek to strengthen the forces of moderation and reconciliation within the Communist world.

INT 294 **RECOGNITION OF COMMUNIST CHINA?** *by Robert Newman, 318pp, 1961, Macmillan, $1.95.* Useful both for its substantive contribution and for its careful examination of how the climate of opinion, the use of evidence, and differing moral, political and legal concerns, influence decisions.

295 CHINA, THE UNITED NATIONS AND UNITED STATES POLICY *by the United Nations Association, 64pp, 1966, United Nations Association, $1.00.* A study of the issues and principal alternatives with recommendations for U.S. policy.

296 MAKING A RATIONAL FOREIGN POLICY NOW *by Robert L. Heilbroner, 8pp, 1968, Harper's Magazine, $.15.* Argues for the efficacy of authoritarian regimes, whether Communist or not, as the vehicle for rapid economic growth which Heibroner considers the central need for the "third world."

297. DEALING WITH COMMUNIST CHINA: Is America's State of Mind Adequate to the Central Problems *by Edward LeFeveur, 7pp, 1966, World Without War Council, $.10.* The author says no and argues for bringing China into the world community as a means of changing her present policies.

TEW   298 A NEW CHINA POLICY—SOME QUAKER PROPOSALS *by the American Friends Service Committee, 68pp, 1965, Yale University Press, $.95.* Outlines the background of present hostility and presents alternatives to U.S. policy designed to open channels of communication, exchange, trade and understanding with China.

299 ANATOMY OF ANTI-COMMUNISM *by the American Friends Service Committee, 138pp, 1968, Hill & Wang, $1.50.* A study of the misuses of anti-Communism which attempts to identify a syndrome of beliefs which, the authors hold, are mythical. The reality of Communist power is addressed grudgingly and several anti-Communist alternatives to anti-Communism are offered.

300 SUPPORT CZECHOSLOVAKIA *by April Carter and others, 64pp, 1968, Housmans, $1.00.* A description of the planning and execution of nonviolent demonstrations in Moscow, Warsaw, Budapest and Sofia to protest the Soviet invasion of Czechoslovakia.

300A   WAR BETWEEN RUSSIA AND CHINA *by Harrison Salisbury, 224pp, 1970, Bantam Books, $1.25.* The author believes that Sino-Soviet differences may well lead to war. He suggests ways the U.S. could help prevent such a war and the possible consequences of U.S. failure.

VII AREA STUDIES, CRISIS PROBLEMS AND ISSUES

Decisions to organize or deploy an army in combat are made in a particular place, at a particular time. Political leaders must at a particular time decide to accept or reject a specific proposal to build new weapons systems or to launch new peace initiatives—decisions which can fundamentally alter the shape of world politics. Most war/peace discussions focus on such specific situations or choice points. In the most concrete sense these war/peace issues and their resolutions are the immediate causes of war.

Conceptual formulations such as those considered in previous chapters are meaningless unless they better enable us to deal with these specific choice points. Most people know this, and enter the war/peace field in response to questions raised by specific war/peace issues. Many are impatient with any attempt to step back from an immediate issue and gain perspective on the larger problem of work to end war. What counts, they say, is where you stand on the issue. Are you for or against building the ABM? Do you want American troops withdrawn from Vietnam or don't you? Should America sell war planes to Jordan and Israel or shouldn't we?

This is a compelling approach. It offers an apparently hardheaded and concrete orientation to a field so often dominated by vague and abstract discussion. It is the way most people prefer to discuss war/peace questions. It is also a mistaken and often self-defeating way to do so.

For it turns out that most decisions on war/peace

issues are not made on the basis of the facts of the particular situation. They are made in response to an overall political analysis and value orientation. These war/peace contexts usually determine, far more than the facts, a person's position on a particular issue. It is important then to understand these alternative war/peace contexts, for though often unexamined they, and not the issue, usually determine where people stand. The introduction to *To End War* discussed these fundamental orientations or contexts and gave examples of how they shape responses to war/peace issues.

An examination of alternative contexts is useful because the requirements of a fully developed peace position may be derived from a study of the inadequacies of other viewpoints. Agreement on fundamental ideas is more important to strengthening the understandings essential to ending war than is agreement on a particular issue. A North Vietnamese leader, a Black Panther leader and one concerned to see America lead in ending war, all oppose President Nixon's military policy in Vietnam. And many will say what difference does it make *why* they oppose it? The answer is *no* difference. No difference unless you want to know whether a particular approach to a particular issue is an aid or obstacle to ending war. In this case, there is a crucial difference between opposition to Washington's military policy because you are committed to Hanoi's military victory or because you oppose "white imperialist pigs," and opposition because you are committed to ending war.

At present, violent conflict rages in Vietnam. 500,000 people have been killed in seven years of war in the Sudan. The Nigerian-Biafran war has just ended and the war in Chad continues. Israel and many of the

Arab countries appear to be on the verge of another major military conflict and skirmishes in the Middle East have never ended. The Russian invasion of Czechoslovakia; intermittent warfare in China; clashes along the 38th parallel in Korea; guerrilla warfare in Guatemala, Peru, Cuba and Bolivia; guerrilla warfare in Rhodesia and elsewhere—all these remind us daily that war is a central fact of our present social lives.

Then, too, there is the violence of an oppressive *status quo* in Greece, South Africa and China—to give only three examples—which pose different problems for the peace seeker, but problems he must attempt to resolve.

In *To End War*, we have therefore sought to identify the elements of a body of thought that can challenge any group's justification for the use of mass political violence. We have tried to identify the policies and understandings that provide alternatives to mass violence in political and social conflict.

But a focus on these larger and more abstract problems should not lead one away from specific war/peace issues currently confronting political leaders and citizens. Work on those issues may, in fact, be the best way to clarify the elements in a genuine approach to ending war; and the resolution of that particular problem may increase the chances or dim the hope of a world without war.

This chapter of the bibliography introduces the reader to ten current war/peace issues, to alternative points of view regarding their resolution and to the background area studies essential to understanding them. Part III H summarizes what you need to know to work thoughtfully on a particular war/peace issue. Part II's discussion of current war/peace contexts and Part III F's outline of how to evaluate a peace organization will also prove useful as you consider which specific war/peace issues you plan to work on and how you will do that work.

The problem of ending a particular war is extremely complex, for all the specificities of history, geography, legal arrangements and power realities intrude. There are, however, some guidelines of use in all wars. In a world of armed camps, the possibility is great that a local conflict can escalate into a regional or world war. It is, therefore, generally important to isolate the military conflict. Secondly, since the world community is threatened by mass violence anywhere, it should accept responsibility for intervening when such violence occurs. These are not contradictory statements. *Military* intervention usually compounds the problem. Given mass political violence within or between political societies, the goal should be to define non-military forms of international intervention that can change the conflict from a violent to a nonviolent one. Any intervention or mediation is, of course, dependent for its success upon the consent of the primary parties to the conflict (# 154–167). The prime question then becomes, what understandings, what pressures are most likely to achieve such consent?

In a particular crisis, one clear way of finding out who prefers violence to the risk of peaceful settlement is to ask: which side is willing to initiate steps (not dependent on negotiated agreement) to end the violence? Other tests of whether a proposal aimed at resolving a particular war deserves to be called a peace proposal are:

1) Does the proposal recognize that all combatants are seeking to impose their will by violence or does it focus only on one side's use of violence?

2) Does the proposal offer an alternative way to resolve the source of the conflict?

3) Does the proposal demand specific initiative acts by one side which give promise of changing the policies of both sides, changing them in a direction which would enable the opponents to contest the issue without violence?

4) Does the proposal strengthen international authority, engaging that authority in resolving the current conflict in a way that aids in the control of future threats to the peace? Does the proposal help strengthen a sense of world community by providing for international reconstruction and economic development of the war-torn country on both sides of the battle lines?

Much of the material presented here on specific crisis areas points to the usefulness of these guidelines. They parallel Adlai Stevenson's argument that the international community has a responsibility to intervene in violent conflicts by 1) sealing the borders of the country involved; 2) calling for a cease-fire; 3) offering international means of arbitration and conflict processing through supervised elections or other nonviolent means for conflict resolution. You may disagree that these guidelines are applicable to a particular area. The key problem is to determine what force can be applied to secure compliance. The withdrawal of support from leaders who prefer to try to impose their will by violence is the most effective nonviolent sanction, but that requires a more universal commitment to ending war than now exists. What is needed is widespread agreement that individual leaders who call for war when alternative ways of resolving conflict are available are enemies of mankind and are to be resisted, not followed.

Intelligent work on a particular war/peace issue or crisis problem also requires specialization. You need to know the subject in depth so as to be able to counter arguments for other positions. Part III provides a checklist of what you need to know to follow the discussion in a particular field. But, whether you develop your knowledge of a special area, such as East Africa, or a special issue, such as ownership of the sea bed, an issue-centered approach is not enough. It is the context within which you consider the problem that is likely to determine whether your work on that issue advances or damages work for a world without war.

Indochina

TEW   301   **VIETNAM PEACE PROPOSALS**, *Robert Woito (ed.), 54pp, 1967, World Without War Council, $.75.* Sets seven criteria for judging escalation, negotiation, withdrawal and American peace initiative proposals. Includes the official peace proposals of the U.S., NLF and North Vietnam. Outlines a strategy of American peace initiatives designed to end the war in Vietnam and foster growth toward the long range goal of a world without war. Reprints policy stands taken by leading American organizations.

301A   SAIGON, U.S.A. *by Alfred Hassler, 291pp, 1970, Richard Baron, $3.25.* A devastating exposition of American complicity in Thieu–Ky governmental repression and the most forceful statement yet of the viability of a Vietnamese third force solution to the war. Hassler argues that the "third force" in Vietnam is strong enough to establish a democratic regime in South Vietnam. If U.S. support is withdrawn from the current government, he argues, such a force would make peace with the NLF but not be destroyed by it.

302   THE SECRET SEARCH FOR PEACE IN VIETNAM *by David Kraslow and Stuart Loory, 247pp, 1968, Random House, $1.95.* An attempt to piece together private and public sources of information to determine if the Johnson Administration exhausted the procedures for achieving meaningful negotiations prior to the Paris talks. The authors conclude that the private actions of the Johnson Administration did not match the public rhetoric.

303 **MISSION TO HANOI** *by Harry Ashmore and William Braggs, 369pp, 1968, Bantam Books, $.95.* An analysis of the U.S. conduct of the Vietnam war which concludes that the U.S. position is one of "an extraordinary exercise in duplicity."

304 **VIETNAM, The Unheard Voices** *by Don Luse and John Sommer, 350pp, 1968, Cornell University Press, $1.95.* Members of the International Voluntary Service who resigned in protest against U.S. policies here argue that the majority of Vietnamese is neither with the Vietcong nor with the Saigon government.

TEW 305 **THE UNITED NATIONS AND VIET-NAM** *by Lincoln P. Bloomfield, 44pp, 1968, Carnegie Endowment, $.60.* An analysis of why the United Nations has had no useful role to play in the Vietnam conflict. Argues for a non-U.N. international presence as part of a peace agreement.

306 **WAR, PEACE AND THE VIET CONG** *by Douglas Pike, 186pp, 1968, MIT Press, hardcover, $5.95.* Examination of the real contenders in the Vietnam war, their precarious hold on small segments of the South Vietnamese population. Argues that a socialist and neutralist South Vietnam, as part of a Federated Indochina, would eliminate the need for dominance of the entire population by one of the minority factions now on the battlefield.

307 **THE EDGE OF CHAOS,** *Michael Kirby (ed.), 72pp, 1968, Center for War/Peace Studies, $.75.* Background readings on the period from 1954 to 1963. Authors include Bernard Fall, Robert Shaplen, Douglas Pike and others.

INF 308 **THE TWO VIET-NAMS: A Political and Military Analysis** *by Bernard Fall, 507pp, 1967 (rev. ed.), Praeger, hardcover, $7.95.* Probably the best single source for unraveling the political and military complexities of the Vietnam conflict by a recognized Vietnam expert.

308A   TIME OUT OF HAND *by Robert Shaplen, 480pp, 1970, Harper & Row, $2.95.* A country-by-country analysis of Southeast Asia and of U.S. and Chinese policies in the region.

308B   THE CAMBODIAN CRISIS, *24pp, 1970, New America, $.25.* Background articles and peace proposals from New America (see Part III G). Describes the background to the Lon Noi coup, North Vietnamese and NLF military movement, U.S. intervention and the widening of the war.

309   PEACE IN VIETNAM, A New Approach in Southeast Asia *by the American Friends Service Committee, 112pp, 1967, Hill & Wang, $1.25.* Historical survey with a ten-point peace proposal.

310   VIETNAM: Lotus in a Sea of Fire *by Thich Nhat Hanh, 115pp, 1967, Hill & Wang, $1.25.* A Buddhist view of Vietnamese history which distinguishes between Vietnamese nationalism and Vietnamese Communism. The author believes that U.S. involvement in Vietnam has damaged a third force capable of offering an alternative to military or Communist rule. Calls for rebuilding such a third force based on Vietnam's religious community.

INT   311   VIETNAM, Document of a Major Crisis, *Marvin Gettleman (ed.), 448pp, 1966, Fawcett, $.95.* Anthology of documents, statements by heads of state, speeches by opponents of American policy.

312   VIETNAM READER, Articles and Documents, *Marcus Raskin and Bernard Fall (eds.), 415pp, 1967 (rev. ed.), Random House, $2.95.* Updated in 1967 to include major peace efforts. A valuable collection.

313   VIETNAM AND INTERNATIONAL LAW *by the Lawyers Committee of the American Bar Association, 160pp, 1967, O'Hara Books, $2.25.* Analysis of U.S. policy which finds it in violation of the U.S. Constitution and International Law. Includes the full State Department rebuttal.

314   THE VIETNAM WAR AND INTERNATIONAL

LAW, *Richard A. Falk (ed.), 633pp, 1968, Princeton, University Press, $3.95.* An anthology of articles presenting different factual and legal judgments.

315 **THE UNITED STATES IN VIETNAM** *by George Kahin and John W. Lewis, 465pp, 1967, Delta Books, $2.95.* An in-depth analysis of U.S. involvement in Vietnam by two critics.

316 **VIETCONG** *by Douglas Pike, 490pp, 1966, MIT Press, $2.95.* A detailed study reflecting official American opinion of the Vietcong, its origins, tactics and organizational strength.

317 **VIETNAM: Crisis of Conscience** *by Robert McAfee Brown, Abraham J. Heschel and Michael Novak, 127pp, 1967, Association Press, $.95.* Three essays by Catholic, Jewish and Protestant theologians arguing against U.S. action in Vietnam.

318 **THE BITTER HERITAGE, Vietnam and American Democracy, 1941–1966** *by Arthur M. Schlesinger, Jr., 128pp, 1967, Fawcett, $.75.* Lucid historical survey with a plan for scaling down the fighting with the aim of achieving a negotiated settlement based on some form of coalition government.

(see also 212, 217, 225, 227, 274 and 270)

Middle East

INT 319 **THE ISRAEL-ARAB READER, A Documentary History of the Middle East Conflict**, *Walter Laquer (ed.), 371pp, 1969, Bantam Books, $1.25.* Includes documents on the background to the British mandate (1922), the development of Palestine, 1920–1947, the establishment of Israeli independence, and the ensuing wars between the Arab states and Israel. An extremely valuable introduction to the agonizing problem of peace and reconciliation in the Middle East.

320 **ISRAEL, THE UNITED STATES AND THE UNITED NATIONS** *by George E. Gruen, 45pp, 1968, American Jewish Committee, $.75.* A discussion of the

role of the U.N. in the period before and after the six-day war and the possibilities of a peaceful settlement by the American Jewish Committee.

321 THE ARAB-ISRAEL CONFLICT *by Fayez A. Sayegh, 64pp, 1968, Arab Information Center, $.50.* A justification of war in the name of justice for the Palestinian people.

322 THE MIDDLE EAST CONFLICT *by Malcolm H. Kerr, 63pp, 1968, Foreign Policy Association, $.85.* A well-balanced analysis of the continuing conflict in the Middle East, stressing the wars of 1948, 1956 and 1967. Kerr suggests that U.S. policy has been too closely tied to Israel.

323 ISRAEL AND WORLD POLITICS, Roots of the Third Arab-Israeli War *by Theodore Draper, 172pp, 1968, Viking Press, $1.95.* Draper relates the 1967 war to larger issues of world politics.

(see also 33)

324 THE UNITED STATES AND THE ARAB WORLD *by William R. Polk, 160pp, 1964, Harvard University Press, hardcover, $5.95.* A survey of the Arab states, their goals and the goal of U.S. foreign policy. The author finds that there are many areas of agreement, although Israel is not one of them.

325 THE ARAB-ISRAELI DILEMMA *by Fred J. Kheurix, 436pp, 1968, Syracuse University Press, $4.25.* A critical analysis of the policies of all sides which discusses the historical background, the Palestine question before the U.N., Arab refugees, armistice complications, the June war and the prospects for peace. The author advocates increased authority for international bodies and a strengthened U.N. peace-keeping mission.

325A SEARCH FOR PEACE IN THE MIDDLE EAST *by the American Friends Service Committee, 72pp, 1970, American Friends Service Committee, $.75.* Calls for new Israeli peace initiatives to overcome the mood of absolute distrust that poisons the entire area. Calls for unilateral

Israeli withdrawal from territories occupied in 1967 in return for unequivocal recognition of Israel's territorial integrity by the Arab states and the Palestinians.

326 THE CYPRUS DILEMMA, Options for Peace *by the Institute for Mediterranean Affairs, 91pp, 1967, Institute for Mediterranean Affairs, $3.50.* Four essays which sketch the background of the present crisis and offer divergent solutions.

India/Pakistan

327 INDIA AND PAKISTAN, A Political Analysis *by Hugh Tinker, 228pp, 1968 (rev. ed.), Norton, $2.25.* Background analysis of the long dispute over Kashmir and the Tashkent conference at which the Soviet Union acted as an intermediary.

328 INDIA AND THE WEST, Pattern for a Common Policy *by Barbara Ward, 295pp, 1961, Norton, $1.45.* An attempt to force the West to see India as a major asset, whether neutral or not. Emphasis on assisting India in demonstrating that a country can achieve sustained economic growth in an atmosphere of political freedom.

Africa

329 THE NEW STATES OF AFRICA *by Arnold Rivkin, 63pp, 1967, Foreign Policy Association, $.85.* A useful introduction to the development of new nation-states along former colonial boundaries against a background of 900 tribal groupings with many different languages, religions and cultures.

330 NATIONS BY DESIGN, Institution-Building in Africa, *Arnold Rivkin (ed.), 386pp, 1968, Doubleday, $1.75.* An anthology discussing the problems of creating national loyalties on a continent where tribal loyalties are often more important. Discusses the creation of legal institutions, political institutions and industrialization with the focus on the need for viable institutions for promoting rapid social change.

331 THE UNKNOWN WAR IN THE SUDAN *by Lawrence Fellows, 10pp, 1968, New York Times, $.10.* Presents the background surrounding the seven-year-old war in the Sudan in which 500,000 lives have been lost.

332 BREADLESS BIAFRA, A People without Hope Caught in the Politics of Starvation *by John Sullivan, 104pp, 1969, Pflaum Press, $1.50.* A newsman's account of the effect of the Nigerian/Biafran war with a short political analysis.

332A THE BIAFRA STORY *by Frederick Forsyth, 236pp, 1969, Penguin Books, $1.45.* A political background and interpretation of the war of succession in Nigeria. Generally sympathetic to Biafra.

333 APARTHEID IN SOUTH AFRICA, a United Nations Report, *36pp, 1966, United Nations, $.50.* Includes a historical background and a description of United Nations efforts to resolve the crisis.

334 THE ANATOMY OF THE APARTHEID, Questions and Answers on the United Nations and Racial Discrimination in South Africa, *22pp, 1967, United Nations, $.15.*

335 RHODESIA, Outline of a Nonviolent Strategy to Resolve the Crisis *by Ralph Bell, 33pp, 1968, Housmans, $.50.* An attempt to prove the relevance of nonviolent tactics to a crisis area. Bell outlines the need for training and using a nonviolent expeditionary force.

336 ATTITUDE OF THE ASIAN-AFRICAN STATES TOWARD CERTAIN PROBLEMS OF INTERNATIONAL LAW *by R. P. Anand, 20pp, 1966, Duke Rule of Law Research Center, $.25.* Argues that the Asian-African states, while diverse, in general seek to cooperate through international organizations as the best means of protection against major power influence.

337 AFRICA AND THE COMMUNIST WORLD, *Zbigniew Brzezinski (ed.), 172pp, 1966. Praeger, $2.65.* An anthology of views examining Russia's foreign policy objectives in Africa.

338 **AFRICA IN SEARCH OF DEMOCRACY** *by K. A. Busia, 189pp, 1967, Praeger, hardcover, $4.25.* One of Ghana's leading intellectuals argues against one-party "guided" democracy and the Communist prescription for "people's democracy" while advocating a pluralistic approach with legal guarantees for minority rights.

(see also 162 and 502)

Latin America

339 **ROOTS OF THE DOMINICAN CRISIS** *by Theodore Draper, 16pp, 1965, League for Industrial Democracy, $.25.* Examines the removal of Juan Bosch from office in the light of its consequences.

340 **COLLISION COURSE, The Cuban Missile Crisis and Coexistence** *by Henry M. Pachter, 261pp, 1964, Praeger, $1.95.* Documents and analysis of brinkmanship.

341 **THIRTEEN DAYS: A Memoir of the Cuban Missile Crisis** *by Robert Kennedy, 224pp, 1968, Mentor Books, $.95.* An important historical document as well as an intensely interesting account of the fateful encounter between the U.S. and the Soviet Union in October 1962.

(see also 83, 84, 85, 87, 90, 249 and 347)

War/Peace Issues: Nuclear Weapons

342 **QUESTIONS AND ANSWERS CONCERNING THE SPREAD OF NUCLEAR WEAPONS** *by Arthur Larson, 82pp, 1968, Duke Rule of Law Research Center, $.25.* Attempts to answer opponents of the Nuclear Non-Proliferation Treaty.

343 **STOPPING THE SPREAD OF NUCLEAR WEAPONS** *by the United Nations Association, 48pp, 1967, United Nations Association, $1.00.* Addresses the problem of seeking to provide new options for security requirements of non-nuclear powers through a strengthened United Nations.

344 **NATIONAL SECURITY AND THE NUCLEAR TEST BAN** *by Jerome Wiesner and Herbert York, 8pp, 1964, Scientific American, $.20.* Two of President Eisen-

hower's former advisors assess the impact of and justification for the nuclear test-ban treaty.

345 A WORLD OF NUCLEAR POWERS, *Alastair Buchan (ed.)*, *176pp*, *1967*, *Prentice-Hall*, *$1.95*. Five authors study nuclear proliferation and its consequences for nuclear and non-nuclear powers. Offers a variety of alternatives to proliferation.

346 THE UNITED STATES AND THE SPREAD OF NUCLEAR WEAPONS *by William Bader*, *176pp*, *1967*, *Pegasus*, *$1.95*. A consultant to the Senate Foreign Relations Committee reviews U.S. nuclear policy since World War II and considers the likelihood of India, Japan, West Germany, Israel and others acquiring nuclear weapons. Bader is highly critical of the U.S. approach to nuclear proliferation, though he believes the Nuclear Non-Proliferation Treaty may provide a framework for further U.S.-Soviet cooperation for nuclear issues.

347 THE DENUCLEARIZATION OF LATIN AMERICA *by Alfonso Robles*, *167pp*, *1967*, *Carnegie Endowment*, *$1.95*. One of the leading proponents of declaring Latin America a nuclear-free zone describes the process by which that result was secured in the Treaty of Tlatelolco.

(see also 9, 13, 29, 30, 31 and 646)

War/Peace Issues: Anti-Ballistic Missiles (ABM)

TEW   348 THE ABM AND A WORLD WITHOUT WAR *by Robert Pickus*, *86pp*, *1969*, *World Without War Council*, *$.95*. Valuable for its background information on the ABM decision, this book's primary focus is on the contextual choices which citizens can set within which any war/peace issue is considered.

349 WHY ABM? Policy Issues in the Missile Defense Controversy, *Johan Holst and William Schneider, Jr. (eds.)*, *321pp*, *1969*, *Pergamon*, *hardcover*, *$6.95*. An anthology defending the development of the ABM and offering alternative rationales for its deployment. Discusses the ABM

in relation to the arms race, European defense and strategic arms control.

INT   350   THE CONTROVERSY OVER U.S. ANTI-BALLISTIC MISSILE SYSTEMS: Pros and Cons *32pp, 1968, Congressional Digest, $1.50*. A useful summary of the issues pairing Senators Russel, Dirksen, Pastore and Thurmond (pro) against Symington, Cooper, McCarthy and McGovern (con).

351   ABM: Yes or No? *147pp, 1969, Center for the Study of Democratic Institutions, pamphlet, $1.00, Hill & Wang, paperback, $1.75*. Arguing for the ABM are Donald Brennan and Leon Johnson, against are Jerome Wiesner and Senator McGovern.

352   ABM: A Guide to the Evaluation of the Safeguard System, *340pp, 1969, New American Library, $.95*. Introduced by Senator Edward Kennedy, this critique of the Nixon Administration proposal includes analysis of the ABM by sixteen scientists and experts. Selections are by Hans Berthe, Arthur Goldberg, Theodore Sorenson, Bill Moyers and others.

353   THE ABM AND THE CHANGED STRATEGIC MILITARY BALANCE—U.S.A. vs. U.S.S.R., *60pp, 1969, American Security Council, $1.75*. A justification of ABM deployment as required by American Security in the face of Russian ABM deployment and development of multiple targeted offensive missiles.

354   MIRV *by the Union of Concerned Scientists, 14pp, 1969, Union of Concerned Scientists, $.25*. The case against both testing and deployment of the Multiple-Independently-Targeted Re-entry Vehicle.

(see also 36)

War/Peace Issues: The Sea Bed

355   USES OF THE SEAS, *Edmund A. Gullien (ed.), 202pp, 1968, Prentice-Hall, $2.45*. Asks whether the rich resources of the seabeds will become an arena of nationalistic rivalry or an area of international cooperation.

356   THE SEA BED *24pp, 1968, War/Peace Report, special issue, $.50.* A study of the possible uses of the newly discovered wealth of the sea in building international cooperation and providing a resource for the world's war on poverty.

War/Peace Issues: Outer Space

357   OUTER SPACE, Prospects for Man and Society, *Lincoln Bloomfield (ed.), 267pp, 1968, Praeger, $2.50.* Studies the impact of space technology and exploration on man and society. Includes the U.S. Senate ratified treaty which proclaims astronauts "envoys of mankind."

Other War/Peace Issues

Recognition of Communist China, see #'s 294, 295, 297, 298

Foreign Aid, see #'s 87, 89, 91, 92, 93, 95, 98, 102

U.N. and World Organizations, see #'s 134, 139

Dealing with the Communist World, see #'s 292–300

The Draft, see #'s 454–459

Berlin, see #'s 232, 233

Human Rights, see #'s 108–112

Connally Reservation, see # 146

Open Seas, see #'s 114, 131, 141, 146

Arms Control and Disarmament, see #'s 35–68

VIII MORAL, RELIGIOUS, PHILOSOPHICAL AND ETHICAL THOUGHT ON WAR

In the matter of the use of mass violence in war, what is right? The contemporary peace seeker may have trouble recognizing the validity of this question, for it is seldom asked today. Yet, it intrudes whatever war/peace problem is under discussion.

Moralistic slogans abound alike in the peace movement and in the statements of governmental leaders, but the question, "What is right?" is seldom seriously considered. Currently dominant ethical views, whether stated in theological or secular terms, argue that it cannot be answered. It cannot be answered, one hears, either because there is no way to justify ethical standards or because all ethical standards are situationally based and change as particular situations change. Some refuse to deal with this question because they feel that the danger of war comes precisely from those who *do* assert that they are right and therefore justified in violently imposing their views on others. Those seeking an end to war need to consider the other side of that argument, for without standards by which conflict can be arbitrated or resolved, there is left only the test of violence. Without standards other than history, i.e., who wins the battles, right becomes identified with might. Thus both the existence of standards for determining what is right and their absence can be considered causes of war.

"Might is right" is one answer to the question. Given the fact that different people and groups think different things are right, and given our search for alternatives to war, what other answers make sense?

We have encountered the question of what is right in each of the previous sections. Questions about the use of violence in political relationships occur throughout religious and philosophical history. There are no simple answers. The use of violence by a state, for example, seems incompatible with the widely accepted moral injunction against murder. But being responsible for the security of a society may in some cases, say some thinkers (# 416), absolve men of responsibility for acts which they would ordinarily consider wrong.

Other ethical questions which we have encountered but which have not been stated are the following:

1. When there is a conflict between the dictates of conscience and acts held to be justified by the common good, how is it to be resolved?

2. What determines the legitimacy of a government and therefore its right to regulate the action of its citizens: the means by which it comes to power, the degree to which it represents the interests of its citizens, the social goals of its rulers, or the extent to which it is continuously authorized by citizen consent?

3. Does a state have the right to threaten the destruction of other states, if not of civilized life, in pursuit of its own security? Does the refusal to use such means require abandoning political responsibility?

4. Do national leaders have an obligation to exhaust all present alternatives to violence before war can be justified? Is war *then* justified or must attempts be made to create new alternatives? Is it morally preferable to resist domination nonviolently rather than risk mutual destruction?

5. What are the limits of our responsibility for each other? How do you rank conflicting responsibilities to family, state, religion, mankind, the person facing you?

6. Given agreement on goals, such as the elimination of poverty, the creation of representative governments or the creation of a national government, or world government, what are the limitations on means? How do you answer that question—by determining what works? Does killing men to achieve just goals necessarily corrupt the goals and those who work for them?

7. Does a community of men have a right to establish and enforce laws for all members of the community? How does a man become a member of such a community? Can he end his membership? What determines the limits of a political community: its power, the geographical territory it controls, the social class, race, or heritage of a minority within a state?

8. Can there be a *universal* declaration of human rights? If human rights are universal, is every man responsible for their enforcement? What institution should be responsible for fulfilling such a responsibility?

All political positions on war/peace questions explicitly or implicitly answer these and similar ethical questions. In fact, it is the answers to these questions that often determine a person's position on specific war/peace issues.

How should we answer them?

For most of modern history the answers to such questions have been sought in religious articles of faith. These are God's laws which require obedience. The increase of secular thought since the eighteenth century has led to two distinctive, non-theistic ways of answering such questions: utilitarianism as defended by John Stuart Mill, and the acceptance of categorical imperatives, or rational, obligatory rules seen as inherent in human nature and beyond empirical proof, as argued by Immanuel Kant. Rejecting both approaches as insufficient in themselves, some modern secular theorists have sought to combine them, defining an ethical obligation as one which is applicable to all men and conducive to human welfare.

Clearly the lack of agreed upon standards by which men can decide what is right in the use of violence is one major obstacle on the road to a world without war.

It is true that some movements, convinced of the absolute righteousness of their cause, have sought to impose their creed on others through violence. But it is also true that other persons believing in the same creeds have sought to spread them through persuasion rather than violence (# 359). It is, it would appear, not the belief in standards but the justification of violent means for imposing them which results in war.

It is essential to recognize that people do differ widely in the opinions, practices and values they believe valid. Such disagreement, however, can often be resolved by appealing to more basic beliefs or, by a common arrangement, to contest areas of difference without violence. Crucial to the problem of ending war is the acceptance of one norm: the use of violence cannot possibly be justified until all alternatives have been exhausted. This obligation can be derived from the democratic tradition which regards men as of equal worth and forbids murder on the ground that it denies the individual an inherent right, or from the religious view that men are of infinite worth.

But when the obligation not to kill comes in conflict with the obligation to do justice or to aid one's community, those committed to such democratic and religious values have often justified war on utilitarian grounds. The moral pacifist argues that the obligation not to kill is absolute (# 371–376). Others have held, consistent with their interpretation of the democratic, Christian or Jewish traditions, that killing is always regrettable, but that sometimes it is a lesser evil (# 386 and # 388) than abandonment of community responsibility or acquiescence in injustice.

The tension between these two important strands of moral thought impose at least the following obligations: a *pacifist*, one who accepts the norm that it is never just to participate in mass violence, must work to establish alternatives to violent conflict in order to avoid standing as witness to murder. The just-war advocate, one who believes human welfare requires, in some situations, joining an army, must work with the pacifist in order to avoid killing. Thus, while a pacifist may reject all violence now, and a just-war advocate may reject submission to others' use of violence, both to be consistent with their ethical commitments must combine with their present practice the obligation to work for a world without war.

There are two other ethical perspectives on war that have served as guidelines for many. But few thoughtful people rest easy today in the traditional patriotic obligation to go to war and to do in war whatever political leaders command. Many are adopting a modern version of another very old perspective on these matters. They focus on the *personal* reality involved, refusing to consider large abstractions, like the nation, communism, or democracy. In this personalized approach the focus is on the individual human being. It is your responsibility to him, to yourself, your family, your friends, the actual human being you encounter that counts; you owe nothing to formally organized political structures. Whether expressed as political anarchism or by ignoring communications from the draft board, it is an attractive perspective to many today. It states an important truth: if we lose our humanity by failing to see the *person* opposite us, if we lose him and our responsibility to him in the larger terms of politics and history, it matters little whether we drop the bomb or are hit, whether we end in concentration camps or guarding them. The personalized approach to war/peace issues thus reveals significant problems. But it will not end war, for in its attempt to deal with the problems, it reduces them to what they only rarely are: a question of personal relationships.

The books in this chapter argue that the question of what is right can be answered. They provide a number of different, sometimes conflicting, grounds for this position: religious, utilitarian, rational and historical. They survey different attitudes toward the use of mass violence, the obligation of the rich nations to the poorer ones, the nature of political obligations, and other central ethical issues.

Past and Present

358 **COMPLETE PLAYS OF ARISTOPHANES**, *M. Hades (ed.), 501pp, 192, Bantam Books, $1.25.* A Greek pacifist and playwright argues against the Peloponnesian War and much more.

INT   359 **CHRISTIAN ATTITUDES TOWARD WAR AND PEACE** *by Roland Bainton, 299pp, 1960, Abingdon, $2.25.* A historical survey and critical appraisal by a well-known historian.

360 **ON WORLD GOVERNMENT** *by Dante Alighieri, 80pp, 1957, Bobbs-Merrill, $.75.* Dante's plan for a world government of Christian powers written in 1317.

361 **THE ESSENTIAL ERASMUS,** *John Dolan (ed.), 397pp, 1964 Mentor Books, $.75.* Erasmus of Rotterdam (1466–1536) found it "incredible to see the tremendous expenditures of work and effort which intelligent beings

put forth in an effort to exchange (peace) for a heap of ruinous evils (war.)" *(The Complaint of Peace)*

362 **ON GOD AND POLITICAL DUTY** *by John Calvin, 102pp, 1956, Bobbs-Merrill, $.75.* Calvin argues that obedience to earthly rulers takes precedence over the freedom which Christianity grants to conscience.

363 **PROLEGOMENA TO THE LAW OF WAR AND PEACE** *by Hugo Grotius, 43pp, 1957, Bobbs-Merrill, $.95.* Grotius set forth the rules for warfare in order that it might be conducted in a more humane manner (1625).

364 **ON PERPETUAL PEACE** *by Immanuel Kant, 59pp, 1957, Bobbs-Merrill, $.75.* Kant foresaw the elimination of war through the development of a world government of republican nations (1795).

INF 365 **THE COMMUNIST MANIFESTO** *by Karl Marx and Friedrich Engels, 48pp, 1968, International Publishers, $.40.* Marx and Engels foresaw the elimination of war by the elimination of class hostilities when one class achieves world domination (1848).

INT 366 **WAR AND CONSCIENCE IN AMERICA** *by Edward Long, Jr., 144pp, 1968, Westminster, $1.65.* A lucid attempt to explain the great variety of attitudes toward war current today. The author treats fairly conscientious participation in and conscientious objection to war.

367 **MODERN WAR AND THE CHURCHES** *by Ralph Moellering, 96pp, 1969, Augsburg, $2.50.* Argues that a Christian must choose either war or peace; after presenting three historical Christian justifications for war, the author concludes that none of them will do today.

368 **CHRISTIAN-MARXIST DIALOGUE,** *Paul Oestreicher (ed.), 156pp, 1969, Macmillan, $1.95.* A discussion between East European Marxists and radical Christians which discusses the similarities and differences between modern, radical theology and Marxism.

369   WAR AND MORAL DISCOURSE by Ralph B. Potter, 128pp, 1968, John Knox, $2.45. Assesses the many ways men determine the rightness or wrongness of a war and examines Christian pacifism, just war (defensive war) and holy crusade (offensive war) doctrines in Christian theology.

370   AMERICAN FOREIGN POLICY AND MORAL RHETORIC, The Example of Vietnam by David Little, 117pp, 1969, Council on Religion and International Affairs (hereafter CRIA), $1.75. Little argues that the liberal critics of American Vietnam policy paradoxically reject moral issues in international relations as irrelevant, while using language which is loaded with unconsidered moral connotations. Both a useful critique of much Vietnam rhetoric and a statement of the inescapable relevance of moral issues to the conduct of international relations.

(see also 517, 533 and 557-567)

Christian Pacifism

371   THE CHRISTIAN CONSCIENCE AND WAR by the Church Peace Mission, 48pp, 1951, Church Peace Mission, $.25. An important pacifist statement which argues that a Christian cannot justify war without violating his commitment.

372   AN ALTERNATIVE TO WAR by Gordon Zahn, 32pp, 1963, CRIA, $.50. Argues that nonviolent resistance to war is an alternative which Catholics should adopt. The best short pamphlet which relates Catholic teachings to nonviolence.

373   BLESSED ARE THE MEEK: The Roots of Christian Nonviolence by Thomas Merton, 12pp, 1967, Catholic Peace Fellowship, $.25. A pacifist statement of the central Christian concepts which support nonviolence.

374   REINHOLD NIEBUHR AND CHRISTIAN PACIFISM by John Yoder, 19pp, 1954, Herald Press, $.25. A critique of Niebuhr by a Mennonite scholar who first sets

forth the areas of agreement with Niebuhr and then gives the reasons why he believes Christianity supports pacifism.

INF **375** **THE NEW TESTAMENT BASIS OF PACIFISM** *by C. H. C. MacGregor, 160pp, 1968, Fellowship Publications, $1.25.* The acceptance of suffering presented as a Christian obligation. A traditional Christian pacifist statement and a careful analysis of the New Testament by a British theologian.

376 **THE DAGGER AND THE CROSS** *by Culbert Rutenber, 138pp, 1965, Fellowship Publications, $1.50.* A careful survey of the Biblical foundations of pacifism written in the context of contemporary Christian thought.

(see also 147, 218, 433, 444, 445, 462, 588, 561 and 564-567)

Christianity and on War: Just War

377 **RELIGION AND PEACE,** *Homer Jack (ed.), 137pp, 1966, Bobbs-Merrill, $1.80.* Papers from the national Inter-Religious Conference on Peace which underline the need for commitment on war/peace issues by the religious community.

378 **WORLD RELIGIONS AND WORLD PEACE,** *Homer Jack (ed.), 208pp, 1968, Beacon Press, $1.95.* Papers of the New Delhi International Inter-Religious Symposium on Peace which brought together leaders of the various world religions to consider and discuss their responsibilities in the war/peace field. Contains an especially useful paper on Gandhi by Shri Ramachandran.

379 **MODERN WAR AND THE PURSUIT OF PEACE** *by Theodore Weber, 36pp, 1968, CRIA, $.50.* A careful consideration of just war doctrine, its assumption that men choose war, its traditional applications and the crucial role of the actors' intentions in present Christian consideration of what constitutes a just and unjust war.

380 **ETHICS AND UNITED STATES FOREIGN POLICY** *by Ernest W. Lefever, 199pp, 1960, Meridian, $2.25.* An attempt to determine the relevance, if any, of ethical considerations to the realities of power politics.

INT 381 **PACEM IN TERRIS, Encyclical Letter of Pope John XXIII,** *48pp, 1963, National Catholic Welfare Conference, $.35.* A vital and influential statement which restates the Catholic Church's responsibility to help achieve peace on earth. It has led many others to consider their own responsibility.

382 **PACEM IN TERRIS,** *Edward Reed (ed.), 259pp, 1965, Pocket Books, $.95.* A symposium of world leaders in response to Pope John's *Pacem In Terris* encyclical. Discusses the question of world government.

383 **RELIGION AND INTERNATIONAL RESPONSIBILITY** *by Robert Gordis, 21pp, 1959, CRIA, $.50.* Argues that the ethical heritage of the Judeo-Christian tradition is both practical and relevant to international affairs.

384 **MORAL TENSIONS IN INTERNATIONAL AFFAIRS** *by John Bennett, 27pp, 1964, CRIA, $.50.* An assessment of the importance of and difficulties in relating moral understandings to political dilemmas.

385 **FOREIGN POLICY IN CHRISTIAN PERSPECTIVE** *by John Bennett, 160pp, 1966, Scribner's, $1.25.* The head of the Union Theological Seminary seeks to improve foreign policy by judging it in the light of his Christian commitment. The author finds that the need to defend one's neighbor makes nonviolent theories inapplicable to international relations.

386 **WAR AND/OR SURVIVAL** *by William O'Brien, 216pp, 1968, Doubleday, hardcover, $4.95.* A study of modern war, the deterrence strategy, revolution and the use of military force as means of settling disputes. The author concludes, after carefully examining the moral issues and assessing the alternatives to war, that war is justified to promote justice and preserve political order.

387 **FAITH AND POLITICS: A Commentary on Religious, Social and Political Thought in a Technological Age,** *essays by Reinhold Neibuhr, edited by Ronald Stone,*

268pp, 1968, Norton, hardcover, $6.50. Includes several valuable essays on international relations.

388 THE JUST WAR, Force and Political Responsibility *by Paul Ramsey*, 554pp, 1968, Scribner's, hardcover, $12.50. Examines the morality of the use of nuclear weapons, just and unjust war conceptions, deterrence and defense theories and argues for the responsible use of force (military) to maintain and achieve justice and political order.

(see also 425, 431, 448 and 449)

Christianity and Foreign Aid

389 PACEM IN TERRIS AND FOREIGN AID *by Richard Collins*, 10pp, 1966, *Committee for World Disarmament and World Economic Development*, $.10. An examination of Pope John's encyclical and its implication for foreign aid.

390 FOREIGN AID: Moral and Political Aspects *by Victor Ferkiss*, 48pp, 1965, CRIA, $.50. Sets standards for judging foreign aid programs.

391 LINE AND PLUMMET *by Richard Dickinson*, 112pp, 1968, *World Council of Churches*, $1.50. A searching analysis of development in human terms which places attitudes toward economic development in a theological perspective. Considers the role the churches should and should not play in the field.

Christianity and Nuclear Weapons

TEW 392 THE MORAL DILEMMA OF NUCLEAR WEAPONS, *William Clancy (ed.)*, 78pp, 1961, CRIA, $1.50. An anthology of works bringing together political scientists, military strategists and journalists. Still the best introduction to the subject.

393 MORALITY AND MODERN WAR *by John Murray*, 23pp, 1967, CRIA, $.50. A non-pacifist study of the

Catholic Church's teaching on war in the light of the development of nuclear weapons.

Judaism and War

394   JUDAISM AND WAR *by Robert Pickus, 40pp, 1968, World Without War Council, $.50.* An anthology of materials on five different perspectives on war encountered within the Jewish tradition. Prepared for high school discussion, useful for adults.

395   I AND THOU *by Martin Buber, 137pp, 1958, Scribner's, $1.25.* Buber believes that the I-Thou relationship is the only ethical one, and he draws from that insight a commitment to nonviolence. A difficult exposition of human relationships.

396   PATHS IN UTOPIA *by Martin Buber, 152pp, 1949, Beacon Press, $1.75.* Critical appraisal of utopian thought by a utopian.

397   GOOD AND EVIL *by Martin Buber, 143pp, 1953, Scribner's, $1.25.* A philosophic attempt to clear up the puzzles which cloud the distinction between good and evil. An important work by a modern Jewish theologian.

398   JEWISH VALUES AND SOCIAL CRISIS: A Casebook for Social Action *by Albert Vorspan, 339pp, 1969, Union of American Hebrew Congregations, $4.00.* A helpful attempt to relate the teachings of Judaism to contemporary problems. Includes sections on "War, Peace and Conscience," "Civil Disobedience" and "Israel and Zionism."

(see also 463)

Philosophic Issues: Mass Violence

TEW   399   NEITHER VICTIMS NOR EXECUTIONERS *by Albert Camus, 28pp, 1968, World Without War Council, $.25.* Camus' classic delineation of the terrible dividing line between those who justify mass violence and those who refuse to do so. Introductory essay by Robert

Pickus discusses how much of the present peace movement blurs that line.

400   THEIR MORALITY AND OURS *by Leon Trotsky, 54pp, 1969, Merit, $.95.* Trotsky denies that there is a valid nonviolent position in a world in revolutionary ferment. He argues that the only choice is between revolutionary violence or the violence of the status quo.

400A   ETHICS, VIOLENCE AND REVOLUTION *by Charles West, 72pp, 1969, CRIA, $1.75.* West, Professor of Christian Ethics at Princeton Theological Seminary, carefully assesses the ethical issues involved.

401   NEW THEOLOGY NO. 6, On Revolution and Non-Revolution, Violence and Non-Violence, Peace and Power, *Martin Marty and Dean Peerman (eds.), 287pp, 1969, Macmillan, $1.95.* Reprinted from *Theological Journal,* these essays indicate both the concern of modern theologians with social issues and the focus of that concern: revolution and violence. Included are selections on the Marxist-Christian dialogue, on pacifism, revolution and the "third world."

402   REVOLUTION IN THE REVOLUTION *by Regis Debray, 126pp, 1968, Grove Press, $.95.* In the context of Latin America, Debray articulates his faith that somewhere among the peasants or workers there must be the purity of intention Marx spoke of. Debray calls for revolutionary violence to create the political forces necessary for achieving The Revolution.

403   THE REBEL *by Albert Camus, 209pp, 1960, Random House, $1.65.* Camus examines the rebel as a social type and concludes with a plea for a philosophy of limits.

404   RESISTANCE, REBELLION AND DEATH *by Albert Camus, 209pp, 1960, Random House, hardcover, $2.45.* An anthology of nineteen essays on nonviolence, rebellion and social obligation selected by the author. One of the best introductions to Albert Camus' thought.

405   **FORCE, ORDER AND JUSTICE** by *Robert Osgood and Robert Tucker,* 374pp, 1967, *Johns Hopkins Press,* hardcover, *$10.00.* Argues against the viability of nonviolent alternatives to war; but recognizes that nuclear weapons have sharpened the apparent paradox between preparation for war and the use of violence to achieve order necessary for the pursuit of justice.

(see also 20)

Rationality and Ethical Relativism

INF   406   **FOUNDATIONS OF THE METAPHYSICS OF MORALS** by *Immanuel Kant,* 92pp, 1959, *Liberal Arts Press,* $.80. Kant's attempt to construct a moral philosophy free from evidence about how people live. The resultant moral laws are universal, must be devoid of self-interested intention and dependent upon experience only in determining their application.

407   **UTILITARIANISM** by *John Stuart Mill,* 350pp, 1962, *Meridian* $1.45. Mill's defense of the greatest happiness for the greatest number as the norm on which a rational ethics can be based.

408   **THEORIES OF ETHICS,** *Philippa Foot,* 187pp, 1967, *Oxford University Press,* $1.50. An anthology focusing on the "naturalistic fallacy" (the impossibility of deriving obligatory rules from descriptive evidence) and utilitarianism through current philosophic disputes. Especially useful is John Searle's "How to Derive the Ought from the Is."

409   **THREE ARGUMENTS CONCERNING THE MORALITY OF WAR** by *Richard Wasserstrom,* 13pp, 1968, *Journal of Philosophy,* $.25. Applies moral considerations to warfare between nation-states and concludes by stating the problems which an argument that it is morally unjustifiable to participate in war must meet.

410   **ETHICAL JUDGMENT,** The Use of Science in Ethics by *Abraham Edel,* 348pp, 1955, *Macmillan,* $2.45.

Edel analyzes seven strands contributing to ethical relativism: morality is man-made, everything changes, doing your own thing, struggle for power, mechanistic psychological and educational theory and linguistic theory. He then studies these strands in modern social science disciplines and concludes that democratic values are well-supported and should be considered the basis for moral criticism.

411 **THE LOGIC OF MORAL DISCOURSE** *by Paul Edwards, 248pp, 1955, Macmillan, $1.95.* A study of the problems encountered in rendering moral judgments which concludes with an argument for their legitimacy and relevance. An important work by the editor of the *Encyclopedia of Philosophy.*

INF   412 **SCIENCE AND HUMAN VALUES** *by J. Bronowski, 118pp, 1965, Harper & Row, $1.25.* Examines the place of value considerations in the pursuit of scientific ends. Includes the author's famous essay, "The Abacus and the Rose."

413 **PRIMARY PHILOSOPHY** *by Michael Scriven, 303pp, 1966, McGraw-Hill, hardcover, $7.95.* Argues that reason can dictate answers to man's primary problems, or when evidence and reason is inconclusive, at least achieve the best interim solution. Concludes that democracy (representative) is probably a prerequisite of a moral society but no guarantee of one.

Political Community and the Legitimation of Governments

414 **THE LEGITIMATION OF GOVERNMENTS,** An Annotated Bibliography *by Peter Cremer, 6pp, 1969, World Without War Council, $.10.* One-paragraph descriptions of what major social theorists have held lends legitimacy to a government.

415 **OBLIGATION AND THE BODY POLITIC** *by Joseph Tussman, 144pp, 1960, Oxford University Press,*

$1.50. Argues that individuals belong to organizations they did not "join" by virtue of the benefits they receive from them. Offers a difficult intellectual challenge to individuals considering conscientious objection, civil disobedience or other forms of appeal to a higher obligation than that of obeying the law.

INF   416   **MORAL MAN AND IMMORAL SOCIETY** *by Reinhold Niebuhr, 248pp, 1960, Scribner's, $2.45.* A book which sets a new modern framework for consideration of fundamental moral and political issues; the individual's relationship to the state, "legitimate" action for social change and the use of force to achieve justice. Niebuhr holds that societies are different entities than individuals, requiring different moral categories for judgment.

417   **MAN'S NATURE AND HIS COMMUNITIES** *by Reinhold Niebuhr, 125pp, 1965, Scribner's, $2.25.* Four essays on the nature of man and the obstacles to world community.

418   **THE IDEA OF WAR AND PEACE IN CONTEMPORARY PHILOSOPHY** *by Irving Horowitz, 224pp, 1957, Paine-Whitman, hardcover, $4.50.* A study of major twentieth century philosophers and their attitudes toward war and peace: metaphysical harmony (Whitehead), Pacifism (Tolstoy and Gandhi), Humanism (Einstein), Universal Individualism (Perry), man against man (Russell), historical vision (Lenin), and others. Concludes with an attempt to develop an "integrated philosophy of peace."

419   **THE CRITIQUE OF WAR, Contemporary Philosophical Explorations,** *Robert Ginsberg (ed.), 360pp, 1969, Henry Regnery Co., $3.95.* An anthology exploring the causes of war, its nature in the modern world and the problem of justifying war today. Examines alternatives to war including law and nonviolent resistance. Useful as a challenge to philosophers to consider war as a distinct problem.

420 THE CASE FOR MODERN MAN *by Charles Frankel, 240pp, 1966, Harper & Row, $1.45.* An important modern philosopher argues that the prophets of doom are always with us.

421 THE POLITICAL COMMUNITY, A Study of Anomie *by Sebastian de Grazia, 258pp, 1948, University of Chicago Press, $1.95.* A study of the relationship of consent and belief systems to democratic social change and of anomie (alienation) to violent change.

422 THE MORALITY OF LAW *by Lon L. Fuller, 202pp, 1964, Yale University Press, $1.45.* Usefully distinguishing between the moralities of duty and of aspiration, the author goes on to examine the relationship between law and morality and state the moral preconditions of law.

423 THE CONCEPT OF LAW *by H. L. A. Hart, 263pp, 1961, Oxford University Press, hardcover, $6.50.* An introduction to the philosophy of law, the bases of law and its worth in adjudicating disputes.

424 THE PHILOSOPHY OF LAW IN HISTORICAL PERSPECTIVE *by Carl J. Friedrich, 297pp, 1957, University of Chicago Press, $1.95.* A study of the different origins of law: divine, social contract, human nature, as required by justice, etc. Concludes with an examination of "Peace and the World Community of Law."

425 DARE TO RECONCILE, Seven Settings for Creating Community *by John Oliver Nelson, 127pp, 1968, Friendship Press, $1.50.* Argues that Christians have a responsibility to reconcile antagonists. Includes several dramatic situations in which the goal is to change conflicting individuals and groups into a community. Deals with war, race, alienation and generational conflict.

426 THE CHILDREN OF LIGHT AND THE CHILDREN OF DARKNESS, A Vindication of Democracy and a Critique of its Traditional Defense *by Reinhold Niebuhr, 190pp, 1944, Scribner's, $1.25.* Argues that democratic ideals often fail to account for the evil which men may do, and that democracy rests on moral attitudes which should be distinguished from those groups who may hold such attitudes for self-interested reasons at a particular time. Defends the idea that democracy is relevant to the emergent world community.

(see also 517-552)

IX CONSCIENTIOUS OBJECTION AND THE DRAFT

One cause of war is individual willingness to join armies, for armies ultimately depend on the cooperation and obedience of individual soldiers. Some conscientious objectors therefore conclude that the withdrawal of their consent is the sole action needed to end war. All mankind need do, they say, is join them, for wars will cease when men refuse to fight. This tautology does not take us very far, however. Most human beings are not C.O.'s; most non-C.O.'s, even though they may hate war's effects, feel that war is sometimes justified. There are, they say, evils greater than war, and in many situations there is no alternative to war or surrender. To get all men to refuse to fight, one must either demonstrate that there is no greater evil than war or that there are alternatives to war or surrender in situations of mass conflict.

Still the C.O.'s choice, or the dilemma faced by any person who considers resisting his country's call to military service, poignantly focuses the abstract issues considered in the previous section. The combination of the Vietnam war and the Selective Service System has forced many young men, and the families, schools and churches involved in their lives, to think deeply about problems of war and conscience and about the rights and obligations of citizenship in a democratic society.

One essential element in a body of knowledge adequate to the problem of ending war involves problems of conscience and war and of conscription for military service. The bibliography of this chapter includes general introductions to these problems as well as studies of particular issues. Books listed in chapters 8, 10 and 11 also bear directly on the matters considered here.

Many regard military service as an essential and honorable duty of the citizens of a democratic society. Others view it as a most objectionable form of tyranny. The concept of a universal military obligation is closely related to the rise of mass democracy. Since Napoleon, military conscription has spread to all the countries of continental Europe and in recent years to virtually the whole world. As Harold Bing, recent chairman of the War Resisters' International, points out (# 444), conscription is looked upon almost as a necessary adjunct of national sovereignty and independence. A general obligation for military service is regarded by some as a fairer and more effective restraint on a military foreign policy than a volunteer professional army. General conscription, the argument goes, touches every family and thus acts as a restraint on political leaders. Like compulsory education and compulsory taxation, it is argued, conscription is an essential requisite of democratic government.

Bing gives three primary reasons for resistance to conscription. First, conscription is an instrument of war preparation and war operation. Far from restraining political leaders, it conditions each generation to accept preparation for war as right and rational. Second, it is the most extreme assertion of the state's power over the free choice of the individual and as such, inculates an attitude of subservience to authority, which undermines the very conception of democracy.

But most fundamentally, military conscription "deprives the individual of personal responsibility in matters of life and death; his own, and more particularly, of others." To compel a man to engage in killing other human beings whom he does not know and with whom he may well have no quarrel, is the "greatest infringement of natural liberty and moral freedom." But a greater "infringement," say some of our authors (# 366) is being killed yourself by a man in someone else's army who has a "quarrel" with the political community to which you belong.

The issue of conscription is a profound one. Nowhere does the perspective of *To End War* make more sense. Only as we succeed in controlling the threat of war do we open a way out of the moral and political ambiguities which conscription for military service poses for those committed to democratic values. That is why the questions raised by the conscientious objector are so important, even to those that do not share the C.O.'s moral or religious belief.

Wars are not only the sum total of numerous decisions by individuals; they are also the product of defective social institutions. Not only individuals must change, but so also must institutions. Many pacifists tend to view problems of conscience and war only in a personal dimension, ignoring the social and political context of choice. The terrible reality confronting the conscientious objector is that even though he says no to war, even though he correctly asserts the importance of each individual's moral choice, he must also recognize that, at least in the short run, war will continue despite his personal refusal to participate. C.O.'s who see this reality know that more is needed than simply a personal withdrawal. They seek ways to make their lives count in building the institutions of peace.

Understanding of the C.O. position begins with one basic concept: a C.O. may regard the *goals* of a war as just (as some see our goals in World War II), but he will never countenance the *means* (warfare) as permissible in reaching these goals. The C.O. usually argues that means must be compatible with ends, or ends will never be achieved. He insists that organized mass violence will never bring peace or achieve justice.

This idea differentiates the C.O. from many other objectors to the draft and the Vietnam war. These latter do not necessarily object to all war. They may, on political grounds (e.g., the U.S. is on the wrong side in Vietnam), selectively object to a particular use of military power. The problem here is agreement or disagreement with the right of the government to make these judgments for the whole society. Others may object to conscription, not to war (# 448). An objection may be that military service compromises one's personal stance ("going into the army is not my style") or one's religious stance (as early Christians rejected service in Rome's army because such service involved idolatrous practices).

Any one or all of these positions may be considered grounds for legally excusing a person from military service in the future, but such *selective* forms of objection implicitly legitimize the use of organized mass violence in some circumstances, and thus do not necessarily contribute to ending war. This is especially true when such objectors feel no obligation to work to develop alternatives to war.

Many other issues are raised by the draft; e.g., questions of administrative fairness and due process, and more general constitutional questions. None of these problems appear basic to the problem of ending war. They are therefore not pursued further here.

Conscription itself, as indicated above, is a central issue for some C.O.'s. But the conscientious objector, while denying that war can be justified, generally recognizes that members of a society incur obligations to the society and may be required to perform some service to it. Many C.O.'s combine this sense of social obligation, which they seek to fulfill in consonance with their conscience, with the realization that most Americans do support war and the draft for purposes they believe legitimate. A conscientious objection to military service is viewed by such C.O.'s as just one step in the long struggle to change men's minds and to develop alternatives to mass violence in the defense of values. We turn to these nonviolent alternatives in the next chapter of *To End War*.

Conscientious Objection: Present

427 DRAFT COUNSELORS KIT, *Steve Bischoff (ed.), 400pp, 1969, World Without War Council, $9.50.* A WWWC kit offering extensive information on draft counselling procedures, especially information on the C.O. classification and the political and value choices involved. Includes all items marked K below.

K   **428 TABLE OF CONTENTS:** Draft Counselors Kit *by Steve Bischoff, 8pp, 1969, World Without War Council, $.10.* An annotated list of materials needed to adequately inform an individual about the conscientious objection position and other problems of draft counselling.

K   **429 HANDBOOK FOR CONSCIENTIOUS OBJECTORS,** *Arlo Tatem (ed.), 100pp, 1970, Central Committee for Conscientious Objectors (hereafter CCCO), $1.00.* The basic handbook containing much of the information needed by individuals considering becoming conscientious objectors to war.

INT   **430 CONSCIENCE AND THE DRAFT:** Intro-
K   ductory Materials, *16pp, 1969, World Without War Council, $.35.* A brief description of the alternative choices facing a young man of draft age (from 1-A to Noncooperation), a sample form 150 (request for classification

as a conscientious objector), and instructions on building a C.O. file, on writing support letters for conscientious objectors and on C.O. procedures.

κ   431 **STATEMENTS OF RELIGIOUS BODIES ON CONSCIENTIOUS OBJECTION** *by the National Interreligious Service Board for Conscientious Objectors (hereafter NISBCO)*, 62pp, 1970, NISBCO, $.75. Official statements of all the major religious denominations on conscientious objection.

432 **QUESTIONS AND ANSWERS ON THE CLASSIFICATION AND ASSIGNMENT OF CONSCIENTIOUS OBJECTORS** *by NISBCO*, 40pp, 1967, $.35. Provides authoritative answers to the questions most frequently asked about becoming a conscientious objector.

κ   433 **CATHOLICS AND CONSCIENTIOUS OBJECTION** *by Jim Forrest*, 12pp, 1966, *Catholic Peace Fellowship*, $.15. A pamphlet prepared especially for Catholics which draws on the traditions of the Catholic Church to support the conscientious objector's position.

κ   434 **WHO IS A C.O.?** *by NISBCO*, 6pp, 1968, $.05. A pamphlet which answers many questions. Thoughtful and concise.

κ   435 **UP TIGHT WITH THE DRAFT?** *by War Resisters League*, 8pp, 1967, $.05. A pamphlet for young men considering conflicting obligations and the possible ways of resolving them.

436 **GUIDELINES FOR EAST BAY DRAFT COUNSELING CENTER** *by Robert Pickus and Steve Bischoff*, 8pp, 1969, *World Without War Council*, $.10. An almost singular example of draft counseling aimed at providing a searching examination of religious and ethical dimensions of draft decisions as well as unbiased information, undertaken with the formal cooperation of community organizations.

κ   437 **WHY WE COUNSEL**: Conscience and War *by Allan Blackman and John Messer*, 20pp, 1967, *World*

Without War Council, $.35. A distinctive approach to problems of draft counselling emphasizing the relation of the individual's objection to war and the problems of ending war.

438 THE CONSCIENTIOUS OBJECTOR AND THE ARMED FORCES *by CCCO, 10pp, 1968, $.15.* Prepared for members of the armed forces who believe they are conscientious objectors to war.

к **439 FACE TO FACE WITH YOUR DRAFT BOARD: A Guide to Personal Appearances** *by Allan Blackman, 96pp, 1969, World Without War Council, $.95.* A description of the procedures, questions and answers encountered when a local draft board probes an individual's claim to a C.O. classification. Indispensable for C.O.'s, a must for draft counselors, valuable for every registrant facing a personal appearance before his draft board.

к **440 ANSWERING SSS FORM 150 KIT** *by World Without War Council, 35pp, 1970, $.50.* Includes a sample form 150, CCCO News Notes on the Seeger decision and a memorandum on answering the questions in SSS Form 150.

к **441 MEMORANDUM CONCERNING 1967 REVISION OF THE DRAFT LAW** *by Allan Blackman and Al Carlson, 6pp, 1969, World Without War Council, $.10.* Describes the new draft law as it affects young men considering the C.O. position.

к **442 ON OBTAINING A C.O. CLASSIFICATION AFTER BEING ISSUED AN INDUCTION NOTICE** *by CCCO, 6pp, 1966, $.05.* Describes what steps can be taken to obtain a C.O. classification after receiving a notice of induction into the armed forces. The burden of proof is much greater for those who wait so long.

442A ADVICE FOR CONSCIENTIOUS OBJECTORS IN THE ARMED FORCES *by Mike Wittels, 147pp, 1970, CCCO, $1.00.* A handbook for men who become C.O.'s after entering the military. Offers advice on a variety of problems a C.O. in the armed forces is likely to encounter.

443   **GUIDE TO ALTERNATIVE SERVICE** *by NISBCO, 86pp, 1970, $.75*. A list of agencies approved by the Selective Service System for alternative service by C.O.'s.

444   **CONSCRIPTION: A World View** *by War Resisters International, 166pp, 1968, Housmans, $2.25*. Examines the status of conscription, and particularly conscientious objection, in nearly every country in the world. An excellent guide to comparative study of this issue.

Conscientious Objection: Past

445   **CONSCIENTIOUS OBJECTION IN THE CIVIL WAR** *by E. Wright, 274pp, 1966, A. S. Barnes, $1.95*. A study of individuals in America in 1861–65 who tried to resolve their conflicting obligations to conscience, the state and social justice.

446   **DIARY OF A SELF-MADE CONVICT** *by Alfred Hassler, 182pp, 1958, Fellowship Publications, $1.50*. A moving account of the author's experience in prison as a non-cooperating C.O. in World War II. Recommended reading for all concerned C.O.'s.

447   **IN SOLITARY WITNESS** *by Gordan Zahn, 277pp, 1968, Beacon Press, $2.95*. Biography of a conscientious objector in Nazi Germany.

447A   **CONSCRIPTION OF CONSCIENCE** *by Mulford Sibley and Philip Jacob, 580pp, 1952, Johnson Reprint, $20.00*. The most complete account of C.O.'s in the World War II period.

Selective Objection

448   **CONFLICT OF LOYALTIES: The Case for Selective Conscientious Objection,** *James Finn (ed.), 288pp, 1968, Pegasus, $1.75*. Thoughtful arguments for governmental recognition of conscientious objection to a par-

ticular war, but not to all war. Sections by Michael Harrington, Mulford Sibley, Arnold Kaufmann and others.

449 CONSCIENCE, WAR AND THE SELECTIVE OBJECTOR *by Richard Niebanck, 8pp, 1968, Board of Social Ministry, Lutheran Church in America, $.60.* A careful argument which attempts to establish the real but limited autonomy of conscience. Examines the conflict between civil authority and selective objection to war based on just-war arguments.

Non-Cooperation and Resistance

450 OF HOLY DISOBEDIENCE *by A. J. Muste, 20pp, 1952, Greenleaf Publications, $.25.* An argument for non-cooperation (a refusal to register for the draft) as morally superior to the C.O. position.

451 HANDBOOK ON NON-PAYMENT OF WAR TAXES, *Ernest Bromley (ed.), 50pp, 1967, $.45.* A manual which describes the procedures to go through if you wish to protest the use of tax revenue for military programs.

451A MANUAL FOR DRAFT AGE IMMIGRANTS TO CANADA, *Mark Satin (ed.), 128pp, 1968, Toronto Anti-Draft Programme, $2.00.* A comprehensive and optimistic handbook for getting in and making it once there.

452 WE WON'T GO, *Alice Lynd (ed.), 331pp, 1968, Beacon Press, $1.95.* Principally composed of statements by draft refusers and resistance members in response to the editor's query "Why won't you go?" The selection reflects the author's interest in non-cooperation (the C.O. position is largely disclaimed). Offers useful insights into some of the present draft opposition.

453 CONSCIENCE IN AMERICA, A Documentary History of Conscientious Objection in America, 1757–1967, *Lillian Schlissel (ed.), 444pp, 1968, Dutton, $2.75.* Anthology of writings which traces the conflict of individual conscience wth the demands of the state concerning warfare. Introduces a wide range of views, too many of which fail to present viable alternatives to violence as a means for achieving security or justice.

The Draft and Selective Service

INT 454 GUIDE TO THE DRAFT *by Arlo Tatum and Joseph Tuchinsky, 281pp, 1969, Beacon Press, $1.95.* Covers the spectrum of alternative responses to the Selective Service System, including civilly disobedient choices and leaving the country. A sound general exposition which refers readers elsewhere for details. Includes twenty-two official forms.

454A CONSCIENCE AND WAR, The Moral Dilemma, *68pp, 1970, Intercom, $1.50.* An issue of Intercom (See Part III G) which provides a thoughtful study of the moral choices posed by national military conscription. Includes the arguments for and against conscription and the range of individual responses. A list of voluntary organizations working in this field, standards for judging them, and a selected bibliography make this a most useful introduction to this problem area.

455 THE DRAFT AND YOU: A Handbook on Selective Service *by Leslie Rothenberg, 322pp, 1968, Doubleday, $1.45.* Analyzing many aspects of Selective Service, Rothenberg attempts to provide a definitive manual for those concerned with the draft. This work is helpful but misleading when it assumes that the Selective Service regulations are identically implemented by each local volunteer board. They are not.

456 THE DRAFT? *by American Friends Service Committee, 111pp, 1968, Hill & Wang, $1.25.* An examination of the draft and various types of draft resistance. Argues against conscription on moral and political grounds.

457 THE DRAFT, A Handbook of Facts and Alternatives, *Sol Tax (ed.), 497pp, 1967, University of Chicago Press, $3.95.* An anthology which presents the full spectrum of views on the draft.

457A THE LOTTERY AND THE DRAFT: Where Do

I Stand? *by David Kendall and Leonard Ross, 159pp, 1970, Harper & Row, $.95.* A descriptive summary of how the lottery works, and an introduction to Selective Service procedures.

458 **THE SELECTIVE SERVICE ACT, A Case Study of the Governmental Process** *by Clyde Jacobs and John Gallagher, 207pp, 1968, Dodd, Mead & Co., $2.50.* Studies the issues considered, the governmental procedures involved and some of the consequences.

459 **LITTLE GROUPS OF NEIGHBORS: The Selective Service System** *by James Davis and Kenneth Dolbeare, 276pp, 1968, Markham, $3.95.* Two political scientists analyze in detail the workings of the Selective Service System in Wisconsin. This policy study is extremely valuable in understanding both how the system works and the causes of some of its problems. The authors were especially interested in the direct participation of volunteer citizens in government through draft boards.

X SOCIAL CHANGE:
THE NONVIOLENT APPROACH

The fact, the pervasive fact, of conflict occurs again and again throughout this book. This is not a book on peace that finds love and trust a sufficient answer, or even a very helpful answer to problems of international conflict. International conflict is not viewed as simply a problem of clearing up misunderstandings. It is seen, in many instances, as real, important and likely to be resolved by war until alternative institutions for resolving it are established because men insist that war end.

To End War has discussed law as such an institution; but law, unless imposed by a conqueror, requires consent and a sense of community to sustain it. War is the *denial* of community; it breaks the unity that is essential to non-tyrannical law. Any approach, therefore, that seeks in the midst of conflict to knit the break in the sense of community, whose fracture is both a cause and a result of war, is worth careful study.

The term "nonviolence" covers a variety of such approaches, some of enormous importance to those seeking an end to war, some seriously misleading. We treat nonviolence as one important element in a body of knowledge that can end war because it is a way to prosecute conflict that builds, instead of destroys, community. Though usually presented in pacifist guise or in the context of Gandhi's experience in India and South Africa (# 494–511), the history of the idea of nonviolence touches a wide range of religious and political traditions. In addition to the Judeo-Christian statements, it involves religious texts as old as the Chhandogya Upanishad of ancient Hinduism and the Chinese Tao Te Ching, and essays from syndicalist, liberal democratic and classical sources of political philosophy.

Within the nonviolent tradition one encounters passive acceptance, nonresistance, a mystical orientation to human experience, but also a dynamic basis for active movements of social change such as those led by Gandhi and Martin Luther King, Jr. The latter are built around the idea of the power of socially organized withdrawals of consent as presented, for example, in Etienne de la Boétie, *Discours de la Servitude Volontaire* (ca. 1548).

We focus here on this Gandhian conception of nonviolence: nonviolent social organization as a way of forcing change, or prosecuting conflict. This is related to, but an important extension of, the long tradition of religious and political challenge to proponents of violent conflict (# 463–465).

Our focus is not on the case *against* violence but on thought and experience that demonstrate what nonviolence can do to defend values and force change in ways that build, instead of destroy, men's sense of responsibility for each other.

In the post-World War II period there has been a broadening interest in nonviolence so conceived. Gandhi's success in achieving independence for India through nonviolence (# 507) is one source of this interest, as is widespread recognition of the terrible facts of nuclear weapons. The interest behavioral and other social scientists have taken in conflict (# 470–472) is another current of thought feeding the discussion of nonviolence, as is the continuing theological and ethical examination of the relation of violence to the conflicting claims of love and justice. The need to find ways of achieving rapid social change which do not violate the central intention of those working for such change has drawn many young people to the study of nonviolence.

Advocates of nonviolence have varied in their judgment of the areas in which they thought nonviolent conflict was possible, in their justification for nonviolence, in their reasons for preferring nonviolent to violent conflict and in their objectives. For example, most Americans, by and large, accept nonviolence in child rearing, in the punishment of criminals and in the waging of civil conflicts, but reject nonviolence in international affairs. It is not that they prefer violence to support for nonviolent diplomacy, economic assistance or even proposals for nonviolent self-defense. Rather, most Americans find themselves justifying violence because there are values they see threatened by military organizations, and because they have not been persuaded that any of the approaches suggested are viable alternatives to violence in international relations.

Advocates of nonviolence generally agree that nonviolence is preferable to violence because, when successful, its achievements are lasting (# 460 and 461). They do not deny that violence is sometimes successful in achieving political ends, although many doubt that violence has ever achieved progressive ends, particularly so when progress is defined as movement toward an "egalitarian society." As Mulford Sibley warns today's revolutionaries, "the utilization of violence tends to set up a kind of social logic which enhances class differentiation; promotes inequality; destroys the possibility of reconciliation; and in general undercuts revolutionary objectives" (# 486).

There is a major division within the ranks of individuals who believe in nonviolence which centers on the relation of *nonviolence to democracy*. On the one hand, some argue that representative democracy is "institutionalized nonviolence." They believe that representative democracy incorporates the best insights of the nonviolent tradition into everyday practice, i.e. a commitment to rationality, to supportive action for one's opposition through protection of minority rights, and through agreement about how a minority can gain power without violence (by persuading others and becoming a majority) (# 473). According to this view, *civil disobedience* when correctly practiced, is an extension of democracy, offering a way to apply democratic values to situations where only the withdrawal of consent, within a framework of respect for law, allows people to nonviolently challenge centralized and bureaucratized power.

A contrary view held by some describing themselves as committed to nonviolence holds that representative democracy has little to do with nonviolence. Arguing from a variety of viewpoints, sometimes anarchist (Thoreau), sometimes Marxist, sometimes neither, these advocates of nonviolence and revolution reject present democratic institutions as corrupt. In this context, the term civil disobedience is applied to action undertaken as dissociation from, not commitment to, a society. It is applied to action which seeks to evade, not accept the law's penalty, and which, far from rejecting violence, is designed to further a climate that will engender it. Here civil disobedience teaches not respect for law but the most extreme hostility to it and to those responsible for its enforcement. Such action, despite demurs, is often an attempt to impose a minority's will rather than to persuade a majority (# 466). It is an ally of, rather than an alternative to, the organization of violence for political ends. It contributes to that which it claims

to abhor—mass violence. Rejecting the sense of social
obligation to the majority, this view eliminates the
crucial element in nonviolent conflict resolution: support for the opponent one is trying to change.

Genuinely nonviolent civil disobedience can be seen
as an instrument essential to the proper function of
democracy in a mass society. But even those holding
this view must meet the argument that nonviolent
acts can destroy respect for law and thus the essential
consent that makes democratic government possible.
Clearly there are many times when a minority should
obey laws with which they disagree while working
to change them.

Another division among contemporary nonviolent
theorists is evident when questions of international
relations and revolution are discussed. The division
is usually along the same lines as the controversy over
the relation of nonviolence to democracy. Those who
see nonviolent civil disobedience as an extension of
democracy frequently support nonviolent means of
prosecuting international conflict: such as an international peace brigade (a group trained in nonviolence willing to interpose themselves between violent
armies), or a strategy of concrete, peace initiative
acts (steps a nation can take to demonstrate its willingness to resolve conflicts peacefully) while strengthening international institutions into viable instruments
for nonviolent conflict resolution. Those who primarily
identify with revolutionary movement undertaken in
the name of oppressed peoples, usually support the
revolutionaries in spirit if not in practice, but seek to
"humanize" the revolution by making it as nonviolent
as possible. For the latter, international conflict is
generally seen as another form of class conflict and
they sometimes put their conception of justice in that
conflict ahead of their commitment to work for non-

violence. Across this division, charges like "apologists for murder" and advocates of a "coalition with the marines" are heard. The issues here are the same that divide those committed to nonviolence from those supporting national armies: differing judgments as to the practicability of nonviolent strategies and the morality of the use or the refusal to use violence in the interest of what is deemed just. In addition there is disagreement over the validity of the claim to loyalty of national units vs. ideological or class groupings.

What appears at first as a single coherent body of thought is soon recognized as involving a variety of often contradictory tendencies. One must ask those committed to nonviolence, as one asks those committed to "peace," to explain what they mean.

The nonviolent tradition commended here is the effort to maintain unity among men.

It relies upon love rather than hate, and though it involves a willingness to accept rather than inflict suffering, it is neither passive nor cowardly.

It offers a way of meeting evil without relying on the ability to cause pain to the human being through whom evil is expressed. It seeks to change the attitude of the opponent rather than to force his submission through violence.

It is, in short, the practical effort to overcome evil with good.[1]

The essence of this kind of nonviolence lies in its ability to prosecute conflict without destroying community between those on opposite sides of the battle lines. From this base one can build a distinctive approach to politics. The central problem for advocates

[1] *Speak Truth to Power*, Cary, Mayer, Gilmore, Pickus, Rustin, Whitney, *et al.* (Philadelphia: American Friends Service Committee, 1955), p. 35.

of political nonviolence is how to counter the violence others will use; the problem is how to force needed change without becoming an executioner. A thoughtful advocate of nonviolence faces the facts of evil, of aggression, in human affairs and prepares nonviolently to defend his values and change his opponents. He thinks, then, about ways of prosecuting conflict, not of avoiding it, but of prosecuting it in ways that build instead of destroy community. He is then thinking to the right purpose, for the problem of world peace, stated most simply and most fundamentally, is the problem of achieving community in the midst of conflict.

The currently exotic body of belief called nonviolence has much to contribute to thought about ending war, not least in what may currently be deemed unrealistic thought about nonviolent resistance to external aggression. Far from unrealistic, say many who have written of these ideas, it has again and again been demonstrated to be practicable even, in some situations, against the Nazis (# 465).

The bibliography presents a range of thought about nonviolence in theory and practice, in relation to problems of democracy and revolution and as an alternative to military defense.

Nonviolence: Theory and Practice

TEW   460   CONQUEST OF VIOLENCE—The Gandhian Philosophy of Conflict *by Joan V. Bondurant, 261pp, 1965, University of California Press, $1.95.* An important contribution to conflict theory and the best exposition of Gandhi's ideas using concrete examples. Criticizes the frequent identification of power with military force, given Gandhi's success in transforming his "enemies."

INF   461   THE POWER OF NONVIOLENCE *by Richard B. Gregg, 187pp, 1966, Schocken, $1.75.* A classic statement by an experienced advocate of nonviolence. Includes examples from India, the United States and other countries.

462 NONVIOLENCE, A Christian Interpretation *by William R. Miller, 380pp, 1964, Schocken, $2.45.* A comprehensive, carefully written analysis which finds the root values underlying nonviolence in the Christian ethical tradition.

INT   463 THE PACIFIST CONSCIENCE, *Peter Mayer (ed.), 447pp, 1966, Henry Regnery Co., $2.65; Holt, Rinehart and Winston, hardcover, $7.95.* Anthology of writings from Lao-Tzu to Camus with extensive bibliography. Demonstrates the wide variety of thought which has been called pacifist.

464 INSTEAD OF VIOLENCE, *Arthur and Lila Weinberg (eds.), 474pp, 1963, Beacon Press, $2.75.* Anthology of statements from ancient and contemporary sources by individuals who have applied the basic nonviolent insight to a wide variety of circumstances.

TEW   465 THE QUIET BATTLE, *Mulford Q. Sibley (ed.), 377pp, 1968, Beacon Press, $2.95.* An anthology of essays discussing instances when nonviolent means have been used to achieve desired ends.

466 NONVIOLENCE IN AMERICA, *Staughton Lynd (ed.), 530pp, 1966, Bobbs-Merrill, $3.45.* Examples of the use of nonviolence by unions, Quakers, abolitionists and others in American history.

467 THIRTY-ONE HOURS *by Theodore Olson and Gordon Christiansen, 349pp, 1963, Grindstone Press, $2.00.* A deeply moving account of an experiment in civilian defense performed in 1963 when committed pacifists attempted to apply their convictions in a staged invasion/ defense. Their failure and the lessons they learned about the levels of conflict, the relationship between violent and nonviolent conflict, and the problems of remaining nonviolent are instructive.

468   NONVIOLENT ACTION, Theory and Practice, A *Selected Bibliography by April Carter, David Hoggett and Adam Roberts,* 83pp, 1970, Housmans, $1.50. Extremely useful compilation of both theoretical works and case studies. Probably the most complete listing of instances when groups have chosen to defend themselves nonviolently.

469   NONVIOLENT DIRECT ACTION: American Cases: Social-Psychological Analyses, A. *Paul Hare and Herbert H. Blumberg (eds.),* 575pp, 1968, Corpus Books, hardcover, $10.00. Case studies of civil rights and peace demonstrators' use of civil disobedience with analysis by Joan Bondurant, Erik Erikson, Gene Sharp, Pitirim Sorokin and others.

470   CONFLICT: Violence and Nonviolence, *Joan V. Bondurant (ed.),* 200pp, 1970, Atherton Press, $2.45; hardcover $6.95. An introduction to the study of conflict which considers both familiar forms of nonviolence (pacifism, civil disobedience, democracy) and the forms and uses of violence. Considers the ways in which the concept of violence enters political theory and explores alternatives to violence in international relations. Selections by Gene Sharp, Thomas Schelling, Ernest Jones and others.

471   THE FUNCTIONS OF SOCIAL CONFLICT by *Lewis Coser,* 188pp, 1964, Macmillan, $1.95. A behavioral scientist's approach to the various forms of social conflict.

INF   472   CONFLICT AND DEFENSE: A General Theory by *Kenneth Boulding,* 349pp, 1963, Harper & Row, $1.95. An important theoretical work which examines conflict from the personal to the international level.

(see also 218, 300, 399, 649, 659 and 661)

Nonviolence and Democracy

473   DEMOCRACY AND NONVIOLENCE, The Role of the Individual in World Crisis by *Ralph T. Templin,* 434pp, 1965, Porter Sargent, hardcover, $4.00. Templin argues that democratic governments, human values, individual rights and due process of law are destroyed by violent conflict. Citing Gandhi as an example, the author concludes that socially organized nonviolence can both defend and extend democratic institutions and practices.

474 STRIDE TOWARD FREEDOM by *Martin Luther King, Jr.*, 230pp, 1968, Harper & Row, $.75. King describes the Montgomery bus boycott and the moral basis of his nonviolence. He explains why he believes that when nonviolence failed it was because not enough nonviolence was tried.

475 ALTERNATIVES TO VIOLENCE: A Stimulus to Dialogue, *Larry Ng (ed.)*, 100pp, 1968, Time-Life, $1.00. An anthology which probes the basis of violence and reflects on alternatives to violence. Essays by Erich Fromm, Arthur Koestler, Harold Lasswell, Robert S. McNamara and Harvey Wheeler are included.

Civil Disobedience

476 CIVIL DISOBEDIENCE IN A DEMOCRACY by *Gene Sharp*, 17pp, 1968, Housmans, $.15. Since acquiescence to injustice and armed insurrection are both destructive of democracy, nonviolent civil disobedience is seen as one essential form of dissent which aims to advance democracy. Lists the characteristics of civil disobedience and suggests how governments should respond.

477 THEORY AND PRACTICE OF CIVIL DISOBEDIENCE by *Arthur Harvey*, 29pp, 1961, Greenleaf Publications, $.25. A dedicated Gandhian explicates the concept of civil disobedience by describing how and why the best way to get rid of an enemy is to make him a friend. Includes a lawyers' case for civil disobedience which holds that civil disobedience is, when properly carried out, a means of fulfilling the law.

478 CIVIL DISOBEDIENCE, 32pp, 1966, *Center for the Study of Democratic Institutions*, $1.00. An attempt by Bayard Rustin, Richard Wasserstrom and others to determine when civil disobedience is justified. They also describe when it fulfills and when it is detrimental to democratic institutions and practices.

479 **CONCERNING DISSENT AND CIVIL DISOBEDIENCE** *by Abe Fortas, 128pp, 1968, Fawcett, $.50.* A prominent judge argues for civil disobedience as a means of conducting conflict without violence. Fortas argues that those truly committed to *civil* disobedience must also be committed to accepting the legal consequences and must make clear precisely what law or practice they hope to change through this tactic.

480 **DISOBEDIENCE AND DEMOCRACY: Nine Fallacies of Law and Order** *by Howard Zinn, 124pp, 1968, Random House, $1.45.* Attacks the Fortas book on the grounds that civil disobedience is a check on majority decisions and need not concern itself with respect for law or use of constitutional means.

TEW 481 **CIVIL DISOBEDIENCE AND INSURRECTIONARY VIOLENCE** *by Robert Pickus, 5pp, 1969, World Without War Council, $.15.* A reprint from *Dissent* which makes the distinction clear and applies it to current confusions in the peace movement.

481A **THE OBLIGATION TO DISOBEY, CONSCIENCE AND THE LAW** *by Mulford Sibley, pp, 1970, CRIA, $1.75.* A committed advocate of nonviolence, argues that civil disobedience is required of the morally concerned individual when governmental leaders exceed their authority or abuse their power.

482 **TOLSTOY ON CIVIL DISOBEDIENCE AND NONVIOLENCE** *by Leo Tolstoy, 302pp, 1968, Signet, $.95.* An anthology of Tolstoy's writings, including "The Kingdom of God," "On the Emigration of the Dukhobors" and "A Letter to the Peace Conference."

483 **ANARCHISM: A History of Libertarian Ideas and Movements** *by George Woodcock, 504pp, 1968, Meridian, $2.95.* A history of major anarchist writers and of anarchism as a political movement which demonstrates its

libertarian character, which is rightly identified with complete opposition to legality and the state only occasionally.

484 CIVIL DISOBEDIENCE: Theory and Practice, *Hugo Bedau (ed.), 288pp, 1969, Pegasus, $1.95.* An anthology of over seventeen selections which seeks to answer the question: "When is civil disobedience justified in a democracy?" Includes the extremely valuable article by Richard Wasserstrom, "The Obligation to Obey the Law," plus selections by Martin Luther King, Jr., Lewis Feuer, Noam Chomsky, A. J. Muste, Irving Kristol and others.

485 SELECT BIBLIOGRAPHY ON CIVIL DISOBEDIENCE AND THE AMERICAN DEMOCRATIC TRADITION, *5pp, 1964, World Without War Council, $.05.*

Nonviolence and Revolution

486 REVOLUTION AND VIOLENCE *by Mulford Q. Sibley, 8pp, 1964, Peace News Reprint, $.10.* Argues that revolutionary violence is an impediment to achieving democratic and humane goals: a radical's rejection of the current New Left case for violence.

487 REVOLUTION: Violent and Nonviolent *by Barbara Deming and Regis Debray, 28pp, 1968, Liberation Reprint, $.35.* Two separate justifications for revolution: Deming argues that nonviolent revolution is both possible and preferable on moral and practical grounds; Debray argues that violent revolution alone can create the class consciousness needed for a successful revolution.

488 ON REVOLUTION *by Hannah Arendt, 344pp, 1963, Viking Press, $1.65.* Examines revolution as a phenomenon, considering its cost to human liberty and human happiness, and the loss of political community associated with violence.

488A ON VIOLENCE *by Hanna Arendt, 106pp, 1970, Harcourt, Brace and World, hardcover, $4.75.* While power creates positive values, violence can only destroy; another distinctive and thoughtful statement.

489   VIOLENCE AND SOCIAL CHANGE *by Henry Bienen, 119pp, 1968, University of Chicago Press, $1.25.* A study of the relationship of violence to social change— attempts to answer the question of whether violence impedes or accelerates the achievement of social change. How does the use of violence affect the type of change achieved?

489A   WHY MEN REBEL? *by Ted Gurr, 421pp, 1970, Princeton University Press, hardcover, $12.50.* An important contribution to thought about collective violence, which charts the conditions—relating primarily to the gap between what people believe to be theirs by right and what they actually have—of its appearance in history. Focuses primarily on urban and colonial revolutions. Written for an academic audience.

490   THE POLITICS OF VIOLENCE: Revolution in the Modern World *by Carl Leiden and Karl Schmitt, 244pp, 1968, Prentice-Hall, $2.45.* A study of Cuba, Mexico, Turkey and Egypt which attempts to establish the preconditions of revolution, the function of ideology, the stages and relations of violence to revolution.

INF   491   REFLECTIONS ON VIOLENCE *by Georges Sorel, 286pp, 1967, Macmillan, $1.50.* The classic of revolutionary syndicalism (1906), its apology for working class violence, visible again in current justifications of street and university violence. Why not read the original?

492   WRETCHED OF THE EARTH *by Franz Fanon, 225pp, 1963, Grove Press, $1.25.* A psychological argument that violence in the ex-colonial countries is necessary to the achievement of true dignity and selfhood. Equates dignity with the dominance of others and ends by denouncing the cities as neo-colonial strongholds. In addition to the difficulties in this argument, Fanon sets no limits to his justification of violence. As a consequence his argument is valid against anyone in power.

493   A BIBLIOGRAPHY ON REVOLUTION *by D. E. Russell Ekman, 11pp, 1968, World Without War Council,*

$.10. A useful listing and categorization of 171 works on revolution.

Gandhianism—A New Form of Conflict

TEW 494 **GANDHI, His Relevance for Our Times,** *G. Ramachandran and T. K. Mahadevan (eds.), 303pp, 1970, World Without War Council, $2.95*. A modern attempt to reevaluate and apply Gandhi's successes to present problems. A valuable book including selections by Joan Bondurant, Kenneth E. Boulding, Richard Gregg, R. R. Diwaker, Gene Sharp and others.

495 **REVOLUTIONARY SARVODAYA** *by A. Vinoba Bhave, 54pp, 1962, Greenleaf Publications, $.95*. A study of Gandhian techniques of achieving revolutionary change without violence.

496 **FOR PACIFISTS** *by M. K. Gandhi, 113pp, 1949, Greenleaf Publications, $.95*. A collection of Gandhi's writings on pacifism.

497 **SELECTIONS FROM GANDHI,** *N. K. Bose (ed.), 320pp, 1948, Greenleaf Publications, $2.50*. An excellent anthology of Gandhi's writings imported from India (in English).

498 **WAR WITHOUT VIOLENCE** *by Krishnalal Shridarni, 380pp, 1962, rev. ed. Greenleaf Publications, $1.50*. Recognizes that conflict is inevitable, without concluding that violence can resolve it.

499 **GANDHI AND MARX** *by K. G. Mashruwala, 119pp, 1951, Greenleaf Publications, $.95*. An examination of the two ideologies in the context of the need for rapid economic development.

500 **MY AUTOBIOGRAPHY, The Story of My Experiment with Truth** *by M. K. Gandhi, 390pp, 1957, Beacon Press, $2.75*. Gandhi describes his early life, his commitment to nonviolence and his techniques for transforming an enemy through love and the acceptance of suffering, while making clear what it is you want.

INT **501 LIFE OF GANDHI** *by Louis Fischer,* *189pp, 1954, Mentor Books, $.75.* A short biography of Gandhi which offers an excellent introduction to his ideas and techniques.

502 SATYAGRAHA IN SOUTH AFRICA *by M. K. Gandhi, 321pp, 1964, Greenleaf Publications, $2.00.* Gandhi's description of the nonviolent campaign for equality in South Africa.

503 THE SCIENCE OF SATYAGRAHA *by M. K. Gandhi, 253pp, 1968, Greenleaf Publications, $.70.* A clear exposition of Gandhi's central concept.

504 ALL MEN ARE BROTHERS *by M. K. Gandhi, 253pp, 1968, Greenleaf Publications, $1.95.* Compiled and edited by UNESCO, this anthology includes selections from many of Gandhi's better writings.

505 GANDHI *by Geoffrey Ashe, 494pp, 1968, Stein & Day, $2.75.* A biography of Gandhi which provides a detailed historical analysis.

506 NONVIOLENT RESISTANCE *by M. K. Gandhi, 404pp, 1961, Schocken, $1.95.* An anthology which covers a wide range of Gandhi's thought on nonviolence.

INT **507 A BIOGRAPHY OF GANDHI** *by B. R. Nanda, 272pp, 1969, Barron's Educational Series, $.95.* An excellent introduction to Gandhi, his thought and action.

508 NONVIOLENCE AND AGGRESSION, A Study of Gandhi's *Moral Equivalent of War by H. J. N. Horsburgh, 207pp, 1968, Oxford University Press, $5.60.* A scholarly study of Gandhian Satyagraha which argues that nonviolence is a morally preferable and comparably efficient method of achieving ends which others hold warfare achieves. Offers a useful set of criteria for judging the effectiveness of defense systems.

INF **509 GANDHI'S TRUTH, On the Origins of Militant Nonviolence** *by Erik H. Erikson, 510pp, 1969, Norton, $2.95.* A leading psychoanalyst's study of the inevitability of conflict and Gandhi's contribution toward making such conflict creative through the development of non-violent techniques of coercion and support for one's opponent.

510 **THE POLITICS OF NONVIOLENCE** *by Gene Sharp, forthcoming in 1970.* This soon to be published book promises to be an important contribution to the field. Sharp provides one of the most comprehensive analyses of different types of nonviolent action and relates them to democratic decision making.

511 **COLLECTED WORKS OF MAHATMA GANDHI** A projected 60-volume collection, 25 volumes now available. Published by the Government of India. *$6.00 each.*

Civilian Defense (Nonviolent Resistance to Foreign Invasion)

512 **THE POLITICAL EQUIVALENT OF WAR— CIVILIAN DEFENSE** *by Gene Sharp, 65pp, 1965, Carnegie Endowment, $.60.* An attempt to answer William James' call for a moral alternative to war. Civilian defense (*not* civil defense) is offered as a means by which the civilian population can be trained in techniques of non-violent defense. An excellent introduction to the subject.

513 **CIVILIAN DEFENSE** *by Gene Sharp and others, 70pp, 1964, Peace News, $.70.* An explication of the idea of civilian defense as opposed to military defense, which demonstrates the tremendous power of a united citizenry.

514 **IN PLACE OF WAR** *by American Friends Service Committee, 115pp, 1967, Grossman, $1.45.* Argues that nonviolent means of national defense are not only more appropriate than military means but more effective and that the techniques for successfully implementing them are, with effort, acquirable.

515 **CIVILIAN DEFENSE, An Introduction,** *T. K. Mahadevan, Adam Roberts, and Gene Sharp (eds.), 265pp, 1967, hardcover, $5.95.* Published in India, these essays by

Laes Prosholt, Theodore Ebert, Arne Naess and the editors treat the central problems of nonviolent resistance theory, often in the Indian context.

516 CIVILIAN RESISTANCE AS A NATIONAL DE-FENSE, Nonviolent Action Against Aggression, *Adam Roberts (ed.), 320pp, 1968, Penguin Books, $1.65.* An important study which faces the hard objections to the idea of civilian defense and which states the political and educational prerequisites of successful nonviolent resistance.

(see also 58, 59 and 63)

XI POLITICAL PROCESSES AND THE PEACE EFFORT

Wars have occurred in the past when disputes could not be resolved within a given institutional framework. The American Civil War, for example, was caused in part by the inability of democratic institutions to resolve the questions of slavery and secession. Many critics of democratic institutions today argue that democracy is viable only within consensus groupings, e.g., the bourgeoisie, the whites or the national community. These critics maintain that conflicts between classes, races or nations cannot be resolved by democratic political institutions. Only violence, they say, can resolve such disputes. One may therefore consider the limitations of democratic institutions— our most effective alternative to the violent resolution of political differences—to be a major problem for the peace seeker.

How limited are democratic institutions? How can they be improved?

The features which distinguish democratic from other forms of government are the free circulation of ideas, electoral processes, usually based on universal suffrage, whereby representative leaders are kept responsible to those they govern, the legitimacy of an organized opposition, and a conception of inalienable human rights insuring equality before the law and protection from the arbitrary use of state power. These fundamental features of democratic government have frequently been attacked from the right. Today critics on the student and intellectual left have joined the traditional enemies of democratic government. They reject the notion of a loyal opposition; in this view one is limited to two choices, you are either an enemy of the system or an apologist for it. Some views, they say, are considered too reprehensible to be allowed expression (# 525). In this political tradition "participatory democracy" is raised as a slogan challenging the legitimacy of representative institutions.

The explosive issues of race and war have fed emotions that sustain forms of political belief and action inimical to democratic values. Nonviolence, equality before the law, the right to the majority to rule while protecting the minorities' right to strive to become the majority: all have been disputed and denounced by some elements of the intellectual left or undermined by reactions to it and by currents of guilt flowing from past failures of democratic institutions.

A defense of democratic political processes and democratic norms begins with an examination of the alternative political systems. On what values are they based? What are their goals? How have they worked? A defense of democratic theory does not require defense of past policies in a democratic society. Democracy does not assure wise policy. It does assure that if a policy is unwise and if its consequences affect many people, the policy can be changed without violence.

It is the ability of democratic governments to change without mass violence which is of prime significance. For democratic governments do not suppress political opposition, they protect it. Current American critics of democracy on the right and the left deny this pointing to the experience of the Black Panthers (or the Minutemen). But both groups have and exercise the right to organize politically, to publish and to disseminate their views. It is when resistance to arrest, incitement to murder, unlawful possession of weapons and paramilitary organization and arsenals enter the scene that government protection ceases and governmental repression (not always just) begins.

Democratic governments provide a legal means for a minority to become a majority: electoral politics. Perhaps even more importantly, the full democratic political process, with its complex of independent organization and communication, is a sensitive and remarkably flexible way to process change without violence. While no party in power can legally violate constitutional rights, the constitution can be changed. Thus democracy alone makes possible even its own liquidation—if you can persuade a majority that the system is evil. And that should be easy if the evils of American society are as great as the anti-democratic ideologists would have it.

Advocates of a world without war need to understand democratic theory and practice. They may disagree on capitalist or socialist forms of economic organization, for one could change the present American economic system enough to be accurate in calling it either capitalist or socialist and not fundamentally affect the chances for war or peace. But if democratic institutions are weakened, one effective instrument for the nonviolent resolution of conflict is damaged. Increasing the effectiveness of democratic institutions is one important part of work for a world without war because democratic political processes recognize the inevitability of conflict while institutionalizing some of the crucial insights of nonviolent conflict resolution discussed in the previous chapter.

Because peace activity in America swings between opening and improving democratic channels and on occasion severely damaging them, *To End War* lists a variety of books concerning democratic and anti-democratic theory and practice.

THE PEACE EFFORT

Those interested in ending war will also want to study the peace effort—those organizations whose stated purpose is work to end war. Historians have generally considered the "peace movement" to be composed of advocates of disarmament, world economic development, world community, strengthened international authority, nonviolence or pacifism, rather than advocates of violent revolution, military deterrence or national interest diplomacy. As such, the peace movement has attracted only a small minority of the population whose numbers in a crisis will sometimes swell, but who have had little lasting political influence.

Members of the peace movement generally agree that they lack political power but differ on what to do about it. At least three different conceptions of responsibility are variously advocated: 1) personal witness, a withdrawal from political life in order to preserve and demonstrate the integrity of one's convictions; 2) revolution, seizing the instruments of power and forcing others to assent to one's will; 3) conversion, attempting to become a majority through persuasion.

Steps toward ending war involve political action, a fact which even those committed to moral witness must recognize (# 544). Advocates of revolution and conversion may agree on the need for radical change but hold fundamentally different attitudes toward representative democracy. Those considering democracy a fraud see violent confrontation, threat, polarization and, if necessary, civil warfare as the only effective way to force change. Advocates of representative democracy are opposed to dictatorships, whether of the right or left, and believe that social institutions

can and should be based on consent. They thus regard
the revolutionaries' means to power as unacceptable
and destructive even when they succeed (# 537).
They are destructive because while channels for processing change perpetuate some evils, they prevent
many others. If radical change is to be realized, viable
democratic institutions for contesting and institutionalizing such change must be maintained. In short, representative democracy is probably a present precondition of a more just society, but certainly no guarantee
of one (# 414).

But what organizational form should a democratic
peace effort take?

There is currently a wide variety of groups which
count work for a world without war as one of their
reasons for existence. These include primary community organizations (religious, economic, etc.), world
affairs educational groups (e.g., the Foreign Policy
Association), peace research centers, and the peace
groups themselves. There are three distinct categories
of peace groups. *Ad hoc* groups which spring up in
reaction to a particular issue (e.g., North Dakotans
concerned about the ABM), *functional* peace groups
focused not on ideas but on a particular task (e.g.,
student exchange or volunteers for international development) and the thirty or forty *established* peace
education and action organizations distinguished from
ad hoc groups by longevity, explicit procedures for
determining internal leadership and policy and by a
developed set of understandings shared by members
of the organization. They exist to further ideas, attitudes and/or policies which they feel, if widely accepted, would help in preventing or ending war. The
weaknesses and strengths of each of these types of
organizations and a guide to evaluating individual
organizations is presented in Part III.

There is a need for a peace movement which can
(1) focus public attention on particular issues, (2)
develop the understandings and the policies capable
of ending war and (3) obtain majority support for
such policies. No one form of organization is adequate
to these tasks. *Ad hoc* peace groups frequently focus
attention on key war/peace issues, but often in a way
that makes gaining majority support for alternatives
to military policies unlikely. Peace research organizations have developed a sophisticated body of
knowledge but have no organizational vehicle to
carry these understandings into the public policy
process. Primary community organizations have the
requisite political influence but rarely significantly
commit themselves to war/peace issues because these
issues are divisive and complex.

We have a long way to go in building an effective
non-governmental peace effort in America. We will
never build an effective constituency for peace without
considerably greater clarity as to the values, the political understandings and the programs that distinguish such a constituency.

Simple, even passionate, opposition to Washington's
military policies is not sufficient ground on which to
build a peace constituency. Nor is constant reiteration
of the horror of war. One would think the melancholy
history of the peace movement before World War II
was proof of that.

A movement that is wrong in its view of international realities, that posits a single villain in world
affairs is of no aid in building the institutions and
understandings that can control the threat of war.
But much of the present American anti-war movement, tired of hating the Communists, has simply
found a new villain: America.

Such a movement, whatever its origin in genuine

anti-war feeling, becomes simply a movement to withdraw American power from world politics. When such a movement is strongly influenced by isolationist assumptions, or the tag ends of a vulgarized Marxism, or a cultural revolt which measures health by psychological distance from America, the result may be a powerful social force. But it is not a force capable of turning America or the world toward peace.

The answer to the question, "How do you build an effective constituency for peace?" begins by answering the question, "What kind of vision are you pursuing?" A genuine peace constituency will seek to end war. Not conflict or even all violence (we are not, as Camus put it, "so mad as that") but the mass organized violence of war. Such a constituency will be clear on the elements of a body of thought and policy capable of achieving that end. In rejecting reliance on national military power, it will offer alternative ways of defending legitimate security and value concerns.

We do not help work for a world without war by failing to distinguish such a constituency from those who in rejecting American violence opt instead for Mao's or Guevara's.

Given clarity on the vision pursued and on the policies that can fulfill it, some of the major elements needed for a more effective peace constituency in America can be listed:

(1) a strong and sound radical wing; people committed to active opposition to American militarism, but opposition set in the context of resistance to the use of mass violence by other nations and ideologies as well.

(2) a significant peace research effort.

(3) a national planning, catalytic, and communication structure for both peace education and

action organizations and those mainstream organizations of the community that want to work for a world without war. Such a structure must also relate national and regional and community work. The World Without War Council is probably the most ambitious current attempt to build such a center.

(4) mainstream community organizations of this country that have gone beyond an occasional resolution into a commitment to work seriously to end war.

(5) a recruiting and training program for professionals in this field.

(6) a serious approach to the mass media.

(7) a coherent group within Congress and the Senate committed to this work.

(8) an international, morally authoritative voice serving functions similar to three above and capable of reaching all political camps but prisoner of none.

(9) a series of flexible organizational structures capable of focusing maximum strength on specific issues.

(10) a program for fundamental work on our schools, now often an obstacle to work for a world without war.

(11) a national fund capable of raising the kind of money needed and applying standards for serious work to the whole range of instrumentalities involved.

There is a considerable difference between building a strong peace movement and actually changing attitudes and policies in our country. A peace movement deemed successful in terms of money, adherents and visibility may simply succeed in polarizing attitudes and strengthening previously nascent opposition. Those interested in lasting change need more than a majority. They must consider more than problems of effective protest or movement building. They must think through ways of bringing those in disagreement into a new consensus on policies for peace.

The books on the peace effort listed here trace the history of the international and American peace efforts. They address some of the organizational problems of the peace effort and examine the variety of approaches taken by peace groups at different times and places. Those who wish to work effectively for a world without war need to think carefully about how to do so.

Democracy and Its Critics

INT 517 **THE DEVELOPMENT OF THE DEMOCRATIC IDEA,** Readings from Pericles to the Present, *Charles Sherover (ed.), 604pp, 1968, Washington Square Press, $1.45.* An anthology bringing together the foundations of democratic theory. Includes selections by Cicero, Montesquieu, Madison, Mill, Dewey, Hook, Karl Jaspers and others. An excellent introduction to democratic theory, the values on which democracy is based and the ends democracy is designed to make possible.

518 **THE DEMOCRATIC EXPERIENCE,** Past and Prospects *by Reinhold Niebuhr and Paul Sigmund, 202pp, 1969, Praeger, $2.25.* Niebuhr analyzes the history of democracy in the West, Sigmund discusses democracy's relevance to the new nations of today. Argues for the viability of the democratic prospect.

INF 519 **PATTERNS OF ANTI-DEMOCRATIC THOUGHT** *by David Spitz, 295pp, 1965, Macmillan, $2.45.* An attempt to distinguish what forces and attitudes reinforce and which undermine democratic processes.

520 **POLITICAL OPPOSITION IN WESTERN DEMOCRACIES** *by Robert Dahl, 458pp, 1966, Yale University Press, $2.95.* A study of the function of political opposition in eleven democratic countries.

521 **A PREFACE TO DEMOCRATIC THEORY** *by Robert Dahl, 154pp, 1966, University of Chicago Press,*

$1.50. An abstruse, almost mathematical, argument which attempts to demonstrate why traditional theoretical justifications of popular sovereignty fail, and which attempts to develop an alternative model.

522   OPIUM OF THE INTELLECTUALS *by Raymond Aron, 320pp, 1959, Norton, $1.75.* Examines intellectuals' tendency to impose the most exacting standards on democratic practices while justifying anything that can be called revolutionary. Aron focuses on the inability of Marxism to describe twentieth century industrial society and on the gap between theoretical and actual emancipation of labor in Communist societies.

INF   523   DEMOCRACY IN AMERICA *by Alex deTocqueville, 317pp, 1956, Mentor Books, $.95.* The classic study of the development of democracy in the United States, which points to the dangers of tyranny by the majority.

INF   524   ON LIBERTY *by John Stuart Mill, 141pp, 1960, Bobbs-Merrill, $.75.* Still the classic argument for and justification of individual liberty against state and social pressures. Liberty is not a luxury for Mill, but a necessary requisite of achieving a true view of a problem and the different means of resolving it.

525   CRITIQUE OF PURE TOLERANCE *by Herbert Marcuse, Barrington Moore, Jr. and Robert Wolff, 123pp, 1969, Beacon Press, $1.85.* Argues against Mill's *On Liberty* on the grounds that certain views, not their own, are too loathsome to be tolerated.

526   THE POLITICAL THEORY OF POSSESSIVE INDIVIDUALISM *by C. B. MacPherson, 310pp, 1962, Oxford University Press, $2.50.* A critical critique of seventeenth and eighteenth century political theory which argues that its common assumptions no longer fit today's realities. Assumes that individualism is inherently possessive and that socialism is more democratic than welfare capitalism.

527   ON PURE TOLERANCE: A Critique of Criticism *by David Spitz, 16pp, 1966, Dissent Reprint, $.25.* A leading advocate of freedom of speech, tolerance of all views, no matter how loathsome, so long as they do not deprive others of basic rights, responds to Wolff, Marcuse and Moore (# 525).

527A THE DECLINE OF THE NEW by *Irving Howe, 326pp, 1970, Harcourt, Brace and World, hardcover, $7.50.* Howe defends the politics of democratic radicalism, the norms of rationality and intelligence and the life of the mind as a humane dedication in this book of essays on literary themes. Includes a number of thoughtful responses to current movement attacks on democratic values and practices.

528 ONE DIMENSIONAL MAN by *Herbert Marcuse, 260pp, 1967, Beacon Press, $2.25.* Argues that industrial society leads to some form of authoritarianism or totalitarianism. Assumes that societies are social entities which cannot be changed piece-meal but must be wholly replaced, without being clear about how one gets outside of a society in order to develop a new one.

529 ONE DIMENSIONAL PESSIMISM, A critique of Herbert Marcuse's theories by *Allen Graubard, 13pp, 1968, Dissent Reprint, $.25.* A careful critique of Marcuse's authoritarianism, his sense of despair and his method of social analysis.

530 THE RADICAL RIGHT, *Daniel Bell (ed.), 446pp, 1965, Doubleday, $1.45.* Anthology of analytic descriptions on the resurgence of the right-wing in America.

INF   531 THE POWER ELITE by *C. Wright Mills, 423pp, 1956, Oxford University Press, $2.25.* A sociological analysis of American society which concludes that this society is dominated by a self-perpetuating, unresponsive elite who controls the major news media, political organizations and economic institutions.

532 COMMUNITY POWER by *Nelson Polsby, 144pp, 1963, Yale University Press, $1.45.* Argues against Mills on the grounds that there is a variety of countervailing centers of power operating within a democratic framework in the U.S.

533   DECISION-MAKING IN THE WHITE HOUSE *by Theodore Sorensen, 94pp, 1963, Columbia University Press, $1.25.* An advisor to John F. Kennedy argues that the President must listen to public opinion but not be bound by it. Public opinion limits the president but he influences public opinion.

INF   534   THE LIVING U.S. CONSTITUTION *by Saul K. Padover, 386pp, 1968, Meridian, $.95.* The basic study of the American Constitutional tradition complete with thirty-five crucial Supreme Court decisions. An excellent introduction to the ability of law to change and adjust while providing the framework for social change.

534A   THE NEW LEFT: A Documentary History, *Massimo Teodori (ed.), 501pp, 1969, Bobbs-Merrill, $4.95.* Brings together the major writings of New Left theoreticians and students in the 1960's. A useful source book.

TEW   535   THE POWER STRUCTURE, Political Process in American Society *by Arnold Rose, 506pp, 1967, Oxford University Press, $2.95.* A study of American political process, the influence of pressure groups, the power of America's many voluntary organizations and the military-industrial complex. Maintains that the U.S. power structure retains the essential features of a democratic polity: the structure is open to new talent, new ideas and is accountable to the electorate.

536   PUBLIC OPINION AND AMERICAN DEMOCRACY *by V. O. Key, Jr., 566pp, 1961, Knopf, hardcover, $7.95.* A study of public opinion which finds that both political activists (broadly defined) and the masses significantly shape policy-making in a democracy. Key argues that the political activist plays a crucial role in developing new ideas but that public opinion formulates boundaries within which elected officials must act.

537   DEMOCRACY AND THE STUDENT LEFT *by George F. Kennan, 208pp, 1968, Bantam Books, $1.25.*

An exchange between Kennan and student activists on the values of democratic decision-making, rationality in debate and constructive opposition: one which combines a denouncing of current policies with thoughtful alternatives.

TEW **538 EDUCATION AND THE BARRICADES** *by Charles Frankel, 90pp, 1968, Norton, $1.50.* Frankel examines the arguments for student power, confrontation politics and structural reform of universities and concludes that the latter is needed while student power does exist without majority rule in institutions with a purpose: education. A defense of learning against University Luddites which takes the 1968 Columbia University violence as a starting point.

539 THE POLITICS OF PROTEST *by Jerome Skolnick, 419pp, 1969, Ballantine Books, $1.25.* A study of the violence which grew out of anti-war demonstrations, student confrontations, black militant demonstrations and police responses. Argues that the protests arise out of the frustration at achieving needed changes without carefully distinguishing what are needed changes and what are rhetorical demands.

540 VIOLENCE IN AMERICA, Historical and Comparative Perspective *by H. D. Graham and Ted Gurr, 795pp, 1969, New American Library, $1.25.* The complete official report to the National Commission on the Causes and Prevention of Violence which examines political violence in the U.S. and Europe, working class protest, racial conflict, crime, international conflict and rebellions.

INF **541 THE AUTOBIOGRAPHY OF MALCOLM X** *by Malcolm X, 460pp, 1964, Grove Press, $1.25.* A moving account of Malcolm X's odyssey from a poor negro in the ghettos of Boston and New York to guest lecturer at Harvard University, his political development in prison and after. Once a black Muslim, Malcolm X moved toward a Marxist critic of American society, while at times advocating the organization of blacks within the democratic process as an interest group analogous to labor unions, religious organizations and corporate interests.

542   **SOUL ON ICE** *by Eldridge Cleaver, 210pp, 1968, Delta Books, $1.95.* Cleaver's earlier writings on the need for black identity and a description of his movement toward the politics of violence.

543   **FROM PROTEST TO POLITICS** *by Bayard Rustin, 16pp, 1966, Commentary reprint, $.25.* Rustin, a leader since the 1940's in the struggle for nonviolent social change, argues persuasively for the need to challenge many democratically derived policies in ways which maintain democratic political processes.

544   **ANTI-POLITICS IN AMERICA, Reflections on the Anti-Political Temper and Its Distortions of the Democratic Process** *by John Bunzel, 291pp, 1967, Vintage, $1.95.* The author's experience in 1968 at San Francisco State College confirmed his 1967 thesis: many Americans are insensitive to the ultimate value of democratic politics. A searching analysis of why so many of the left and right and religious sects fail to understand democratic nonviolent politics and why they so often act to make them impossible.

545   **AMERICAN MILITARISM 1970,** *editors of The Progressive, 150pp, 1969, Viking Press, $.95.* An anthology which argues that American foreign policy is decided largely by the Pentagon and its defense contract suppliers, the CIA and other special interest groups outside of the control of elected officials.

545A   **MILITARY-INDUSTRIAL COMPLEX** *by Sidney Lens, 145pp, 1970, Pilgrim, $2.95.* An explanation of the growth of the military-industrial complex to its present state: in the author's judgment unchecked by civilian authority, unaffected by international politics.

546   **THE AMERICAN PEOPLE AND FOREIGN POLICY** *by Gabriel Almond, 269pp, 1960, Praeger, $2.75.* An assessment of American attitudes and their impact on foreign policy decision-making. Argues that there is a consensus among Americans in favor of U.S. participation in international organizations.

547 DISSENT, DEMOCRACY AND FOREIGN POL-ICY, A Symposium with Oscar Handlin, Hans Morgenthau, Saul Padover and others, *47pp, 1968, Foreign Policy Association, $.85.* Examines the nature of democracy and the responsibility of dissenters within it.

548 PATTERNS OF ANARCHY, *Leonard Krimerman and Lewis Perz (eds.), 571pp, 1966, Doubleday, $1.95.* A historical overview demonstrating the rich variety of libertarian, individualistic, anti-state, pro-state ideas which have been called anarchy.

549 THE RADICAL PAPERS, Essays in Democratic Socialism, *Irving Howe (ed.), 391pp, 1966, Doubleday, $1.45.* A range of essays arguing that democratic values can only be preserved in a corporation-dominated economy by enlarging the role of social ownership and control. Includes several essays advocating a democratic foreign policy.

550 TOWARD A DEMOCRATIC LEFT *by Michael Harrington, 314pp, 1968, Penguin Books, $1.25.* Presents the case for a reorganization of the Democratic Party by dropping current Southern Democrats and adding liberal Republicans, while adopting a policy of increased government involvement in the war on poverty, in regulation of service industries, and in developing a democratic foreign policy.

551 WORLD REVOLUTIONARY ELITES: Studies in Coercive Ideological Movements, *Harold Lasswell and Daniel Lerner (eds.), 478pp, 1965, MIT Press, $3.95.* Examines the literature of the elites which led the Politburo in Russia, the Nazis in Germany, the Kuomintang and Communists in China and the Fascists in Italy.

TEW   552 THE CHALLENGE OF DEMOCRACY *by John Strachey, 45pp, 1963, Encounter, $.60.* Argument for democracy as the form of government most capable of discovering and resolving acute social problems, most consistent with individual freedoms, and most likely to characterize economically and socially developed countries.

(see also 200, 217, 414-426, 476, 477-481, 484, 485)

The Peace Movement: General

553 POWER AND THE PURSUIT OF PEACE: Theory and Practice in the History of Relations between States *by F. H. Hinsley, 416pp, 1963, Cambridge University Press, $2.95*. A history of the ideas and organizations associated with past peace efforts. The author examines past attempts to resolve the apparent identity between violence and power by developing international institutions, but concludes that the problem cannot be resolved in that way because world government would condemn the developing areas to perpetual backwardness.

TEW   554 PEACE IS POSSIBLE, A Reader for Laymen, *Elizabeth Hollis (ed.), 354pp, 1967, Grossman, $2.95*. A survey of the ideas which have dominated the on-going American peace movement in the post–World War II period. Includes essays by Paul Tillich, Robert Pickus, Grenville Clark, Hans Morgenthau and others. With accompanying study guide this book offers an excellent introduction to the field.

555 THE WAR/PEACE ESTABLISHMENT *by Arthur Herzog, 271pp, 1965, Harper & Row, hardcover, $5.95*. A sometimes perceptive analysis of the range of organizations, individuals and ideas involved in full time work on war/peace issues. Includes a description of Air Force related organizations, Communist peace organizations, pacifist groups, unilateral disarmers, multilateral disarmers and others.

556 TOWARD A PEACEMAKERS ACADEMY, A Proposal for a First Step Toward a United Nations Transnational Peacemaking Force *by Arthur Waskow, 42pp, 1967, World Association of World Federalists, $.50*. A study of the political need, curriculum and institutionalization process of an academy designed to train an international civil service in the art of peacemaking and peacekeeping.

The American Peace Movement

557 PEACE OR WAR: The American Struggle 1636– 1936 *by Merle Curti, 374pp, 1959, Canner, hardcover, $7.50.* An important history of the various strands in the struggle for peace: religious pacifists, internationalists and liberals who found violence incompatible with democratic values.

558 PACIFISM IN THE UNITED STATES, From the Colonial Era to the First World War *by Peter Brock, 1,005pp, 1968, Princeton University Press, hardcover, $18.50; or abridged paperback, 298pp, 1968, $2.95.* A detailed history of both religious pacifism and those sections of the peace movement which repudiated all war. The author argues that the failure to relate the quest for international peace with the attainment of justice and freedom within the national community was fatal to the peace efforts of that time.

559 ELEVEN AGAINST WAR, Studies in American Internationalist Thought 1898–1921 *by Sondra Herman, 264pp, 1969, Hoover Institution Press, $2.95.* A study of two strands of internationalist thought: one represented by Woodrow Wilson, Elihu Root and others, sought to abolish war through international political organization; the other sought the same end through economic abundance.

560 OPPONENTS OF WAR, 1917–1918 *by H. C. Peterson and Gilbert Fite, 424pp, 1968, Washington University Press, $2.95.* A summary of the various types of opposition to World War I and the response to such opposition by the American public and government.

561 PEACE PROPHET—American Pacifist Thought, 1919–1941 *by John Nelson, 192pp, 1968, University of North Carolina Press, $4.50.* Demonstrates that the divergent types of pacifist thought (from those who consider all conflict sinful to those who consider it healthy) often spring from a common religious perspective. Sharply critical of the political alliances and mistaken political judgments made by pacifists between World War I and World War II.

562   TO END WAR, The Story of the National Council for Prevention of War *by Frederick Libby, 188pp, 1969, Fellowship Publications, hardcover, $5.00.* The executive secretary describes the efforts of his organization to mobilize American voluntary organizations for peace from 1921 to 1954. Portrays the shift in emphasis within the peace movement from support for world organizations in 1921 to neutrality in foreign wars in the 1930's without apparent recognition of the difference. An important document on the peace movement.

562A   IN PURSUIT OF PEACE AND JUSTICE, Pacifists in the American Peace Movement, 1914–1941 *by Charles Chatfield,   pp, 1971, University of Tennessee Press, hardcover.* A thorough and supremely relevant study of pacifist attempts to develop a political coalition capable of translating their ideal into reality. A careful, analytic interpretation of the ideas and organizational philosophy of the peace movement prior to World War II.

563   REBELS AGAINST WAR, The American Peace Movement 1941–1960 *by Laurence Whittner, 339pp, 1969, Columbia University Press, hardcover, $10.00.* A study of the backbone of the American peace movement in the post–World War II period. Sympathetic treatment of many divergent groups.

564   REBEL PASSION *by Vera Brittain, 240pp, 1964, Fellowship Publications, hardcover, $5.00.* A study of various leaders of the international pacifist peace movement. Concentrates on the past leaders of the Fellowship of Reconciliation: Norman Thomas, Martin Niemoller, J. Nevin Sayre and others.

565   WOMEN'S INTERNATIONAL LEAGUE FOR PEACE AND FREEDOM, 1915–1965 *by Gertrude Bussey and Margaret Time, 255pp, 1965, George Allen & Unwin*

Ltd, hardcover, $6.75. A detailed record of the origins and development of the WILPF including officers, policy stands and organizational activity.

566 **FOR MORE THAN BREAD, An Autobiographical Account of Twenty-Two Year's Work with the American Friends Service Committee** *by Clarence E. Pickett, 433pp, 1953, Little, Brown, hardcover, $5.00.* A detailed account of the AFSC's peace and related activities during the 1930's and 1940's.

567 **PROTEST: Pacifism and Politics,** *James Finn (ed.), 511pp, 1968, Random House, $2.45.* Interviews with a wide variety of pacifist and radical opponents of American violence which demonstrates the diversity of thought in the peace movement in 1966–1967. How quickly fashions change.

(see also 473, 474 and 475)

The Democratic Peace Movement: What Basis for Organizing?

568 **PEACE POLITICS, THE NEW LEFT AND THE PITY OF IT ALL** *by Robert Pickus and Carl Landauer, 16pp, 1966, World Without War Council, $.25.* Argues that rejecting America's cold war and Vietnam war policies does not by itself substantiate an individual's or organization's claim to be for peace.

569 **THE PROBLEM OF THE NEW LEFT** *by Tom Kahn, 16pp, 1966, League for Industrial Democracy, $.25.* Examines the New Left, its political and social programs and concludes that it is likely to be destructive to democratic institutions while raising issues which need to be discussed.

570 **ON THE NATURE OF COMMUNISM AND RELATIONS WITH COMMUNISTS** *by Irving Howe, 10pp, 1965, League for Industrial Democracy, $.25.* Howe considers that while anti-Communism is in itself an inadequate political position, anyone committed to democratic values

will often find himself opposing Communist organizations and powers.

571   DOES THE PEACE MOVEMENT NEED THE COMMUNISTS? *by Michael Harrington, 6pp, 1966, Village Voice, $.10.* Harrington argues that his commitment to democratic values forces him to oppose both U.S. support of the Saigon government and the policies of Hanoi/NLF.

572   HOMAGE TO CATALONIA *by George Orwell, 232pp, 1967, Beacon Press, $1.75.* The failure of a united front examined by the author of *1984* and a participant in the Spanish civil war. Underlines the difficulties in cooperating in a united front with antithetical political objectives and only one common denominator—an enemy.

Peace and Voluntary Organizations

573   A NATION OF JOINERS *by Arthur M. Schlesinger, 27pp, 1954, Macmillan, $.25.* Describes the historical importance of America's voluntary organizations as the moving structure in American politics.

574   STANDARDS OF RESPONSIBILITY FOR VOLUNTARY ORGANIZATIONS WISHING TO BE OF AID IN ACHIEVING A WORLD WITHOUT WAR *by Robert Pickus, 8pp, 1968, World Without War Council, $.10.* Meets criticism against voluntary organizations putting war/peace issues on their agenda by demonstrating how they can deal with such issues constructively.

575   CRISIS IN THE SOCIAL ACTION COMMITTEE *by David Luse, 16pp, 1966, World Without War Council, $.25.* A fifteen minute play dramatizing the difficulties of peace activity in voluntary organizations.

**INT   576   WORKING FOR A WORLD WITHOUT
TEW   WAR IN YOUR COMMUNITY, A Study Kit** *by Robert Pickus, 300pp, 1968, World Without War Council, $4.75.* This mimeographed study guide is designed for use with nine one-half hour films (rental copies available on request). It offers in summary form a complete answer to

the question: what do I need to know to work effectively for a world without war in my community?

577 VOLUNTARY ORGANIZATIONS IN WORLD AFFAIRS, *Virginia Saurwein (ed.), 72pp, 1969, Center for War/Peace Studies, $1.50.* A special issue of *Intercom* devoted to the voluntary organizations, their leaders, addresses and activities, currently engaged in world affairs. A valuable introduction to the voluntary organization world.

(see also 181 and 545)

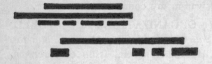

To match men's hope for peace with knowledge of why wars occur is the mission of peace research. Today scholars from a broad spectrum of disciplines are engaged in analyzing the causes of war and possible cures. A short ten years ago it was hard to find academic centers working on problems other than those related to traditional problems of diplomacy and military strategy. Today we can list eighteen institutions (see also # 578) seeking validated knowledge of aid in controlling the threat of war. Theory and research methodology have become increasingly sophisticated, to the point where some claim the minimum conditions for a science of the causes of war exist (# 579).

In an embarrassingly simplified, but we believe defensible fashion, *To End War* has attempted to identify the causes of war and to explore alternatives which could either eliminate the cause in question or channel its propensity for producing violent conflict into nonviolent processes of conflict resolution. But our argument is faulty. We have not identified, much less eliminated, *all* the causes. The plausibility of our argument, however, remains high if the web of alternatives we have sketched can be made strong enough to catch the causal factors we have not identified.

The identification of other causes is one task on which peace researchers are working. Among those of particular importance are the nature of man as an aggressor. The misperception by national leaders of threat, over-reaction to it and other communication failures; self-fulfilling prophecies; belief in the inevitability of war; the self-interest of domestic beneficiaries of war and war preparation; hostility and irrationality as a characteristic of mass ego's; patterns in the responses of elite decision makers to problems of national security in situations involving international tension, i.e. arming or psychologically preparing for war, increased tension and finally hostile acts; domestic political scapegoating; the substitution of a foreign enemy for domestic ones. All of these and others, as well as the major causes considered in Part I of *To End War* deserve and are receiving further study.

If our emphasis here has been on a line of argument sustaining a certain approach to foreign policy problems, it is not because of any assurance that all the evidence is in, but rather because of the requirement to act now on the best evidence and thought available while continuing to search for better answers.

Throughout *To End War* we have challenged approaches which assert a single law under which all the causes of war can be subsumed. We have instead tried to deal with a list of discrete causes, rather than obtain a single general law. The advocacy of a single cause approach may remove one cause of war while increasing the likelihood that some other factor will then become decisive. Part of our purpose throughout this book has been to demonstrate that it is possible to face the *multiple* causes of war and yet sustain the argument that ending war is a practicable goal.

Much extremely valuable peace research is now being done. The UNESCO publication, *International Repertory of Institutions Specializing in Research on*

Peace and Disarmament (# 578) introduces over 125 research institutes from all over the world. The National Council on Peace Strategy, an outgrowth of the World Without War Council work in the sixties, attempted to serve as a bridge between peace research institutes and the work of peace organizations, but much remains to be done to achieve this essential linkage.

The peace research movement has crystallized in the last decade. The establishment of the *Journal of Conflict Resolution* (1957, p. 241) and the *Journal of Peace Research* (p. 241) along with the creation of an international organization for scholars in the field and of a number of institutes both in the United States and elsewhere are indicative of the professionalization of the field. Dean Pruitt and Richard Snyder mark Quincy Wright's *A Study of War* (# 2, 1942) as the Peace Research movement's intellectual precursor. Wright treated war as a subject for empirical interdisciplinary scholarship and clearly differentiated between the demanding scholarly work needed and past practice. By 1960, one heard frequent references to a "science of peace" as a consequence of interdisciplinary governmental research like Project Michelson, analytical studies focusing on the nature of strategic encounters in a thermonuclear age, and a variety of approaches to a general theory of international relations and to improved research methodology.

Ten years later, skeptics may dubiously regard the likely product of an emphasis on "science" and may, in any case, reasonably doubt the claim to scientific validation over a very significant area. One can still appreciate the potential importance of work underway. Current work includes the development of simulation techniques for studying international rivalry at the International Relations Program, Northwestern University. Stanford Studies in International Conflict and Integration at Stanford University is using computers, content analysis techniques and other quantifying devices for measuring variables in the patterns of conflict that lead to war. The World Law Fund, New York City, is in the midst of a Model World Orders Project which seeks to develop eight to ten model world orders based on different views of an acceptable world government. The Duke Rule of Law Center, Duke University, Durham, N.C., conducts research on international institutions and world law; the Institute for the Study of International Relations, Berkeley, California, emphasizes a functional approach to problems of international political community.

Those interested in following current research will be interested in the work of the Canadian Peace Research Institute, Clarkson, Ontario, which publishes abstracts on a wide variety of peace research subjects. The Arms Control and Disarmament Agency publishes a quarterly covering periodicals and research reports related to disarmament and arms control.

The books in this chapter provide only an introduction to work now underway. More extensive bibliographies are available in the books marked B below.

Peace Research and Analysis

578 INTERNATIONAL REPERTORY OF INSTITUTIONS SPECIALIZING IN RESEARCH ON PEACE AND DISARMAMENT, UNESCO, *79pp, 1967, UNESCO Publications, $1.25.* An examination of the peace research field with a listing of agencies, their budgets, important publications and activities.

579 THEORY AND RESEARCH ON THE CAUSES OF

WAR, *Dean G. Pruitt and Richard C. Snyder (eds.), 314pp, 1969, Prentice-Hall, $4.95.* A study of the different causes of war seen primarily as international conflict. A valuable introduction to much of the current research including computer simulation techniques.

B 580 THE GREAT IDEAS: A *Syntopicon* of Great Books of the Western World, *Mortimer Adler et al., Vol. II. pp. 1010–1037, 1952, Encyclopaedia Britanica.* "War and Peace" offers a helpful division of the subject matter and an introduction to the basic ideas.

B 581 WAR, Studies from Psychology, Sociology, Anthropology, *Leon Bramson and George Goethals (eds.), 434pp, 1968, Basic Books, $4.95.* Examines the failure of any single cause approach to the study of war and argues for the need for a comprehensive list of the causes of war for those interested in its prevention.

582 THE MEANING OF THE TWENTIETH CENTURY: The Great Transition *by Kenneth Boulding, 199pp, 1964, Harper & Row, $1.60.* An examination of the transition from civilization to "post-civilization" (technological society). Calls for research on the problems of war and overpopulation which are seen as the main obstacles to the successful transition.

583 PEACE RESEARCH AROUND THE WORLD *by Hanna and Alan Newcombe, 204pp, 1968, Canadian Peace Research Institute, $3.00.* A survey of peace research informational and substantive now being conducted.

584 PEACE RESEARCH REVIEWS: Volume I. 1969, *Canadian Peace Research Institute, $7.00.* Essays on alternative approaches to world government, the history of disarmament negotiations, political violence, games theory and the simulation of disarmament and deterrence strategies in world politics. Includes essays by Theodore F. Lentz, Anatol Rapaport, Hanna Newcombe and others. (Write Canadian Peace Research Institute, 514 Chartwell Road, Oakville, Ontario, Canada for a description of subsequent volumes.)

585 **DIALOGUE ON PEACE RESEARCH** *by Milton Mayer and Kenneth Boulding, 30pp, 1967, Pendle Hill, $.45.* Two Quakers discuss peace research and agree that "love is not enough."

586 **A TIME TO SPEAK—ON HUMAN VALUES AND SOCIAL RESEARCH** *by Herbert C. Kelman, 368pp, 1968, Jessey-Bass Inc., hardcover, $9.50.* A study of the role of the social scientist as a producer of social forces, as an experimenter and as a participant in social action. Argues for the relevance of nonviolent action and sets forth alternative foreign policy perspectives.

(see also 1-8)

International Relations

587 **INTERNATIONAL CONFLICT FOR BEGINNERS** *by Roger Fisher, 231pp, 1969, Harper & Row, hardcover, $5.95.* Depicts how an adversary looks at a conflict situation, the opinions open to the parties and how different moves and initiative acts can help achieve nonviolent resolution of a conflict.

588 **APPROACHES TO THE STUDY OF POLITICS,** *Roland Young (ed.), 382pp, 1969, Northwestern University Press, $3.00.* A useful study of value choices, political power, political identifications and related ideas by political scientists, sociologists and psychologists.

589 **APPROACHES TO COMPARATIVE AND INTERNATIONAL POLITICS,** *Barry Farrell (ed.), 368pp, 1966, Northwestern University Press, $3.95.* Includes essays by twelve leading political scientists on the relationship between domestic and foreign policy, between developed and underdeveloped countries and open and closed decision-making processes, as well as suggestions for future research.

590 **THE ANALYSIS OF INTERNATIONAL RELATIONS** *by Karl W. Deutsch, 214pp, 1968, Prentice-Hall, $2.95.* A useful introuction to the study of international relations using games theory, communication patterns, quantitative data and conflict theory.

591 CONFLICT AND PEACE IN THE MODERN IN-TERNATIONAL SYSTEM by Evan Luard, 343pp, 1968, Little, Brown, $3.95. A study of previous and present state systems (ancient China and Greece are used as precursors), which examines the bipolar balance of power and deterrence systems of maintaining peace. Stresses the crucial role of domestic conflicts in producing international wars.

B **592 NEW APPROACHES TO INTERNATIONAL RELATIONS**, Morton A. Kaplan (ed.), 400pp, 1968, St. Martin's Press, hardcover, $10.00. A study of new behavior science techniques for studying international relations, including use of computers, game theory, alternative world futures, systems approaches, historical comparisons and quantitative approaches.

INF **593 NATIONALISM AND SOCIAL COMMU-NICATION: An Inquiry into the Foundations of Nationalism** by Karl W. Deutsch, 292pp, 1953, MIT Press, $3.95.

594 NOBODY WANTED WAR: Misperception in Vietnam and Other Wars by Ralph K. White, 346pp, 1968, Random House, hardcover, $5.95. A study of the complex of emotions and prejudices which, the author holds, causes international conflicts. From a study of World War I, World War II and the Vietnam war, the author concludes that misperceptions produce tensions which can lead to wars.

595 INTERNATIONAL RELATIONS RESEARCH: Problems of Evaluation and Advancement by Raymond Platig, 177pp, 1966, Carnegie Endowment, $1.00. A guide to evaluating research which emphasizes the importance of international interdependence.

(see also 143 and 553)

Anthropology

596 WAR: The Anthropology of Armed Conflict and Aggression, Morton Fried, Marvin Harris and Robert Murphy (eds.), 262pp, 1968, Natural History Press, $2.95.

A symposium on the contribution which anthropology can make to the understanding and prevention of war. Divergent views are presented on such topics as man's "innate" aggression, the social function of war and its impact on social structure.

597 **THE TERRITORIAL IMPERATIVE** *by Robert Ardrey, 390pp, 1966, Delta Books, $2.45.* Ardrey argues that there is an instinctive drive in man and animals to acquire and defend territory which must be understood by those seeking an end to war.

598 **ON AGGRESSION** *by Konrad Lorenz, 306pp, 1967, Bantam Books, $1.25.* Lorenz argues that man is instinctively violent and that he is overly violent because his development of weapons has far outstripped the development of cultural inhibitions against the use of violence within the species.

599 **MAN AND AGGRESSION** *by M. F. Ashley Montague, 178pp, 1968, Oxford University Press, $1.95.* Critical essays on Lorenz's and Ardrey's view of man as instinctively violent. Montague argues that man is capable of love as well as hate—although neither is an instinct.

(see also 3)

Political Science

INF   600 **THE ORIGINS OF TOTALITARIANISM** *by Hannah Arendt, 520pp, 1958, Beacon Press, $2.95.* A brilliant study of the origins and roots of totalitarian movements. Argues for the need to safeguard the rights of man against such movements and for recognition of human dignity throughout the world as a precondition for peace.

601 **TODAY'S ISMS: Communism, Fascism, Capitalism, Socialism** *by William Ebenstein, 267pp, 1970, sixth edition, Doubleday $3.50.* An examination of two different ways of life—totalitarianism and democracy in their twentieth century manifestations.

602 **THE WAR MYTH** *by Donald A. Wells, 288pp,*

1967, Pegasus, $1.75. Traces Western philosophical, theological and institutional justifications for war.

INF   603   THE NATURE OF PREJUDICE *by Gordon W. Allport, 456pp, 1958, Doubleday, $1.95.* One of the basic studies of the nature of prejudice, its origins, manifestations and consequences.

604   THE YEAR 2000, A Framework for Speculation on the Next Thirty-Three Years *by Herman Kahn and Anthony J. Wiener, 431pp, 1967, MacMillan, hardcover, $9.95.* An attempt to extend trend lines in order to speculate about alternative future worlds.

Psychology

605   WAR WITHIN MAN *by Erich Fromm, 56pp, 1963, American Friends Service Committee, $.35.* A psychological inquiry into the roots of destructiveness.

606   SANITY AND SURVIVAL, Psychiatric Aspects of War and Peace *by Jerome Frank, 330pp, 1967, Random House, $1.95.* A study of the facts of human nature which need to be accounted for if we want to end war. Argues against theories of immutable violent conflict. By the author of *A Non-Violent Alternative*.

607   INTERNATIONAL BEHAVIOR, A Social-Psychological Analysis, *Herbert Kelman (ed.), 626pp, 1965, Holt, Rinehart and Winston, hardcover, $12.95.* A symposium of prominent psychologists discussing the psychological causes of war.

608   MAY MAN PREVAIL? *by Erich Fromm, 257pp, 1964, Doubleday, $1.45.* This question is asked in the light of a psychiatrist's understanding of man's need to dominate others and the contemporary weapons technology. Fromm concludes that one precondition for survival is a willingness to recognize *that it is just that which is at stake: survival.*

609   THE PSYCHOLOGY OF POWER *by Ronald V. Sampson, 247pp, 1965, Random House, $1.95.* A study of the acquisition of power and its effect on those who acquire it.

610 CHILDHOOD AND SOCIETY *by Erik H. Erikson, 445pp, 1963, rev. ed., Norton, $2.95.* A noted psychiatrist studies individual identity crises and their relationship to political identifications with nation-states.

TEW   611 PSYCHIATRIC ASPECTS OF THE PREVENTION OF NUCLEAR WAR, *Group for the Advancement of Psychiatry, 96pp, 1963, hardcover, $3.00.* A study of the consequences of long periods of "cold war" on social attitudes toward the other side. Underlines the effect of military deterrence in stereotyping and reinforcing hostile images of the opponent. Concludes with some considerations related to the conduct of international conflict without violence.

612 IMAGE AND REALITY IN WORLD POLITICS, *John C. Farrell and Asa P. Smith (eds.), 140pp, 1968, Columbia University Press, $2.25.* An anthology on the effect of misperceptions, myths, and images of "enemies" in world politics. Selections by Kenneth Boulding, Reinhold Niebuhr, John Stoessinger, Benjamin Schwartz, Robert North and others.

613 WORLD POLITICS AND PERSONAL INSECURITY *by Harold D. Lasswell, 238pp, 1965, Macmillan, $2.45.* A psychological study of many "beyond the fringe" problems: the possibility of astro-politics, the manipulation of symbols of world unity, the demands for peace and justice and their relationship to personal insecurity.

History and Literature

B   614 BIBLIOGRAPHY ON PEACE RESEARCH IN HISTORY *by Blanche Cook, 72pp, 1969, Clio Press, $6.50.* A research guide for historians including archival holdings, current and out of print books and peace organization record depositories. Emphasizes international relations, disarmament, nonviolence and world law.

615 THE RESPONSIBILITY OF POWER, *Leonard Krieger and Fritz Stern (eds.), 499pp, 1969, Doubleday, $1.95.* Twenty-four leading American historians examine the ways in which various men and nations have interpreted their purposes and the use of political power during the past 500 years. Included are studies of Machiavelli, Lenin and the internationalism of the U.S. in the twentieth century.

616 WAR AND HUMAN PROGRESS *by John U. Nef, 464pp, 1963, Harper & Row, $2.45.* Argues that material and scientific progress have not relied on the stimulus of war, but flourish most in peace time. The moral neutrality of science and technology and their use in the development of industrial societies have weakened many of the moral, aesthetic and cultural restraints on war.

617 THE ILIAD, or the Poem of Force *by Simone Weil, 39pp, 1957, Pendle Hill, $.45.* Uses the Homeric epic to discuss the effect of violence on those who use it.

618 WAR: An Anthology, *Edward and Elizabeth Huberman (eds.), 304pp, 1969, Washington Square Press, $1.25.* Brings together poets' and authors' descriptions and condemnations of human suffering in war.

619 MAN AND WARFARE *by William F. Irscher, 340pp, 1964, Little, Brown, $2.95.* A study of the treatment of warfare in works of fiction.

620 THE PLAGUE *by Albert Camus, 278pp, 1948, Random House, $2.45.* Does adversity bring out the worst or the best in man? Camus says that despite the plague (War? the Human Condition? Totalitarianism?) there is something irreducible in man's striving for what is right.

621 THE FACE OF VIOLENCE, An Essay with a Play *by J. Bronowski, 166pp, 1967, Meridian, $2.25.* A scientist explores the theme of violence and concludes it is a gesture against the constraints of society.

INF **622 THE PELOPONNESIAN WAR** *by Thu-*

cydides, 516pp, 1951, Random House, $2.45. An indictment of war, expressed in the history of the ascendancy of Athens in ancient Greece. A classic of Greek history with many ethical and political analogies to subsequent history.

(see also 192, 260, 261 and 477)

Science

623 SCIENCE IN THE CAUSE OF PEACE *by Gerard Piel, 358pp, 1964, Random House, $1.65.* The publisher of *Scientific American* studies the usefulness of dispassionate inquiry, scientific thought and the drawing of valid inferences from limited data for the problems of peace, particularly disarmament.

624 TOWARDS A SCIENCE OF PEACE *by Theodore Lenz, 193pp, 1955, Halcyon Press, $3.00.* Advocates utilization of science to eliminate war.

625 EINSTEIN ON PEACE *by Albert Einstein, 710pp, 1968, Schocken, $2.95.* Through Einstein's essays and letters, this work demonstrates the concern and courage of one of the century's leading scientists. Included are the famous Einstein-Freud exchanges on war and world government.

626 THE SUBVERSIVE SCIENCE, Essays Toward an Ecology of Man, *Paul Shepard and Daniel McKinley (eds.), 451pp, 1969, Houghton-Mifflin, $5.95.* Ecology, the study of man's biological make-up in his natural environment, has become a popular science. This reader demonstrates the relevance of considering biological issues in more traditional subject matter: population, sociology, urbanization, and ethics.

626A TECHNOLOGY AND WORLD POWER *by Victor Basiuk, 63pp, 1970, Foreign Policy Association, $1.00.* A valuable study of the impact of technological innovation on the social institutions of national societies. Explores the impact of rapid technological achievement on international relations both between the U.S. and the U.S.S.R. and between the rich nations and the poor.

Peace Research Organizations

The following is a selective listing of peace research centers. For a more detailed listing, including an analysis of the peace research effort, see the *UNESCO Reports and Papers in the Social Sciences*, publication #23, entitled "International Repertory of Institutions Specializing in Research on Peace and Disarmament," or contact the International Peace Research Association (address below) which has the responsibility for maintaining this directory.

INTERNATIONAL PEACE RESEARCH ASSOCIATION (IPRA)

Ubbo Emmiussingel 19, Groningen, Netherlands
An association which accepts as members institutions and individuals of adequate professional standing with a professed interest in peace research. The purpose of the association is to stimulate peace research through peace research centers, conferences and publications.
Journal: *International Peace Research Newsletter*, 1100 East Washington St., Ann Arbor, Michigan 48108.

INTERNATIONAL INSTITUTE FOR PEACE

Mollwaldsplatz 5, Vienna IV, Austria. Cable: Paxinstitu
An independent institution; research focuses on economic development, disarmament, and international relations.
Journal: *Active Coexistence*, in English, Spanish, and French.
Peace and the Sciences, in English, German, and French.

CANADIAN PEACE RESEARCH INSTITUTE (CPRI)

Clarkson, Ontario, Canada.
An independent institution concerned with the eco-

nomic consequences of disarmament; public opinion on foreign affairs; U.N. peace-keeping operations; cross-cultural studies of war-mindedness in relation to other aspects of culture.

Journal: *Peace Research Abstracts Journal,* monthly, English.

Canadian Peace Research Institute News Report, quarterly, English.

Peace Research Review, bi-monthly, English.

HIROSHIMA INSTITUTE OF PEACE SCIENCE (HIPS)

Central P.O. Box 99, Hiroshima, Japan.

An independent institution concerned with cultural conflict in periods of change; experimental small group studies of conflict; effects of nuclear war.

INSTITUTT FOR FREDSFORSKNING

(International Peace Research Institute, Oslo) (PRIO)

Gydas vei 8, P.O. Box 5052, Oslo 3, Norway. Cable: Peace Research.

Private organization concerned with general conflict theory; social aspects of technical assistance; race relations; nonviolence as a method of defense; effects of student exchange on attitudes.

Journal: *Journal of Peace Research,* quarterly, English, summaries in Russian.

CENTER FOR RESEARCH ON CONFLICT RESOLUTION (CRCR)

University of Michigan, 1100 E. Washington St., Ann Arbor, Michigan 48108

A division of the university concerned with general conflict theory; economic development; race relations; cultural conflict in periods of change; disarmament; arms control; analysis of historical examples of prolonged peaceful relations between nations.

Journal: *Journal of Conflict Resolution,* quarterly, English.

STANFORD STUDIES IN INTERNATIONAL CONFLICT AND INTEGRATION
Stanford University, 549 Salvatierra Street, Stanford, California 94305.
A division of the university concerned with general conflict theory; balance of power; diplomacy; ethnocentrism; simulation of international conflict; economic and geographic factors in international relations; the decision-making process in foreign relations; sources and components of nationalism.
Journal: *Progress Report*, 25 issues a year, English.

INSTITUTE FOR STRATEGIC STUDIES (ISS)
18 Adam Street, London W.C.s, England.
An independent institution concerned with general conflict theory; balance of power; U.N. peace-keeping operations; general military strategy; arms control.
Journal: *Survival*, every two months, English.

CENTER FOR INTERNATIONAL STUDIES (CENIS)
M.I.T., 30 Wadsworth St., Cambridge, Mass. 02139.
A division of the institute concerned with social aspects of technical assistance; economic development in general; race relations; cultural conflict in periods of change; class conflict; balance of power; sources and components of nationalism; effects of economic pressures on international relations; factors in successful federation of people with diverse cultures.

CENTER FOR THE STUDY OF AMERICAN FOREIGN AND MILITARY POLICY (CSAFMP)
1126 E. 59th St., Chicago 37, Illinois 60637.
A division of the University of Chicago concerned with the balance of power; diplomacy; nonviolence as a method of defense; general military strategy; effects of modern warfare on popular ethical standards; analysis of historical examples of prolonged peaceful relations between nations.

INSTITUTE FOR POLICY STUDIES
1900 Florida Ave., N.W., Washington, D.C. 20009.

Independent institution concerned with general conflict theory; social aspects of technical assistance; economic development; disarmament; arms control; emergence of individual responsibility in international law; public perception of the intentions of other nations; channels of communication and influence on foreign policy issues.

INSTITUTE FOR RESEARCH ON INTERNATIONAL BEHAVIOR (IRIB)

San Francisco State College, San Francisco, Calif. 94127. A division of the Frederic Burke Foundation for Education, San Francisco State College, concerned with general conflict theory; experimental small groups studies of conflict; simulation of international conflict; arms control; economic models of conflict; evaluation of educational programs on international organization. Journal: *Background* (official organ of International Studies Association), quarterly, English.

INTERNATIONAL RELATIONS PROGRAM, NORTHWESTERN UNIVERSITY

1834 Sheridan Road, Evanston, Illinois 60201. A division of the Political Science Department of the university concerned with general conflict theory; diplomacy; public opinion on foreign affairs; conference techniques; ethnocentrism; general military strategy; attitudes toward other nations and toward war as a function of socialization experiences; comparison of industrial conflict with international conflict; experimental studies of aggression, threat, and intergroup conflict.

WESTERN BEHAVIORAL SCIENCES INSTITUTE (WBSI)

1121 Torrey Pines Road, La Jolla, California 92037. Independent institution concerned with general conflict theory; conference techniques; ethnocentrism; experimental small group studies of conflict; simulation of international conflict; effects of modern war on popular ethical standards; methods of communicating social science findings to decision-makers and the general public; public perception of the intentions of other nations.

WORLD RULE OF LAW CENTER
Duke University, Durham, North Carolina, 27706.
A division of Duke University. Its principal activity is research and publication on questions of law and international organization bearing on security, peace, disarmament, and world order.

CARNEGIE ENDOWMENT FOR INTERNATIONAL PEACE (CEIP)
United Nations Plaza, 46th Street, New York, N.Y. 10007.
Established to seek practical paths to peace. Income from the original endowment has been devoted to research and education in this field. The institution operates normally as a programme foundation. Most of its funds, and grants to it from other foundations, are expended for programmes developed by its own staff.
Journal: *International Conciliation,* five issues a year, English.

FEDERATION FOR THE ADVANCEMENT OF PEACE RESEARCH
100 East Washington St., Ann Arbor, Michigan 48108.
An association of organizations and individuals concerned with the advancement of peace research and related studies. The Federation operates as an objective, professional, scholarly organization without political, ideological, financial or nationalistic bias. Its main objectives are to foster exchange of ideas, promote studies and analyze the problems of peace. It encourages utilization of methods, concepts, analytical techniques and theoretical frameworks designed specifically for peace research.

UNITED STATES ARMS CONTROL AND DISARMAMENT AGENCY (ACDA)
2201 C St., N.W., Washington, D.C. 20541

A U.S. Government institution, with the following subdivisions: International Relations Bureau, Economics Bureau, Science and Technology Bureau, Weapons Evaluation and Control Bureau, Disarmament Advisory Staff, Reference Research Staff, General Counsel, Public Affairs Advisor, Executive Director.

part two

A CONTEXT FOR ACTION

Introduction

In Part I we introduced the reader to the war/ peace field, surveying the state of the discussion in various parts of the field and identifying the books that best present the major points of view. We also constructed an argument. In each chapter we suggested the approach we believe of most aid to ending war.

Part II gathers the strands of that argument into one coherent statement which is set against a discussion of alternative moral and political contexts. Chapter 13 describes these other perspectives which play an important role in the contemporary discussion. That chapter ends with an assessment of the elements of these perspectives which are helpful in the construction of a very different moral and political context believed more adequate to the problem of ending war.

Chapter 14 is a statement of that context. It clarifies the assumptions on which a *To End War* context rests. It summarizes the goals and political analysis of such an approach and explicates the idea of American peace initiatives, which provide the context's distinctive dynamics.

Part III then turns to the problem of intelligent peace activity; activity that can make these ideas, or others you prefer, the public policy of our country.

A context is that which comes before and after a statement and fixes its meaning. In the war/peace field, what comes before a statement of position on an issue is a set of values, goals and political beliefs that do more than surround the position taken; they often determine its content. The statement, "I oppose Washington's policy in Vietnam" for example, could have the following meanings: "I am a pacifist and oppose all military programs"; "I am a Communist and want a Communist government in Saigon"; "I am a mayor and want funds for urban problems"; "I am a musician and do not want to be drafted"; "I am a general and oppose our country getting into land wars in Asia." From the point of view of those committed to work to end war, the ideas and attitudes lying behind these individual statements are more important than the common opposition to U.S. policy in Vietnam; for it is the context from which a person speaks that ultimately makes him an aid or an obstacle to ending war.

In one contemporary usage the term *context* refers to the particular *situation* in which an action takes place. We use it here with quite a different meaning; i.e., that body of thought and belief which, though external to a particular situation, significantly affects the action taken in it. Given this definition, one can see why *To End War* has emphasized the importance of the different political and moral contexts that dominate the war/peace discussion and has given relatively little time to the detailed discussion of particular issues. Although few citizens are experts on war/peace issues, everyone—consciously or not—has a moral and political context that shapes his attitudes on foreign policy. Taken collectively, these underlying contexts set limits to what the country's foreign policy decision makers can do.

In Chapter 7 we demonstrated how contexts influence the discussion of war/peace issues. We turn now to an attempt to summarize and understand these contexts. In their inadequacy lies a primary obstacle to American leadership for a world without war.

SEVEN CURRENT CONTEXTS

Probably the easiest way to appreciate the importance of contexts is to contrast the treatment of three or four specific war/peace issues (e.g., the ABM, Vietnam, the foreign aid budget, the Middle East) in magazines with widely differing political contexts; e.g., *The National Review, Orbis, U.S. News & World Report, The New York Times, Ramparts, The New York Review of Books, The World Marxist Review, Fellowship,* and *Intercom* (see Part III G).

The seven contexts summarized below have dominated the war/peace discussion in America. Within each you will find varying emphases. But each has a clearly identifiable central thrust.

They are:

1) *Win:* a policy for achieving peace through the military defeat of Communism.

2) *The Standard American Approach:* a policy for maintaining peace through a preponderance of American military power.

3) *The Revised Standard Version:* a policy of

achieving peace through military deterrence while strengthening international institutions and pursuing the other requisites of a stable peace.

4) *Reactive Politics:* a *potpourri* of political and apolitical views arguing that America is the single villain in world affairs and/or that stopping the U.S. from intervening in other countries will bring peace.

5) *Marxist:* peace through Communist world domination.

6) *Traditional Pacifism:* peace through a commitment to nonviolence.

7) *Priorities:* the new withdrawal of America from attempts to shape world politics. This context, which can be acclimated to political views as diverse as President Nixon's and the mass media defined anti-war movement, is the context coming to increasing prominence in the seventies.

The summaries below offer the barest précis of alternative war/peace contexts. All are fundamentally different from the approach described as a developed peace position which is discussed last.

I. WIN: A POLICY FOR ACHIEVING PEACE THROUGH THE MILITARY DEFEAT OF COMMUNISM

At the heart of this view is the perception of Communism as evil and the threat, given its expansionist nature, that Communism (whether in China, the Soviet Union, or Cuba) poses to American values and American interests. The distinctive characteristic of the *Win* context is its adherents' conception of "realism." The reasoning goes something like this in, for example, the case of China: the Chinese have the bomb. They will soon have intercontinental ballistic missiles. They have said our society is monstrously evil and should be destroyed. We have the power to destroy them now, and should, since future conflict is inevitable and time works for them.

In this context patriotism is the central virtue and the inevitability of war the key assumption. In this view negotiated agreements, trade with Communist countries, or cooperation with them in international organizations is pernicious and undermines our security.

Elements of this pre-emptive military approach now have some influence in Soviet discussions of what to do about Chinese nuclear installations. It is clearly a minority position within the United States and must work against prevailing ethical conceptions. But, given sufficient frustration, fear and self-righteousness, its logic could become compelling for many Americans.

II. Standard American: Peace through a Preponderance of Military Power

Proponents of this view argue that Communist power does pose a threat but deny that it is necessary to destroy Communism. Instead they argue that a strong military deterrent—usually defined as military superiority at all possible levels of combat, from guerrilla to space warfare—is the essential requisite of peace. Resisting the spread of Communist totalitarianism is seen as a moral and practical responsibility and military power is regarded as the essential instrument for doing so. Adherents of this view see themselves as peace proponents because, they argue, if we use our military power wisely, we will contain small wars and prevent nuclear war, because we do not intend to start one and "they" would not dare. Those denying the validity of these understandings are often seen as either fools or Communists. Some attention is paid to problems of economic growth, trade and political factors, but it is clearly a dominantly military response. Little faith is placed in negotiated agreements with Communist countries or work through international institutions, because agreements are considered possible only in areas of mutual self-interest, narrowly conceived, and will last only so long as such an interest lasts.

Challenged now by a variety of currents sustaining the argument for an American withdrawal from world affairs, this was formerly the dominant point of view in most of the country. The experience of the Vietnam war has profoundly shaken confidence in this context. Many, dubious about the validity of this point of view have, until recently, believed there was nothing they could do about it. It is now being vigorously challenged, but often from points of view no more adequate to the problem of preventing war.

III. Revised Standard Version: A Policy of Achieving Peace through Military Deterrence while Building the International Structural, Economic and Legal Conditions for a Stable Peace

Leaders of American political life have frequently been charged with holding one of the two views above. Few, in fact, have. Since 1948 all our Presidents, for example, have agreed that Communist power is aggressive and a threat to American values and interests. They agreed that a strong American military deterrent was essential to the peace but they saw that deterrent as a negative factor, a requisite for preventing war now, but incapable of building the peace. They saw military deterrence as the protective wall behind which time would produce change in the Communist world. Meanwhile, they believed a vigorous, constructive American policy must, in an increasingly interrelated world, lay the foundation for a stable peace. With varying degrees of understanding and commitment they worked for enlightened trade and foreign aid policies and for strengthened international institutions. They explored the possibility of disarmament agreements and had some success. They distinguished among various states and policies in the Communist world.

Still, we title this context the Revised Standard Version for in *practice* it is almost the same book as the perspective summarized above. When the requirements of a military response conflict with any of the stated constructive goals, it is the latter which gives. This is to be expected since the worst thing you can do in an arms race is plan to come in second. The level and extent of your response is determined by your opponent's strategy and therefore, despite good intentions, the result is and has been a dominantly military foreign policy.

The three positions above, in different ways, see Communist power as a problem, military means as essential to the solution, and the defense of the American national interest by an extended American engagement in world affairs as an essential requisite of sound policy. They differ significantly in the level of sophistication with which they view Communist states and political movements, in their military strategies and in the importance they place on non-military approaches to controlling the threat of war.

Those who break with the perspectives just summarized cross a very important line. They view America's engagement in world affairs differently. They no longer put the requisites of national military power first. They often adopt one of the following three perspectives. For very different reasons these perspectives are regarded here as no more of an aid to ending war than those above.

IV. REACTIVE POLITICS: A POTPOURRI OF POLITICAL AND APOLITICAL VIEWS ARGUING THAT AMERICA IS THE SINGLE VILLAIN IN WORLD AFFAIRS AND/OR THAT STOPPING THE U.S. FROM INTERVENING IN OTHER COUNTRIES WILL BRING PEACE

This is in many respects simply the obverse of the Standard American position. In this view it is not permissible to hate the Communist: you hate LBJ or Nixon or the American military-industrial complex instead. American cold war clichés are hotly rejected; those of favored elements in the Communist world are often substituted.

This context is composed of a number of irreconcilable views which share one idea: opposition to present American policy and, in many cases, to present-day American society. The currents of thought moving people to this position vary all the way from an orthodox and thought-through Marxist position to totally apolitical views. Many are simply reactions to the distortions and half-truths of the Win or Standard American positions. One may arrive at these politics via anguish over the horror being visited on Vietnamese by American bombs or over distress at the black person's experience in America. This context may grow out of literary or cultural revulsion at mass, urban, industrialized, TV-dominated America or from a pacifist moral rejection of American violence. But its common elements are clear.

One element relates to the evil of America (racist, exploitive, "anti-human") and a parallel anti-anti-Communism; another focuses on the evil America does abroad; a third is a conformist anti-establishmentarianism that measures virtue by psychological distance from America. The central task, the final element for all acting within this context, is to stop/destroy/change America.

Depending on what version of this context a person adopts he may be led to revolutionary violence, to calling for nonviolent but radical change in America, to an isolationist view, to a decentralist, apolitical, cultural revolt, or to some version of contemporary Communist politics. Most persons acting within this context make no case for the Communist world but they often adopt its slogans and analysis because of its anti-American content and because so much of the character of this reactive context is emotional and in need of a defined body of thought. Vulgarized Marxist thought is often the most available.

Whatever the distinctive entry point or the resultant politics, the central thrust of this position is withdrawal of American power from world affairs. It demonstrates little interest in international institutions. In sum, it usually leads to the gradual replacement of a commitment to peace with a priority for domestic change and/or support for a variety of internal (e.g., black, drug, youth) or third world revolutionary perspectives.

V. Marxist: Peace through Communist World Domination

It is easy to summarize the main line of orthodox Marxist thought: Communism is the only just form of social organization to which all other forms are prior stages. All societies composed of social classes necessarily have governments which reflect the interests of the dominant class. Representative democracy is the governmental system which reflects bourgeois social and economic interests and is, in fact, a form of class dictatorship. Violent conflict is inevitable between opposed economic classes. Agreements are not lasting between nation-states composed of differing class interests but should be sought when they will advance the interest of Communist states. Economic growth is the instrument of progress. He who controls the means of production will also control the governmental, social, and intellectual life of the society. Economic growth is always at the expense of the laboring classes in pre-Communist societies. The most important identity-giving unit is one's social class. International institutions may be developed within which international relations can be adjudicated while the interests of the working class are advanced within each nation. Capitalism and imperialist expansion is the cause of twentieth century warfare. When capitalism is eliminated in all its forms, war will end.

Such a summary of the main lines of Marxist thought which define a war/peace context does not, however, do justice to the many conflicting strands of thought within Marxism or to the impact of Communist nationalism on Marxist thought. Nor does it cover the curious admixture of Marxism and anarchism that characterizes the contemporary New Left. Neither does it accurately reflect some Soviet Marx-

ists' support of peaceful coexistence, a position hotly
rejected by Chinese, Albanian and some New Left
theoreticians. But some things are clear. Like the Reactive Politics summarized above, most Communist
approaches turn out to be the obverse of the Win
context in that a single villain is identified and work
for a world without war is simply not the point.

VI. TRADITIONAL PACIFIST POSITION: PEACE THROUGH A COMMITMENT TO NONVIOLENCE

The traditional pacifist position is usually oriented
inward to fundamental religious or ethical beliefs
rather than outward to a political situation. This view
puts rejection of reliance on violence *first.* Pacifists
emphasize the possibility of agreement across ideological barriers, the importance of economic development and of growth toward a sense of world community; their faith is most easily conveyed in personal
terms, i.e. in meetings between diplomats, student exchange and work camp experiences and in personal
resistance to military conscription. Sometimes support
for international institutions and a nonviolent international peace force are advocated as means to eliminate war. Most pacifists recognize that there are
elements in Communist society which violate pacifist
ethical concerns but these are usually seen as prod-
ucts of, or reflections of, the Western world's bellicose
foreign policies. The focus, in any case, say many
pacifists, should be on the individual men within each
society, not on the institutions of the society. Other
pacifists disagree and though influenced by this basic
orientation, do act politically seeking nonviolent forms
of social action and organization.

Again, there are many currents of thought in this

context. Some see conflict itself as wrong or rooted simply in misunderstanding. Others emphasize a commitment to forcing change and defending values but insist on nonviolent means. Some are apolitical and choose simply to witness to their rejection of violence. Some adopt the Reactive Politics described above in response to militarist or Communist devil theory politics once so popular in America. Some go on to the developed peace position described below.

Pacifist thought reached an influential high in America when Martin Luther King, Jr. led the civil rights movement and in the early days of the anti-Vietnam War movement. A very different situation now prevails. In coalition with the Reactive Politics described above, many pacifists have adopted its priorities and have turned away from work for a world without war.

These brief descriptions do not do justice to the complexity of these positions or their rationales. Many people, for example, who describe themselves as Pacifist or Marxist would not agree with all the propositions as stated. In addition, different combinations of separate contexts are encountered.

VII. PRIORITIES

A new context has gained increasing influence in response to the Vietnam war. In some cases it combines elements of the Reactive Politics with the Standard American context. While refusing to be anti-Communist, the new context takes a narrow conception of the American national interest as the central criteria for judging a foreign policy decision. It is a familiar context, in many ways expressing one continuing current in American foreign policy thought. It is limited in its goals, focused on the national interest and essentially isolationist in its tone if not always in its policy recommendations. It is, to put it mildly, skeptical of "moral" missions abroad, either because such idealism is regarded as a false mask for U.S. imperialism or, from another point of the political spectrum advancing this context, because it demonstrates a mistaken understanding of the realities of world politics.

The neo-isolationist context argues that the U.S. has more than enough problems at home, that it has overextended itself abroad and that, whatever foreign policy goals are articulated later, for now we should withdraw from attempts to influence the developing nations or to resist the expansion of Communist power. It regards attempts to strengthen international authority as mistaken. The central thrust of this position is that the U.S. cannot and should not seek to impose its values on the rest of the world. As in the other positions, there is a spectrum of overlapping views within a context, in this case regarding the desirable level of American engagement in world politics. Some elements of this view, a cool pragmatic lowering of goals, may be discerned in President Nixon's foreign policy report to the Congress, "A New Strategy For Peace" (1970). The President addressed a nation profoundly shaken by its experience in Vietnam, preoccupied with internal problems and suspicious of world oriented goals.

President Nixon's policy posits peace as the goal; but it's approach to achieving that end is defensive. The burden of initiating constructive change rests with others. Given the cost of America's recent, predominantly military, engagement in the world one can welcome the elements of cautious realism in the President's statement. But a passive strategy continuing reliance on military strength, stressing negotiations but subject to the intentions of those with whom we are in conflict, may prove to be a recipe for a different kind of failure in the pursuit of peace.

Since President Nixon's report, the reaction to the American intervention in Cambodia, Senate efforts to limit Presidential war-making powers, and the shooting of students at Kent State and at Jackson State College have intensified the climate of opinion that originally influenced the report. That climate has overshadowed *any* discussion of a new strategy for peace, not only in the administration but also at the other end of the political spectrum: in many parts of the peace movement. There, the single-minded focus is on Vietnam and exclusively on getting America out, not on ending the killing or on laying the groundwork for control of the threat of war.

Those calling for "new priorities" thus often give a very low priority to work for a world without war: in the Administration, returning gradually to traditional, national interest policies; in elements of the peace movement adopting many of the themes of the Reactive Politics described above.

The summaries above do, we believe, identify main currents of thought in the contemporary war/peace discussion. We have argued that the contexts they describe determine most people's position on specific war/peace issues. We have argued, further, that none of them is adequate to the problem of ending war. The first three positions continue to place primary reliance on national military power for security, thus most likely assuring the continuation of war. The next three challenge American military power but rarely go beyond it, and sometimes make that challenge in the interest of another power center. The developing retreat from world political engagement simply opts out of the attempt to achieve a world without war.

Most of these contexts do not, in fact, count such work among their purposes.

An approach to a more careful analysis of these positions is suggested in Part III F, where a series of questions designed to be of aid in understanding different peace organizations are detailed. Many of these questions regard attitudes, for example, toward rapid economic growth in the developing nations, toward international institutions, toward possibilities of agreement between competing ideological systems. They are helpful in more fully and accurately defining the contexts discussed here. Just defining the politics of a context—its view of the good society, of existing power centers, of the place of violence in politics, of current war/peace issues—is complex. But putting these questions and others regarding the cause of war, the source of legitimacy in government, etc., to the various contexts that now dominate the discussion is an enormously helpful way to formulate one's own position.

VIII. A Developed Peace Position

We return now to a context believed more adequate to the problem than those discussed thus far. A developed peace position is more adequately summarized in Chapter 14. This position rejects each context's (except the pacifist) conception of the necessary evil of war. It takes from each position some element of truth. It takes from the Win position a perception of the reality and importance of conflict—of the need to confront the fact and threat of power in various elements of the Communist world—but points out that even without Communist states *or* America this would still be a world with war. Single villain theories are rejected in a thoughtful approach to peace.

It takes from the Standard American position a commitment to defend democratic values, but regards with considerable scepticism the efficacy of national military power as an instrument for that purpose.

The Developed Peace Position borrows from the traditional pacifist the rejection of reliance on mass violence for security, but adds an insistence on alternative ways to defend values and prosecute a conflict that may be real and important. From the pacifist it also takes an inward sense of obligation to work for an end to war, seeking to link this moral concern to the realities of world politics.

The developed peace position takes from the Reactive and Marxist views the perception that America is part of the problem of war today rather than part of the solution, but sees that that statement applies to the Communist world as well. It believes this country can lead in work to end war.

All these elements, linked to the constructive goals of the Revised Standard Version, make for a developed peace position. To this *To End War* context we now turn.

It recognizes the urgency of domestic needs and joins those calling for new priorities in challenging a dominantly military foreign policy; but it opposes one more futile attempt at American withdrawal from world problems. It disagrees with those who regard such problems as "none of our business."

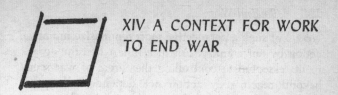

XIV A CONTEXT FOR WORK TO END WAR

Every context sustaining an approach to international conflict involves a number of assumptions.[1] We have made some of the most important of ours explicit here.

ASSUMPTIONS

1) Something is wrong in a world in which war is accepted as a right and reasonable instrument of national policy. A world in which nations train men for mass violence is a world that should be changed.

2) Conflict among men *is* in the nature of things; organized mass violence is not. We will not rid the world of hatred or of individual and small group violence, but we can end war.

3) Ending war is not contingent on achieving a world of perfect justice and harmony, nor does it require a fundamental alteration in human souls or psyches. Ending war does not require resolving all the tensions that lead to conflict.

4) A perspective on foreign policy adequate to present international reality will recognize and meet the threat to our nation's security and to democratic values posed by power organized in other national and ideological camps. It will therefore seek changes of understanding and policy in *those* power centers as well as in America.

[1] Much of the following essay originally appeared in Robert Pickus' *The ABM and a World Without War*. It has been revised for inclusion here.

5) But such a perspective must emphasize initiative action by our country. For in a time when the agreements essential to controlling the threat of war seem beyond reach, only action not dependent on prior agreement can change the situation and make agreement possible. There are initiatives our government could take which are more likely to lead the world toward a stable peace than our present, dominantly military policy, or the current most visible alternative —an attempted withdrawal from world affairs.

6) Work for a world without war which takes intelligent account of threats to democratic values and institutions posed by other power centers is in the best interest of our country and expresses the best in our traditions. It is not a threat to them.

7) Responsibility for such work rests with individual citizens as well as political leaders. Laymen as well as experts have a critical role to play in making our country a leader in work for a world without war.

8) But government provides the process by which a world without war may be both achieved and sustained. Our commitment is to representative, democratic government by which majorities rule and to conceptions of individual and minority rights, which set limits to and legitimize governmental authority.

9) Man can reason and should. With all its shortcomings, a commitment to rationality is an essential requisite in the process by which we will end war.

10) Whatever the odds, we are required to try.

We make no formal argument for the validity of all the assumptions stated. To do so would involve a long and difficult analysis of alternative assumptions and an attempt to establish the superiority of those we have accepted. Some evidence for the validity of some of these assumptions has been provided in other sections, but a full argument cannot be made within the confines of this book. We have, therefore, simply stated the ideas believed to be true which undergird the political statement that follows.

ESTABLISHING THE GOAL

Working to bring an end to war requires establishing alternative means through which nations can resolve their conflicts and defend their values as they act on their presently divergent views of what constitutes justice and security. The obstacles to ending war are not simply in the domain of geography and power—that is, of geo-politics—but also in the domain of psycho-politics, the current crisis of mind and will.

In the shadow of Hiroshima the will to work for an end to war was manifest. It is no longer. Instead, new and old justifications for war urge mankind to disaster. At the heart of the context presented here is a reaffirmation of the right goal: ending war.

Elements in our American heritage turn us to this goal. Our religious traditions teach man's innate dignity and worth. From them has emerged a gradually developing concept of law that protects us from the arbitrary use of power and insists that the state is the servant and not the master of men.

Our own recognition of contemporary threats to these values dictates acceptance of the goal of ending war, for the power of other states is not the only threat to this tradition. It is also threatened by the inexorable requirements of organization for modern war and by the tragic parallel rejection of a non-violent democratic process by many of our own young people, caught in the moral and political contradictions of an America that is waging war.

The root values of our political tradition, the flexible

pluralism of our nation, its immense power—all make possible a significant contribution to attempts to end war. One can recognize the limitations of what the United States can do, while still rejecting many voices now calling for a lowering of goals. The perspective presented here rejects a withdrawal from international responsibility, as it rejects the belief that a dominantly military policy can fulfill that responsibility or secure our own future.

THE ESSENTIAL OBJECTIVES

What are the essential objectives of those committed to achieving a world without war?

A world without war is a world in which agreement on universal, complete and enforceable disarmament has been achieved and put into effect. But disarmament alone is not a sufficient objective, for it cannot be maintained without alternative procedures for resolving conflict and establishing justice in world affairs. It cannot be maintained without law. Achieving disarmament and establishing law are, therefore, the first two objectives. But there can be no law without a sense of world community. If a disarmed world under law is to be based on consent, instead of imposed by violence, there must be a developed sense of unity and mutual responsibility among men. The third objective is, therefore, a strengthened sense of world community.

Most men, however, do not want law and stability if that entails keeping things as they are. They live under conditions of deprivation or exploitation, and they want change. In Asia, Africa and Latin America, economic, political and social change can come with or without mass violence, but it will come. A fourth objective, then, for those committed to work for a world without war is to provide peaceful channels and well-conceived programs for needed change and development.

Those seeking to commit this nation to leadership in achieving a just and stable peace must also find ways to change those attitudes and policies of other nations that block the road to peace. The single-minded focus on the Communist enemy that for so long gave cohesion, whether sensible or not, to U.S. policy has given way to a new realization of a rapidly changing world, one in which sixty-six of the 141 nations on our State Department's list are new nations which have achieved independence in this generation. The primary concern of these new nations is to establish national unity and a national character. Their desire to project their new identity adds new problems to the obstacles posed by the older nationalisms. In this explosive scene it is more important than ever to assess realistically the power and purpose of key elements in the Communist world. Such an assessment rejects both the view of Communism as a demonic, unchanging, monolithic force, and also the unwarranted optimism which ignores the threat to democratic values and world peace posed by some current attitudes and policies of Communist nations and political forces. A fifth objective, then, is to move other nations to join us in pursuit of a disarmed world under law—one in which change can come without chaos, and hopeful trends toward material well-being, education and freedom for all men can be encouraged.

Since values must be defended and needed change is often rejected, those who turn away from mass violence must propose other means by which conflict can be resolved and change achieved in the Communist world in the developing nations and in the West. Thus peace research, particularly the application of the theory of nonviolence to international conflict, and experimentation with nonviolent techniques for conflict resolution, is another essential requisite of progress on the road to a world without war.

Finally, progress in the achievement of the other six objectives is unlikely unless men and nations are impelled to work for them. That recognition of obligation comes when men touch those root values which assert the brotherhood of all men or encounter that knowledge or authority which sustains the commandment "Thou shalt not kill." Whether based on a humanistic ethic or a religious dictum, widespread understanding of *why* men should turn from war, and action consonant with that understanding, is a seventh essential requirement if governments are to lead in ending war.

Seven objectives, then, together make up a world without war approach to foreign policy discussion:[1]

1. General, complete and enforceable disarmament
2. Growth toward world law
3. World community
4. World economic and political development
5. Bringing other nations into agreement on the pursuit of these goals
6. Enabling change without violence
7. Affirming fundamental values

A Dynamic

How can the perspective outlined above provide standards for judgment when a specific war/peace

[1] A detailed summary of current obstacles and recent achievements on the road to each of these objectives is available from the World Without War Council.

issue is encountered? Before deriving those standards from the discussion thus far, we must first note a limitation of the approach outlined. It is a weakness that is widely recognized and that explains in part why so many thoughtful people are no longer interested in universal disarmament or world law statements: to be meaningful each of the objectives requires agreement. And the primary lesson from twenty-four years of international negotiations is that we cannot reach agreement. The fifth objective thus encompasses and is the prerequisite to most of the others.

Is there a policy which begins with today's reality, which can act in situations where agreement has *not* been achieved, and act to produce new incentives and pressures that make agreement more likely?

There is such a policy perspective. It is a policy of American Initiatives.

AMERICAN INITIATIVES

A policy of American initiatives is based on the belief that a dominantly military U.S. foreign policy cannot produce growth toward a world without war or develop successful opposition to the spread of totalitarian political systems. A favorable judgment of the feasibility of an initiative policy does not require an optimistic assessment of the realities of power and policy in the Soviet Union or China. One can, for example, be profoundly pessimistic about present policy in Peking and yet come to the conclusion that initiative proposals for U.S.-China policy involve less risk and greater promise for improvement than does continued isolation and potential military confrontation. The heart of the initiative approach lies in the very different question it seeks to answer: instead of,

"How can our military power best influence their political and military policy," a peace initiative approach asks, "What non-military acts can we take that give promise of producing the change in their attitude and policies that must come if we are to reach agreement on disarmament and world law?"

The initiative approach works with the processes of change. It rejects acquiescence to an opponent's will as it refuses to seek his destruction. It seeks instead to change him. A policy of peace initiatives is distinguished by its goals—world disarmament and world law—from the more familiar military initiatives that constitute an arms race. But its method is a very similar one. It does not wait for agreement. It pursues its purpose by unilateral actions. A peace initiatives policy recognizes that any final settlement must be based on common consent, but asserts that there are situations (Vietnam is clearly one) in which only independent action taken without prior agreement can create a situation in which agreement becomes possible. A peace initiatives policy seeks to form vectors of influence on and within an opposing political system that could move that system toward agreement on world disarmament and world law.[1]

[1] Those interested in exploring the initiatives idea further should read: *American Initiatives in a Turn Toward Peace* (1961), a discussion outline and supplementary materials; *Report of the Fourth Conference to Plan a Strategy for Peace* (1963), a sophisticated introduction to the idea; Charles Osgood, *An Alternative to War or Surrender* (Urbana: University of Illinois Press, 1962), the most influential introduction to the idea by a former president of the American Psychological Association; Richard Gardner (ed.), *Blueprint for Peace* (New York: McGraw-Hill, 1966), contains many possible initiative acts; Mulford Sibley, *Unilateral Initiatives and Disarmament* (Philadelphia: American Friends Service Committee, 1962), presents a pacifist approach to the initiatives idea; Robert Woito (ed.), *Vietnam Peace Proposals* (Berkeley: World Without War Council, 1967) and Robert Pickus, *The ABM and a*

CONDITIONS FOR A SUCCESSFUL
INITIATIVES POLICY

How can initiative acts create the conditions that change behavior?

a. By changing the environment within which the leaders of opposing political systems act.

The principle here is the same one that urges a continuation of the arms race: men respond to their environments. An initiative policy seeks to create an environment which increases internal pressure on Russian and Chinese leaders to respond to peace initiatives. Similarly, an initiative policy focuses external forces and world opinion on the need for change in these leaders' military policies, as well as in our own.

b. By changing the balance of political forces within the opposing systems' leadership.

Proponents and opponents of ABM deployment, of "thick" and "thin" systems and all the other elements in our ABM or MIRV controversies, surely exist in the Soviet Union. "Dove" and "hawk" camps exist in every nation. U.S. initiatives could vitally affect the outcome of internal arguments over the feasibility of negotiating a general and complete disarmament agreement.

c. By bringing pressure for reciprocal action to bear on and within the opposing system.

The American failure to bring significant pressure to bear on Hanoi and the NLF to end the war in Vietnam is a case in point. Could genuine peace initiatives do what military pressure has failed to do? What would be the impact, for example, of a unilat-

---

World Without War (Berkeley: World Without War Council, 1969), are two works which apply the initiatives idea to recent controversial war/peace issues.

eral American cease-fire (save under attack) combined with political initiatives that opened the way for the NLF to pursue their political objectives by means other than violence?

Most of the people of Vietnam are fighting neither Communist aggression nor American imperialism. They are fighting for their lives. Hanoi and the NLF have felt no pressure from them to end the killing because the U.S. has been successfully identified in the minds of many (in Vietnam and around the world) as the force that makes the killing go on. American initiatives to end the killing and to identify the forces that prefer victory to peace could change the situation. This approach is very different from current discussions of "Vietnamizing" the war, whether presented in the Nixon administration's context or in that of a peace movement that concentrates solely on withdrawing American power instead of on ending the killing. An initiative approach aims at ending the killing in a way that moves us toward control of the threat of war. It defines negative and positive incentives that could move the Vietnamese combatants toward a negotiated settlement (# 301).

Similarly, the arms race is an obstacle to most of the world's population participation in the fruits of industrialization. A strategy of American initiative acts, even if unsuccessful, would bring pressure to bear on the powers which prefer the risks of an arms race to the risks of disarmament; for such powers are obstacles to the new nations' desire for rapid economic development. Turning to internal pressures, today's students are one example of an important group in most of the major powers that would work internally for a positive response to genuine peace initiatives.

*d. By opening alternative nonviolent courses of
action through which an opponent may pursue his
goals.*

An initiatives policy offers hope of regaining a perspective on security and the pursuit of justice that can
turn men from present reliance on mass violence or
national military power. For many, despite thermonuclear weapons, there now appears to be no alternative.
A peace initiative policy would reject and seek to
control violence, even as it accepted and opened channels for political conflict and its nonviolent resolution.

Initiative acts may not be immediately reciprocated
in a given situation but may still be useful and important steps. Properly undertaken they can aid in
establishing the understandings and precedents necessary to contain new stages in the arms race or new
threats of war. Since confusion over who is initiating
a new stage, and who is merely responding to the
other side, is the usual justification for each new
stage, there is enormous value in acts which help
identify and isolate those political forces committed
to continuing the arms race.

BUILDING AN INITIATIVES POLICY

There is nothing new in the idea of unilateral initiatives. The Soviet Union has for years jammed or
stopped jamming the Voice of America as a way of
signaling a change in Soviet attitude. As simple an
act as inviting a foreign head of state to visit this
country, as potentially significant an act as President
Nixon's announcement regarding American cessation
of research and stockpiling of bacteriological weapons,
and even the very limited steps taken recently to
change U.S.-China trade relations are unilateral initiatives. President Kennedy's announcement, in his 1963

American University speech, of a unilateral American cessation of nuclear testing in the atmosphere was an important peace initiative that clearly aided in the successful achievement of agreement on the nuclear test ban treaty.

What would be new would be a *policy* of initiative action to end war. There was a period early in the sixties when attention for a time focused on the initiative idea. Premier Khrushchev called for a policy of "mutual example." The Carnegie Endowment's fiftieth anniversary project in 1961 sought suggestions of unilateral steps the United States could take to improve the prospects of peace. Other research agencies worked on lists of American initiative acts they deemed desirable and feasible.

But no policy was ever enunciated.

Doing so would involve a clear and comprehensive statement of goals essential to achieving a world without war. It would require a planned series of initiative acts—not isolated gestures, but a deliberate, graduated set of initiatives designed to move us toward each goal. Such a policy would include careful thought as to what must be done to create or exploit the conditions (outlined above) that would make reciprocation most likely.

With regard to disarmament, for example, agreement on complete banning of arms in Antarctica and outer space has been achieved. What could be done to extend zonal disarmament to other areas? Could the United States designate a segment of this country—say New England—as a disarmed zone open to international inspection? How could that initiative engage the U.N. and other international agencies? What other acts by our government and private agencies could maximize internal and external pressure on the Soviet Union to reciprocate by naming a single disarmed area within the Soviet Union? How could these zones be extended? What would be the most likely countries in Africa willing to designate a disarmed zone? What approaches should be made to governments there?

Since inspection is a key to the disarmament problem, at what point should the United States authorize "inspection by the people" of all U.S. disarmament initiatives? That is, specifically state the U.S. citizen's moral obligation to report any violation of disarmament initiatives (or any subsequent international agreements) to an international agency. What appeals to specific elites and age groups within the Soviet Union; what Russian traditions, what realities of domestic Soviet politics and what possibilities of pressure from world opinion give promise, if properly exploited, of a favorable response to this initiative? How can the facts of extensive governmental controls within Soviet society and the ideological barriers to a sense of world community, be overcome?

It is this kind of detailed thinking extended to each of the major goals considered above that would be necessary to construct an initiatives *policy*.

Any initiative approach requires a carefully thought out policy involving prior public announcement of the act and its intention and suggested possible reciprocal moves. The degree of risk involved in each step would have to be carefully calculated. What, for example, would we risk if we took seriously the proposal to make the DEW line (Distant Early Warning line) an international guarantor of warning against nuclear attack, a warrant that America seeks security from such an attack, not only for our nation, but for others, or, what would we risk if we tied reduction in our arms budget to problems of capital needs in the developing nations?

An initiatives policy would relate disarmament moves to acts strengthening growth toward world law. There have been, for example, proposals for American initiatives to internationalize control of the Panama Canal. Such an agreement could provide a model for international control of international waterways and thus a step toward eliminating situations that have in the past led to war. Repealing the Connally Reservation (thus ending a situation in which the United States and not the International Court of Justice determines when the Court has jurisdiction in cases involving what the U.S. might regard as a domestic issue) is another example of a unilateral act in the world law area that properly undertaken could encourage reciprocation by other nations committed to growth toward world law. An unarmed World Peace Brigade for service on war-threatened borders; opening selected American editorial columns to Communist Chinese editors (and requesting reciprocation); U.N. chartering of international corporations— there is no shortage of specific ideas of how initiatives by our country could have a beneficial impact on economic and political relations, international law and international organization and problems ranging from population and space research to economic development. We do not attempt here to list these, or to sort the sound from the unsound. Our purpose is to introduce the idea, not to spell out a full policy of American initiatives.

There have been two widely different approaches to a policy of American initiatives. One emphasizes the reduction of international tension and sees as the central problem creating an atmosphere of mutual trust in which agreements, previously thought impossible to achieve, may be reached. Just as an arms race is a form of unilateral but reciprocal tension-

increasing activity, this approach recommends uni-lateral but reciprocated tension-*decreasing* activity. Another initiative approach views more soberly the reality of the conflict that produces the tension, and focuses on the problem of producing sufficient pressure to move recalcitrant national leaders to make the desired reciprocal response. A combination of reduction of threat *and* coercive pressures, both internal and external, to force reciprocation, is the approach recommended here.

We face a situation in which every plan for peace comes up against the fact that it requires agreement and we do not agree. In that situation many say we either surrender to other nations' will, or continue to rely on our military power to prevent them from imposing that will. There is a third choice. It requires that we act in situations where agreement cannot be reached in ways most likely to create a changed situation in which agreement becomes possible. A policy of American initiatives for peace provides the needed dynamics. A policy of American initiatives engages us in the right endeavor: progress on our part toward the right goals and the attempt to define what must change in Soviet, Chinese, and others' attitudes to make possible the achievement of those goals.

Needed change will not come easily. It will not come in response to calls for trust in international affairs (as if nations were men). It will not come at all except in response to pressure for such changes. Some of these pressures are now apparent in our society and in others. A world without war approach calls for an American policy primarily focused on defining and taking the steps we *can* take to maximize the chances for hopeful change.

Such an American initiatives policy could immediately provide the dynamics for at least the minimal goals: no further expansion of the arms race; a serious attempt to begin closing the gap between the very rich and very poor nations of the world; and temporary political settlements to defuse the three key explosive areas of Southeast Asia, the Middle East and Germany. Such a policy, however, goes far beyond initial steps and temporary settlements. It recognizes that the awesome threats to man in the remainder of this century—nuclear war, hunger, population, the poisoning of our environment, the fragmenting new separatisms and the developmental agonies of the new nations—are of such a magnitude that only international cooperation by presently opposed great powers and new world organization can resolve them.

Can we form the will which is the essential requisite for the pursuit of such a policy? Have we a President capable of such an initiative? Are we now a nation capable of responding to such leadership?

One need only examine the character of our present peace movement to see that we do not yet have even a citizens' peace effort with such a perspective, let alone a government committed to it.

WHY?

One must number among the causes of war many of you who read this book, for the essential problem is a failure of the public will and that failure is a consequence of individual inaction. Our failure of will is at root a matter of faith, but it also stems from a failure of energy, of intellectual energy. There is no will to end war, in part because few encounter a body of thought that gives rational sustenance to such a goal. Very different currents would move in American politics were there widely shared ideas of how to pursue the goal of a world order rooted in belief in the dignity and worth of individual men and capable of processing conflict and change without organized violence.

We have tried to state such a perspective, to demonstrate that there *are* understandings that can help in ending war. We believe individuals can help advance those understandings. If it is true that you could act, and that your action could help, it follows that your inaction is also a cause of war.

But are you convinced, as we are, that there *is* a body of thought worth acting on? The problems that might have led you to doubt, if not reject the *To End War* approach have been discussed, we hope, adequately. Many, nevertheless may still regard work against war skeptically, in part because conviction comes from experience and experience relates to the facts—and the facts today are the facts of war, not peace.

Still, if you needed the experience of a world without war to believe it possible, you would not have picked up this book. Conceiving an end to war—as at one time conceiving an end to slavery—requires more than knowledge of past experience. What is needed is the faith that men can pursue high goals and that this pursuit is the best way to discover what is possible for men to achieve.

This book has been written for those who share that faith, and who, whatever the odds, want at this time in history to do something specific and thoughtful to help achieve a world without war.

part three

RESOURCES FOR ACTION

Introduction

To End War is an introduction to the war/peace field. It divides the field into categories considered relevant to the problem of ending war. It presents in summary fashion alternative approaches to the field and introduces the books believed most useful to those who wish to pursue these problems further. By identifying the causes of war and by examining ways of eliminating or controlling them, *To End War* structures an argument for the validity and practicality of the goal of ending war.

We have now completed our survey of the primary requisites to the achievement of that goal: law, disarmament, development, community, human rights and nonviolent change. We have discussed the key actors: the major powers, the international organizations, the developing nations, and the complex of voluntary organizations and concerned individuals in America that affect war/peace decisions. We have examined some of the current, specific war/peace issues and explored the root religious and ethical problems of conscience and war. We have surveyed the frontiers of peace research. We have introduced the reader to various theories of social change and examined how a democratic political process and an American peace movement can help in achieving a world without war.

In Part I we introduced these ideas through a consideration of the arguments and counter arguments for their validity. Part II gathered the moral judgments and political analysis presented thus far into a single statement of a context for action.

Now in this final part of the book we turn to the problem of acting to make these ideas public policy. Although aimed primarily at those in agreement with Part II, many of the tools and resources presented here will be of use whatever your point of view.

Protest is probably the most common form of peace action. Most people act on war/peace problems during a war or just before one. The urgency and dynamism of a protest movement touches them and finally, finally they act. When the particular crisis leaves the headlines they retire from the field.

Most of the materials gathered in this part of *To End War* speak to a different conception of action. They are useful for the person who knows how steady and persistent an effort is needed; for the person who, in the span of his life, wants to make a specific and continuing contribution to one of the great endeavors of our century.

Such a person may first want to choose the audience with which he will work: Catholics, scientists, political leaders, businessmen, teachers, friends . . . it is a long list. In Section A, we give one example of work with a particular audience, perhaps the most important audience of all: children.

In Section B we face the question "What can I do?" as such a person asks it. The questions in Section B can help you assess yourself and intelligently choose a course of action.

In Section C we present twenty-three answers to the question "But what can I do?" Each is a statement by a person who found concrete ways to express his concern for peace in his own community.

Section D introduces you to the kinds of organizations now at work in the war/peace field.

Section E is a select listing of specific organizations, some of which you may want to contact and perhaps support.

Section F lists the questions you need to answer about an organization before you decide if it deserves your support.

Once you have found an organizational channel within which to work, you will want to continue to develop your understanding of the war/peace field. Section G introduces a range of periodicals which offer a level of intelligence, degree of sophistication or point of view seldom encountered in the mass media. You will find it useful to select from among them periodicals with a range of views. Following current issues in this way will help you understand competing perspectives as well as the issues themselves.

Eventually you will want to specialize. Section H uses the disarmament problem to demonstrate what you need to know to act effectively in a particular part of the war/peace field.

More detailed materials on the different forms of action embodied in specific programs aimed at specific audiences are available from World Without War Council offices.

CHOOSING AN
AUDIENCE: AN EXAMPLE

The question "What can I do?" involves a choice of audience, a decision as to *who* you want to reach with the knowledge and beliefs that make up your approach to ending war. Some will want to directly influence political leaders for they are the decision makers; some will want to address that nascent group of people primarily committed to work to end war for they can provide the catalytic force that translates new ideas into new public policies; some will focus on a particular institution (the church or the labor movement, for example); some will want to address students, or the key personnel of the mass media, or scientists, or businessmen.

Who you address is in good part a function of who you are, where you are, the level of sophistication at which you aim and, most of all, the seriousness of your commitment to work on the problem. You'll need to prepare carefully, whatever audience you choose. We choose here a single example of an important audience: children. Our bibliography for this section is a highly selective listing of a variety of approaches.

One approach focuses directly on the child: the games children play, the toys they use, the TV programs they watch. Many educators decry the influence of war toys and television violence on children. They fear brutalizing experiences, a daily ration of the assumption that violence is the way to resolve conflict, and a consequent undermining of whatever progress is made in teaching children the value of nonviolent democratic processes and the goal of ending war. Others have argued that war toys and TV violence provide substitutes for the real thing and, far from damaging, offer acceptance opportunities for expressing impulses that if repressed do psychological harm

(# 647). A number of peace education programs with children offer resources (films, books, projects) for homes and schools; they suggest ways to strengthen a child's sense of responsibility for other men and his confidence in nonviolent approaches to conflict (r, s and t).°

Another approach focuses on the adults of special importance in a child's life. Thus the Child Study Association offers guidelines to help a mother answer her three-year-old's question, "What war?" The Union of American Hebrew Congregations has published material (# 394 and 662) to aid those responsible for religious schools in their approach to teaching about ethics and war. Organizations like Nations Inc. (see q), the American Friends Service Committee (see p. 277) and the United Nations Association (see p. 286), which organize extracurricular projects (e.g., school exchange programs, overseas work camps, model U.N. programs, contact with foreign students studying in this country) are another channel through which those concerned with problems of peace education with young people may work.

In recent years our schools have become more self-conscious regarding their role in shaping children's attitudes and understandings in this field. The Foreign Policy Association has recently published a comprehensive survey of the objectives and needs of international education in American elementary and secondary schools (# 631). They describe a revolution in the social studies that is in part a reaction to the expanding role of the U.S. in world affairs, and in part a necessary response to the enormous increase in information about the world and problems of war and peace with which the mass media bombard us all.

For these and other reasons, programs concentrating on specific countries and geographic areas now exist for all the major areas of the world (e, f, g and h). Curricular materials and resources have been developed for the study of international conflict and the growth of world law (o

°Letters in the text refer to the list of educational organizations at the end of Resources for Action A, page 256.

and u). Problems of citizenship, particularly the thoughtful response to controversial public issues, such as war/peace issues, have been a focus of sophisticated interest (a, j and k).

Perhaps the most important development has come in response to the value questions war/peace issues raise, perhaps most acutely for the young. A number of university centers and education departments are now examining (and prescribing) the teaching of the concepts and values central to problems of foreign policy and conflict resolution (a and c). These projects state desired values and devise curricular approaches which introduce these concepts at different grade levels; often they develop specific situations in which young people approach these value concepts and thoughtfully handle conflicts about their application. Work at this level raises for discussion the most profound issues in the war/peace field. For example, problems of:

1. *Identity:* involving the simultaneous development of a sense of personal integrity and of loyalty to the community and the nation. Dilemma: what do you do when loyalty to your nation conflicts with your sense of responsibility to mankind?

2. *Problems of Nonviolent Conflict Resolution:* the cost of domestic and international violence, the possibilities of extending nonviolent norms to international conflict. Dilemma: given the intention to resolve conflict nonviolently, how do you confront those convinced that their view of justice warrants the use of violence?

3. *Respect for Law:* what happens when legal institutions are weakened or destroyed by misuse or disrespect? Dilemma: faced with a particular law you consider unjust, how do you change it without damaging the commitment to law in general?

4. *Change:* recognizing the inevitability of change and examining violent and nonviolent forms. Dilemma: how do you decide who to aid—those who demand immediate, violent change in the social system to

eradicate a particular evil; those who would reform it or those who say the benefits of present arrangements are superior to the change proposed?

A World Without War Council initiated project for which the Center for War/Peace Studies is now the principal consultant seeks to apply a variety of these research and curricular approaches to school systems in a specific geographic area. In the Diablo Valley (California) Education Project (see s) teachers and administrators of both public and private schools have faced the question: are our schools an aid or obstacle to ending war? Concerned with textbook evaluation, curricular innovation, teacher training and resources, their central focus is on basic values and concepts. The project's careful and thoughtful approach to school community relations is especially noteworthy.

This brief introduction to work with children is intended as an example of the wealth of specific opportunities and needs that appear when the peace seeker focuses on a particular audience. The problems of work to end war undertaken in the labor movement or the Catholic Church, with mental health professionals, scientists, lawyers or weight-lifters are just as complex and offer just as many specific points of entry. One wonders why so many ask, "What can I do?"

As you seek to answer the question for yourself, you will find the Personal Survey on pp. 258–61 helpful. What part of the field, what audience will you focus on as you contribute to helping end war?

The books listed here introduce a variety of approaches to peace education. They focus on the value and concept identification approach outlined above. Included are books for children and young adults.

Peace Education

627 THE REVOLUTION IN PEACE EDUCATION *by Richard Falk, 4pp, 1966, Saturday Review, $.10.* The author believes that various specialized agencies now know what to teach, but educators aren't using their materials.

628 THE WORLD AS TEACHER *by Harold Taylor,*

384pp, 1969, Doubleday, hardcover, $6.95. Given the development of an interdependent globe, teachers should be educated as citizens of an international community.

629 CONFLICT RESOLUTION AND WORLD EDUCATION, *Stuart Mudd (ed.), 294pp, 1967, Indiana University Press, hardcover, $6.75.* An anthology of views on the origins and means of resolving violent conflict. In their discussion of fundamental moral values, the contributors attempt to illustrate the many principles which could help form a world community.

630 INTERNATIONAL EDUCATION FOR THE TWENTY-FIRST CENTURY, *Lewis Todd (ed.), 75pp, 1968, National Council for the Social Studies, $1.00.* Presents a variety of education problems in teaching international relations. Selections by Robert North, Kenneth Boulding, Herbert Kelman and others. A valuable aid to the teacher.

TEW   631 AN EXAMINATION OF OBJECTIVES, NEEDS AND PRIORITIES IN INTERNATIONAL EDUCATION IN U.S. SECONDARY AND ELEMENTARY SCHOOLS *by James Becker, 486pp, 1969, Foreign Policy Association, hardcover, $6.45.* An exceptionally able report on the entire educational process. The author believes that international education should recognize the fact of today's interrelated world and prepare students for life in our "global village." Thoughtful, thorough and timely.

Values and Concepts

632 EXPERIMENT AT BERKELEY *by Joseph Tussman, 139pp, 1969, Oxford University Press, $1.75.* A superb analysis of the ends of a liberal arts education, a justification of the distinction between student and teacher and a description of an experimental educational program. Tussman's approach is more radical than the radicals' for it goes to the root problem: the crisis of values.

633 PERSONAL VALUES IN THE MODERN WORLD *by M. V. C. Jeffreys, 174pp, 1962, Penguin Books, $.95.*

An examination of contemporary educational needs. Defends the belief that individual value choices are important in a world in which mass media, mass culture and technical specialization appear to dominate.

INT 634 **MAJOR CONCEPTS FOR SOCIAL STUDIES** *by Roy Price, Warren Hickman and Gerald Smith, 62pp, 1965, Social Studies Curriculum Center at Syracuse University, $1.50.* A study of the value based approach to education with a useful discussion of the concept of "conflict."

635 **SOCIAL SCIENCE CONCEPTS AND THE CLASSROOM** *by Verna Fancett and others, 64pp, 1968, Syracuse University Press, $1.50.* Attempts to identify what "concepts" are, how they are used in social sciences and how conceptions like multiple causation can be taught.

636 **TEACHING PUBLIC ISSUES IN THE HIGH SCHOOL** *by Donald Oliver and James Shaver, 330pp, 1966, Houghton-Mifflin, $4.50.* Argues that value discussions, value conflict and ethical commitments are the central questions for social studies teaching. Establishes a jurisprudential framework for teaching public issues and concludes with the results of a study designed to test the framework in classroom instruction. (see also 537–539)

Teaching a Problem in the Field: e.g., International Organizations

637 **NEW DIMENSIONS** (A series) *by the Foreign Policy Association, 1969–1970, $1.00 each.* Booklets for teachers including: *Teaching About War and Peace Issues, Comparative Development* and *Comparative Cultures.* Each booklet outlines a context and offers practical suggestions for incorporating it in curriculum units.

TEW 638 **TELLING THE UN STORY,** New Approaches to Teaching about the United Nations and its Related Agencies *by Leonard Kenworthy, 166pp, 1963, UNESCO-Oceana, $2.00.* A brilliant example of how to handle a specific issue in the classroom.

639   **A WORLD TO GAIN: A Guide to International Education Year 1969**, *$1.00*. Co-sponsored by the National Education Association, Department of State and U.S. National Commission for UNESCO, this handbook suggests action programs designed to improve educational curricula along the lines of the U.N. goals for the Educational Year.

640   **INTERNATIONAL DIMENSIONS IN THE SOCIAL STUDIES**, *James Becker and Howard Mehlinger (eds.), 343pp, 1968, National Council for the Social Studies, $4.50*. A survey of current international relations courses, suggestions for including the international dimension in discussion of national policies, plus resources available to teachers.

641   **HOW TO PLAN AND CONDUCT MODEL U.N. MEETINGS**, *127pp, 1961, Oceana, $1.50*. Prepared by the United Nations and UNESCO, this handbook tells how to plan, organize and carry out a model U.N. meeting in secondary schools or colleges.

642   **WHAT'S AHEAD FOR THE CLASSROOM? Teaching World Affairs Tomorrow** *by James Becker, 88pp, 1967, Foreign Policy Association, $1.00*. A survey of world affairs teaching in the U.S., its problems and weaknesses, as well as resources available for improving teaching of world affairs.

For Adults

643   **THE INTIMATE ENEMY** *by George Bach and Peter Wydin, 405pp, 1969, Avon, $1.25*. Describes martial conflict and its effect on the family. The author believes that a family which can fight together will stay together. Included are ground rules for creative conflict and a discussion of illegitimate, coersive and counter-productive threats.

War Toys, TV Violence, and Nuclear War

644   **TELEVISION: How to Use It Wisely with Children** *by Josette Frank, 28pp, 1962, Child Study Association,*

$.25. A discussion of the educational benefits and possible dangers of television viewing. Designed to help parents decide what influence they want television to have on their children.

645 **CHILDREN AND THE THREAT OF NUCLEAR WAR** *by S. Excalona, 27pp, 1964, Child Study Association,* $.50. Offers guidance for parents on how to teach their children about the possibility of nuclear war: Is it inevitable? What do you answer when a child asks, "What is war?"

646 **WE'RE TEACHING OUR CHILDREN THAT VIOLENCE IS FUN** *by Eve Merriam, 2pp, 1964, McCall's Reprint,* $.05. A study of different media's treatment of violence.

647 **WAR TOYS AND T.V. VIOLENCE: Their Effect on Children—A Bibliographical Survey** *by Ruth Reid, 66pp, 1967, World Without War Council,* $.10. An annotated survey of the literature. Includes works which argue that conflict and the portrayal of violence is healthy as well as many studies which point to the opposite conclusion.

Books for Children

648 **BOOKS FOR FRIENDSHIP** *by the American Friends Service Committee and the Anti-Defamation League of B'nai B'rith, 46pp, 1968, American Friends Service Committee,* $1.25. A revised, graded, annotated list of about 300 children's books which foster understanding and appreciation of other, different human beings.

649 **THE NO WAR TOYS BOOK FOR YOUNG WRITERS AND ILLUSTRATORS.** *For ages 4–7, 1968, No War Toys, Inc.,* $3.30. Designed to inspire children to make their own pictures and captions. Stimulates curiosity and encourages self-expression.

650 **WILL I HAVE A FRIEND?** *by Miriam Hoban, 32pp, 1967, Macmillan, hardcover,* $3.50. Full color pictures depicting a child going to school for the first time.

651　THE TOMATO PATCH *by William Wondriska, 36pp, 6–9 years, 1964 Holt, Rinehart and Winston, hardcover, $3.50.* Peaceful competition becomes the order of the day as Alice grows a bigger tomato by moving out of the shadow of war.

652　THE KING, THE MICE AND THE CHEESE *by Nancy and Eric Gurney, 63pp, 3–8 years, 1965 Random House, hardcover, $2.50.* Peaceful co-existence proves a viable alternative to escalation. In English and French.

653　THE MONKEY AND THE WILD, WILD WIND *by Ryerson Johnson, 40pp, 6–10 years, 1961 Abelard-Schuman, hardcover, $2.75.* In the face of adversity, enemies become friends. Why wait for adversity?

654　THE PINKISH, PURPLISH, BLUISH EGG *by Bill Peet, 46pp, 4–8 years, 1963 Houghton-Mifflin, hardcover, $3.00.* The story of a baby griffin who learns to solve his problems nonviolently.

655　CANDLES IN THE DARK, An Anthology of Stories to Be Used in Education for Peace, *Margaret Brinton, Mary McWhirter and Janet Schroeder (eds.), 253pp, 1964, Religious Society of Friends, $1.75.* A variety of short stories demonstrating the power of love to overcome racial, national, generational and other differences.

656　TO LIGHT CANDLES IN THE DARK, A Study Guide *by Mary McWhirter, Caroline Pineo and Janet Schroeder, 175pp, 1968, Religious Society of Friends, $1.50.* A companion volume to #655, providing supplementary materials, suggested activities and a discussion guide on the stories' themes: courage, love, forgiveness, building trust, God and friendship.

Books for High School Students

657　THE FIRST BOOK OF ETHICS *by Algernon D. Black, 66pp, 1965, Franklin Watts, hardcover, $2.95.* Introduces the basic ethical values which underlie democratic institutions and practices, religious teachings and world citizenship. An excellent introduction to a range of ethical issues for young people 8 to 18.

658 THE TRUE STORY OF GANDHI: Man of Peace *by Reginald Reynolds, 142pp, 1964, Children's Press,* $3.95. For young adults, this book depicts Gandhi's growth into manhood as preparation for his nonviolent leadership of India.

659 COURAGE IN BOTH HANDS (Instead of Cowardice or Hate) *by Allan A. Hunter, 159pp, 1962, Ballentine Books,* $.50. A collection of 56 case histories of men and women who encountered violence and reacted to it nonviolently—advocates "taking courage in both hands and flinging it in a new and creative direction."

660 WHAT DO YOU MEAN NONVIOLENCE? The Story of Wars with Peaceful Weapons *by Sue Gottfried, 31pp, 1964, Fellowship Publications,* $.50. Written for high school young people, this pamphlet introduces nonviolence in theory and practice through a concise history of various nonviolent movements.

661 LET US EXAMINE OUR ATTITUDES TOWARD PEACE, *Betty Reardon and Priscilla Griffith (eds.), 47pp, 1968, World Law Fund,* $1.00. Introduces high school students to a range of views on the problems of peace. Includes selections by John F. Kennedy, George Kennan, and others.

662 TO DO JUSTLY, A Junior Casebook for Social Action *by Albert Vorspan, 162pp, 1970, Union of American Hebrew Congregations,* $1.95 (est.). An attempt to relate the teaching of Judaism to contemporary problems. A thoughtful study of race relations, violence, Israel, Jews in Russia and liberty for young adults.

663 A MATTER OF LIFE AND DEATH *by Albert Z. Carr, 178pp, 1966, Viking Press, hardcover,* $4.50. A valuable introduction to the issues which surround war/peace questions. The book was written for young people and includes a discussion guide and a variety of viewpoints.

A Selected List of Sources for School War/Peace Education Projects, Teacher Training, Curricular and Extra-Curricular Materials

a. Harvard Social Studies Project, Harvard Graduate School of Education, 210 Longfellow Hall, Appian Way, Cambridge, Massachusetts 02138

b. Center for the Studying of Teaching about Peace and War, Wayne State University, 784 Grosberg Religious Center, Detroit, Michigan 48202

c. Social Studies Curriculum Center (especially key concepts), 4409 Maxwell Hall, Syracuse University, Syracuse, New York 13210

d. Supervisor of Teacher Training in the Social Sciences, Department of Education, University of California, Berkeley, California 94720

e. Asian Studies Project, College of Education, Ohio State University, 1945 North High Street, Columbus, Ohio 43210

f. Asian Studies Curriculum Project, School of Education, Tolman Hall, University of California, Berkeley, California 94720

g. Latin American Teaching Guidelines, University of Texas, 403 Sutton Hall, Austin, Texas 78712

h. Project Africa, Baker Hall, Carnegie-Mellon University, Schenley Park, Pittsburgh, Pennsylvania 15213

i. Center for Teaching International Relations, Graduate School of International Studies, University of Denver, Denver, Colorado 80210

j. Department of Education, Michigan State University, East Lansing, Michigan 48823

k. Bureau of Educational Research, Utah State University, Logan, Utah 84321

l. Marin Social Studies Project (excellent current list of curriculum development projects). 201 Tamal Vista Blvd., Corte Madera, California 94925

m. Western Behavioral Science Institute, 1121 Torrey Pines Road, LaJolla, California 92037

n. National Council for the Social Studies (publishes *Social Education*) 1201 16th Street N.W., Washington, D.C. 20036

o. United Nations Association of the United States of America, Model U.N. High School Programs, 345 East 46th Street, New York, New York 10017

p. University of Oregon, International Relations Seminars, Education Department, Eugene, Oregon 97403

q. Nations Inc., 2428 Hillside Avenue, Berkeley, California 94704

r. Peace Education with Children Program, World Without War Council, 1730 Grove Street, Berkeley, California 94709

s. Center for War/Peace Studies, Western Area Office, Diablo Valley Education Project, 50 Vashell Way, Suite 50, Orinda, California 94563

t. Peace Education With Children, American Friends Service Committee, 160 North 15th Street, Philadelphia, Pennsylvania 19102

u. World Law Fund, Children's Program, 11 West 42nd Street, New York, New York 10036

v. Foreign Policy Association Schools Project (for the most comprehensive survey of projects, problems and materials), 345 East 46th Street, New York, New York 10017

BUT WHAT CAN I DO?:
A SELF-SURVEY

Many people say, "What can I do?" as though it were an answer, one way of asserting that nothing *can* be done. Those putting the question as a question, will find that a meaningful answer requires a careful self assessment. The World Without War Council has used the questionnaire below to aid individuals seeking an appropriate and effective way to help on work to end war.

I. *Who Am I?*
    -Educational and vocational background
    -Family and other primary responsibilities
    -Personality: Do I prefer to take key responsibility or to help those that do?
        To do the overall planning or follow through on the details?
        To do the background work or frontline persuasion?
    -In the Community?
        Organizations I belong to: business, labor, professional, public affairs, religious, education, peace . . . other.
        Circles I move in: conservative, liberal, radical, middle-of-the-road, Catholic, Jewish, Protestant, academic, youth, weightlifter, psychiatric, . . . other.

II. *What Part of the War/Peace Problem Interests Me Most?*
    -U.N. and growth toward world law
    -Challenge of world economic and social development
    -Building a sense of world community
    -Morality, conscience and war

-Current crisis problems: e.g., Vietnam, the Middle East
-Weapons issues, e.g., Nuclear proliferation, MIRV
-Understanding the Communist world
-Forcing change and defending values without violence
-Other:
-I need more information before deciding

III. *What Do I Now Believe?*
-How do I describe my peace position?
   Federalist? pacifist? strengthen the U.N. while maintaining a strong military deterrent? defend the American national interest? just peace concerned? plain confused?
-What motivates me?
   Why do I now (or why do I intend to) give time or money to work for a world without war?

IV. *What Part of the War/Peace Field Do I Know:*
   Rate yourself from 1 (what a good undergraduate course teaches) to 5 (I read the local paper) on each of the twelve chapters into which Part 1 of *To End War* divides the war/peace field.
-How sophisticated am I?
   Have I thought past the obvious need for peace to the hard realities of power and politics which if not faced can result in work in the name of peace doing more harm than good?

V. *What Special Skills or Talents Do I Have?*
-Speaking, organizing, writing, money raising, office skills, leading discussion, research, art, graphics, beauty?

VI.   *How Much Time Will I Give?*
        -A few hours a month, one or two days a week,
        full time?

VII.   *Will I Take Time For Training?*

VIII.   *What Reward/Results Must I Have For Con-
        tinued Work?*
        -Money, sense of accomplishment, visible
        change, appreciation, a good group to work
        with?

IX.   *Where Should I Work?*
        -From which base in the community do I want
        to work?
        a. Major voluntary organizations: church,
            professional organization, political party,
            public affairs group, veterans' organiza-
            tion, labor group, business association,
            service club?
        b. Major institution: school, library, social
            welfare agency, university, private busi-
            ness?
        c. Peace cause organization which is next-
            step foreign policy oriented, U.N. sup-
            portive, pacifist, world federalist, focused
            on world affairs education, *ad hoc* protest,
            special issue, research?
        d. Neighborhood: PTA, community center,
            church or temple, discussion with friends,
            local businesses?
        -What audience do I want to reach?
        National decision makers, local political lead-
        ers, children, Catholics, mass media, peace
        groups, college students, minorities, business-
        men, labor, opinion leaders, other.
        -With what tools do I want to work?
        Campaigns (e.g., petitions, letter writing),

literature, films and tapes, organizational programming consultation, art and display, public events (e.g., speakers, benefits, fairs), demonstrations, and symbolic acts, political organization, personal contact, research and development of new ideas, office work, etc.

X.   *What Will I Actually Do?*

The need for serious and specific community work is infinite. The problem is selecting work that is appropriate for you. Write for *Specific Tasks You Can Do In Your Community* (available from Council offices) for a wide range of suggestions of work which needs to be done in every community and in many different organizational settings.

If you still need help, don't hesitate to ask for it from leaders in organizations you've joined. The simple act of asking for help on expressing your concern for peace is often in itself a significant act for peace.

WHAT CAN I DO?:
TWENTY-THREE ANSWERS

Here are twenty-three examples written in the first person because they are summaries of actual individual experiences.

Work with the Mass Media

1. I'm a writer and TV producer. Using the skills and channels now open to me obviously makes the most sense. I'm always on the lookout for intelligent peace programming for my "Community Workshop" program. When I hear of a returned Peace Corps volunteer, or a faculty person who's been doing useful work on, say, problems of our relation to change in Latin America, I either use them myself or pass the word on to other producers.

2. I have two small children. I must do most of my work from home. I took on the job of listing every TV and radio interview program in the area. I've written or called the producer and explained from time to time that I would call to their attention a specific person making a contribution to work for a world without war that they might want to interview. I've covered the full range of problems from "how to get disarmament" to "children and war toys." I've placed people like a housewife that scheduled the film *Fate of a Child* before some thirty different women's groups to help them understand what's going on in Latin America, and a minister that in conscience withheld a portion of his income tax last year, contributing it instead to one of the U.N. specialized agencies, and explained his reasons to both the government and his congregation. I've found our mass media open to exploring sensitive and controversial issues. My goal has been to see that the important questions are

raised thoughtfully by people who have actually done something themselves to help advance the discussion.

Reach Opinion Leaders

3. I'm an attorney. I've listed the thirty men that bear the most weight in the legal profession in my area and written a brief note to each. I explained that I didn't want to deluge them with material but that from time to time something came to my attention that I thought they should see. I said they should see it because what they think and do has a significant impact on a much wider circle of people. For example, I mailed them the story of the development within the American Bar Association of the World Peace through Law Project and a series of specific proposals for American peace initiatives that could help move us toward world law. I've just begun to do the same thing with the six columnists writing in local newspapers.

Work through World Affairs Education Organizations

4. I've joined the World Affairs Council and the Foreign Policy Association, two organizations I think are doing a balanced and sophisticated job of education on the realities of world politics. I'm also working on our League of Women Voters U.S.-China relations project, doing a lot of studying on the basis of the excellent materials and methods the League has developed. Now our committee is ready to present a summary for discussion by the members.

Choose an Issue

5. The problem of developing the U.N. as a peace-making agency is the one that's interested me the most. I've been distributing the study kit prepared by the United World Federalists to program chairmen of community organizations and we've been conducting a special seminar to train speakers and discussion leaders to be available to those organizations that decide they'll use this program.

Help with Conscience and War

6. I'm twenty-four years old. I'm not a conscientious objector, but I know a great many young men are beginning to think seriously about this matter of conscience and war. I've helped a number of churches establish a counseling program for such men, drawing on materials from the National Interreligious Service Board for Conscientious Objectors, the Central Committee for Conscientious Objectors and the Selective Service System. My purpose is not to turn out conscientious objectors or to assure those that decide to go into the army that they have made the right choice. I try to see that each counseling group presents the facts on the law and the choices men confront, and then urges them to take the root questions of conscience seriously and think through their own position. I believe Selective Service Form 150—the questionnaire the government addresses to men thinking of taking a conscientious objector position—is one of the great religious and political documents of our time. Whatever answers they give, those answering it have had to think deeply about fundamental problems of ethics and war.

Become an Expert in a Specific Program Area

7. I've become an expert on good peace films. With the help of the World Without War Council, the Fellowship of Reconciliation, the U.N. and our local library, I've put together a descriptive listing of some twenty films available in our area, and have been promoting them with program chairmen of organizations all around the community. My next step will be to try to get discussion leaders who can introduce these films and make the connection between the film and the specific kinds of things that we ought to be doing in this community.

Self Surveys

8. I've used the leaflet questionnaire "Ten Minutes for Peace" put out by the Institute for International Order. It

opens with the question, "Do you think another world war is likely?" It goes on to ask people's judgment about some of the ideas of what could be done to prevent it, and then focuses very specifically on whether that person has found any way to make a contribution to ending war. It's a solid, thoughtful survey which can't be answered without feeling that there's some organization, program, or act in which you ought to be engaged. I gave one to every member of my Rotary Club. There's a lot of ability and energy in that club and I'm sure that three or four of those men are not going to rest easy for another year without doing something about the problem of ending war.

Working Through a Peace Cause Group

9. Finding a group that was working along the specific lines I think make sense and then helping them, seemed to me the most effective way to make my contribution. I've joined the United Nations Association. I'm working particularly on getting U.N. world law materials presented in high schools. A friend of mine believed that a pacifist organization, the Fellowship of Reconciliation, best expressed her views. She is supporting their work.

10. I chose to work with the World Without War Council because I think some kind of linking up of the many groups in the field is essential. The World Without War Council ties together leaders of organizations working for a disarmed world under law in which free societies can grow. I chose them because they are clear about the problem posed by elements in the Communist world which must be met by means other than a military response. I was also impressed with the range of specific and continuing work that the organizations associated with the Council are doing. I have had some office experience and, in effect, am working as a secretary.

Through Ma'or Organizations of the Community

11. I'm skeptical about whether these peace groups ever reach anybody except those who agree with them. I also

flatly disagree with the ideas of most of them. I've decided to work where I am: in the labor movement. It's been incredible to me that almost no labor group has done anything locally that's a contribution to ending war. I'm working on two projects, one on channeling good material on war/peace issues into the various newspapers published by labor groups in the area. Secondly, I'm seeing that some of these foreign policy issues, attitudes toward the U.N., aid to underdeveloped areas, and dealing with the Communist world get into the interviews we conduct with congressional candidates or prospective candidates.

12. I'm a doctor. Medical men have considerable authority in the community. They do not always use it wisely. I want to stimulate clear thinking about an important problem. I plan to introduce a resolution to the board of our local medical society. I will suggest that we contribute the last two year's editions of the AMA Journals to a hospital in Communist China. I'm not a sentimentalist; it was not a gesture of good will that concerned me most. It was that every doctor on that board would have to clear his mind, decide what he really wanted to see as America's future relationship to Communist China, and then decide what acts taken now could best help to bring about that relationship. This will be worth more than fifteen experts making a speech, I think.

13. I'm a Catholic and always impressed with how much our church is a private universe. I did a report on Catholic newspapers and periodicals for the various organizations working in this field, so that they would channel to these publications some of their materials on war/peace questions. Many of those publications are now ready to carry such ideas but they don't often encounter them unless someone makes a special effort.

Aid Existing Constructive Efforts

14. It seemed to me that the work that is really building a sense of world community is the work that UNICEF

is doing. They need money. All children need a sense of living in a world where we care for each other, instead of expecting bombs from each other. I think the UNICEF halloween collection project is magnificent and I've worked to organize it in my community.

Work Through a Political Party

15. I have always felt that working directly through our political parties makes the most sense. I've been active as a Republican precinct committee woman. Largely due to my work, my club and district organizations are on record supporting a range of peace legislative proposals such as a decent budget for the U.S. Arms Control and Disarmament Agency. From this base I've developed a correspondence with my congressman which he seems to treat fairly seriously because of my party work.

Symbolic Acts

16. I have decided that what we need are occasions that are dramatic enough to draw the attention of the whole community and make them stop and think about what we're doing. I helped organize a twenty-four hour vigil at the Episcopal Cathedral in our city. It was an attempt to get wide community support for proposals to end the Vietnam war. More than thirty leaders of different religious groups came in during the vigil to speak their mind, and we got wide press coverage.

Protest

17. It seems to me the most important thing you can do is just say 'no,' period. Just make clear that you don't like the way things are going; that you want answers other than bombs and napalm. I do it with buttons. I must have distributed over a hundred thousand nuclear disarmament peace pins, "Say No to War" and "Make Love Not War" lapel buttons and bumper stickers during the past few years.

Focus on Decision Makers

18. I don't believe there are simple answers. Simple protest does not attract me because I'm convinced that achieving universal, enforceable disarmament and institutions of world law is the key to ending war. I believe Clark and Sohn's book *World Peace through World Law* gives the best set of answers to the question, "What do we need to end war?" I've made it my business to call to the attention of every aspiring political leader with whom I come in contact, the pamphlet edition of the introduction to the book which is a convenient summary of its ideas.

19. I have a brother-in-law closely related to a key State Department official. With his help, material I'm forwarding reaches some of the key decision makers. I regularly clip brief and thoughtful articles on various problems relating to our foreign policy in the developing nations and send them to my brother-in-law for his consideration and possible distribution to others.

Working Through Existing Institutions

20. I've taken the periodicals section of our library as my target. I've used the Reading Man's Filter produced by the World Without War Council and have surveyed the periodicals in the library. After my survey I urged the librarian to consider subscribing to four or five others like *Current*, *Atlas*, the *Friends National Committee on Legislation Newsletter* and others that focus specifically on the war/peace area. I believe these lesser-known periodicals represent a level of intelligence, degree of objectivity or point of view rarely encountered in the mass press, but one which should be made available to more people.

Taking Positions

21. I gathered a portfolio of positions on the Vietnam war taken by major national organizations and asked local leaders first to query their national organizations as to whether they had taken a position and second to provide

an opportunity for their members to hear a range of alternative views of what U.S. policy on Vietnam ought to be.

Support a Professional

22. I'm a member of my church governing board. It seemed to me the most important thing we could do in this complex field would be to free someone who could work full time, learning how to do a thoughtful and responsible job in this field of peace education. After some discussion, the rest of the board agreed and we've set up a Peace Education Fund which offers fellowships for Peace Internes to work in the training program of the World Without War Council while assigned to organizations in this community that want to make a contribution to work for a world without war.

Work with Children

23. I believe that it is important to work with children, so, when a group of youngsters in the temple I attend wanted to learn more about people in other countries, we decided to draw pictures of the way we live and play and exchange them with children in Japan. When the Japanese pictures arrived, the children were delighted and we arranged an exhibit of them in the temple. I want now to arrange an exchange with children in a Communist country.

ORGANIZATIONS IN THE WAR/PEACE FIELD: A CATEGORIZATION

There are thousands of American organizations that count work for peace among their purposes or consider such work as their primary reason for existence. One explanation of why there are so many peace groups—and most of them small, inadequately financed, and short-lived—is that people newly discovering a sense of responsibility to act to prevent war seldom examine the field. Instead they start a new organization. But a serious entry into work for a world without war requires careful thought about the work now being done.

We provide here an overview of the three major categories of organizations working in the field: the primary community organizations, the world affairs education organizations and the peace cause groups. We then examine three kinds of peace cause groups: *Ad hoc* protest groups, usually founded in opposition to a particular governmental policy, functionally oriented groups and the established peace education and action groups, which possess a developed tradition and set of understandings. Chapter 12 discussed still another kind of peace organization: the peace research centers.

Together these different kinds of organizations provide many possible vehicles for advancing the ideas and policies surveyed in Part I. Someone seriously considering work for a world without war would do well to examine carefully the promise and shortcomings of each different form of organization. Such a person will find that thinking clearly about what a particular organization stands for and does in this field is one way of clarifying his own peace position.

Primary Community Organizations

Primary community organizations are the voluntary

organizations which make up the very fabric of community life in this country. Taken as a whole, they express the full range of the community's concerns and interests, outside of direct governmental and commercial activity. They are grouped around a variety of special interests and problems: business, labor, educational, religious, public affairs, professional and others which leave an American community of three thousand with two hundred meetings a week. Many of these groups are organized regionally and nationally and count their membership up into the millions. They significantly influence public affairs problems that touch their special competence.

The national boards and officers of many such organizations have recognized their responsibility for work in the war/peace field, but few have developed serious national programs, let alone programs for their local chapters. These organizations have played a decisive role in many domestic public policy issues; for example, religious organizations in the passage of civil rights legislation. But they have rarely worked effectively on war/peace problems. One measure of progress in work for a world without war is the extent to which these primary community organizations have begun to see their responsibility for creating a climate favorable to governmental action that could help end war. One of the primary tasks for those centering on work to end war is thinking through how responsible and thoughtful work for a world without war can take place in these organizations.

World Affairs Education Organizations

World affairs education organizations operate on the assumption that widespread or special elite education in foreign affairs is the means to a more enlightened American foreign policy. They usually provide no answer to the problem of maintaining peace, other than to become well-informed on the problems involved. They present programs and materials which, at a reasonably high level of sophistication, enable participants to consider foreign and military policy options discussed in Washington and other world capitals. They try to avoid a bias toward any particular policy position. Most ideas considered are, however, within traditional diplomatic and military alternatives.

Their audiences range from selected groups of farmers (Farmers and World Affairs) to a general approach to the entire community (The Foreign Policy Association or a metropolitan World Affairs Council). Their programs usually consist of seminars, conferences, speeches, discussion groups, and study groups. They provide many interesting and thoughtful educational opportunities.

Peace Cause Groups

There are three types of peace cause organizations: *Ad hoc* protest groups, functional peace groups, and established peace education and action organizations.

Ad hoc protest groups are usually organized in response to a particular crisis or to a particular government military policy. Usually the only criterion for participation is a single shared view: opposition to the particular policy involved. Rarely do they develop a full explication of their goals, values, or attitudes toward other issues, power camps or policies, for to do so would split most *ad hoc* groups. For example, advocates of American isolationism, or reordering American priorities, of pacifism, of an NLF victory, and of ecological action could all agree to oppose American policy in Vietnam. Because they are trying to unite people with diverse political assumptions, values and goals, they will usually steer clear of specific policy statements or developed proposals. However, there usually *is* a clear set of values and political views that dominate an *ad hoc* effort. Differences in political views explain, for example, why some rallies protesting American policy in Vietnam take account of Hanoi and the NLF's share of responsibility for the continuation of the killing and some don't; why some opposition efforts express essentially isolationist views in the speakers, literature, and leaflets used, while these materials demonstrate that others want American involvement, but with different means than those presently employed. Political and value differences explain why some protest efforts gain the wholehearted support of certain magazines and individuals while others are ignored. But it is sometimes difficult to recognize these realities because participants in a mass protest may not share the essential political thrust of the effort. They simply want to protest the policy and may not have thought about the subsidiary effects of joining in an effort which is based on values and goals they do not share.

Hundreds of *ad hoc* peace protest efforts arise and disintegrate each year. One reason is disillusionment over the effects of a show of strength in numbers; another is the absence of satisfactory answers to probing questions. Another is simply that issues go out of fashion when mass media attention turns away—the ABM, for example. Thus the basis of *ad hoc* organizational success is usually the emotional currents engendered by a particular governmental policy at a particular time. But there *is* a discernible pattern to *ad hoc* protest efforts. The kind of protest encountered is usually traceable to the major political and value contexts moving at a particular time. One needs to think carefully about such efforts to determine the extent to which, for example, Marxist, isolationist, world law, or a particular variety of pacifist view, has gathered and channeled concern over the particular crisis problem involved.

Protest is not the only kind of *ad hoc* effort. Sometimes *ad hoc* groups form because a single charismatic and strongly motivated individual sees a particular need or because well-rooted organizations decide to join their strength for a specific purpose.

Given the character of our mass media, and the emotional rewards involved, many more individual citizens encounter work on the war/peace problem in the form of an *ad hoc* protest effort than they do through contact with a continuing and well-defined effort. It is therefore common to find peace concerned people unaware of other ways to express their concern for peace. The strength of *ad hoc* efforts lies in their drama and flexibility, their ability to attract and focus attention. They put a crucial war/peace item on the public agenda. Their major weakness is that they often do so in a way that makes it almost impossible to *move* the agenda, to gain majority support or to form a climate for thoughtful discussion in which a consensus may form behind alternatives to military solutions.

Ad hoc organizations are crucial to the life and health of a democratic society and, thoughtfully conducted, they can aid in work for a world without war. Too often they are conducted in a way which creates an envenomed and polarized political climate; one that is least likely to produce wise and generous policy leading to a world without war.

Functional peace groups concentrate on specific tasks rather than political ideas or attitudes. Their work helps strengthen a sense of world community, or paves the way for world institutions, or meets a specific need which unresolved could lead to violence. Most describe their work as contributing to world peace. These citizen groups work on problems as varied as world health, student exchange, refugee problems, population and food problems, and business education. Their strength lies in the obvious needs they serve and the fact that they often organize to serve them across national boundaries and in the interest of all men. Their weakness lies in the rarity with which they operate across those divisions in the world which are most likely to produce war or preparation for war. But they are steadily knitting a sense of world community that is one of the key requisites for a world without war.

The established peace education and action organizations, though much less numerous than the *ad hoc* protest groups, nevertheless involve a bewildering set of initials: FOR, UWF, UNA, SANE, WWWC, WRL, WILPF, AFSC, FCNL, CFLW, FFP, CNVA, CCCO, NISBCO (see Section E) among others. They are distinguished from the *ad hoc* groups by longevity, explicit procedures for determining leadership and policy, and a developed set of understandings shared by members of the organization. They exist to further ideas, attitudes, or policies which they feel, if widely accepted, would help in preventing or ending war. These ideas range from unilateral disarmament based on personal pacifist convictions to support for world law; from faith in the U.N. to next step foreign policy proposals. Their methods range from study seminars and lobbying to public demonstrations.

The specific history of each group is usually peculiar to itself. They sometimes arise out of *ad hoc* activity and institutionalize the ideas and attitudes thought capable of containing the threat of war at a particular time. They necessarily expend considerable energy to build the loyalty, raise the funds and train the leadership that can assure their continuing existence. The total number of staff and the total funds available are usually painfully inadequate to their goals. Constant frustration and failure attends their work but they have sometimes articulated and developed ideas that later become embodied in governmental policy.

The divisions and arguments within what is still largely a private universe, involving actively not more than two hundred thousand people and perhaps two hundred full-time staff positions, are important. They are one of the principal reservoirs in the country of a commitment to end war and of ideas and programs for doing so. Whenever these groups reflect irrational and mistaken views and/or unwisely subordinate their understandings to the mood of the *ad hoc* groups, everyone suffers, for their commitment and freedom from governmental responsibilities provide the opportunity for serious and creative work to develop the programs, resources and services of aid in ending war.

A SELECTED LIST
OF ORGANIZATIONS

This listing is highly selective. It does not include *ad hoc* peace organizations, even though for a season they may dominate the news media's coverage of the peace movement. In any given year one could list somewhere between fifteen hundred and two thousand peace organizations. By the next year almost all of them will have disappeared. Those listed here are, for the most part, a continuing part of the American voluntary organization world. They have staff, well-articulated statements of purpose and policy, clear channels for decision making and continuing program goals.

The organizations listed are representative of the many categories of organizations discussed in the previous section. Most churches and synagogues have national social action and education units that work on war/peace issues. We have chosen only a few examples. Specialized research resources and education agencies focus on the problems of specific geographic areas. Again, only a few examples are given. Functional agencies working on the full range of international problems are covered in the same way. A more complete listing is available in the May-June 1969 issue of *Intercom* entitled U.S. Voluntary Organizations and World Affairs (# 577).

A person seriously considering working for one or more peace organization should write, requesting a descriptive brochure, information about current programs, policies and possible work opportunities. It is best to consider different organizations carefully before committing your time or money to their activity. The guide to evaluating peace activity presented in the preceding section should help you decide which of the following peace and world affairs organizations deserve your support.

**Ad Hoc Committee on Human Rights and
Genocide Treaties**
25 East 78th Street, New York, N.Y. 10021

A relatively permanent *ad hoc* organization whose purpose is securing Congressional ratification of U.N. Human Rights Treaties and Conventions.

American Academy of Political and Social Science
3937 Chestnut Street, Philadelphia, Pa. 19104

A membership organization for scholars interested in current political and social issues. Holds national and international meetings on critical problems. Publishes *The Annals* (bi-monthly).

American Association of University Women
2401 Virginia Avenue N.W., Washington, D.C. 20037

Develops program materials for discussion of international affairs issues in clubs composed of women graduates of colleges and universities.

American Field Service
313 East 43rd Street, New York, N.Y. 10017

Promotes international understanding through school year exchanges of high school students in different countries.

American Freedom from Hunger Foundation
1717 H Street N.W., Room 437, Washington, D.C. 20006

Sponsors the world wide Freedom From Hunger Campaign in the United States. Seeks through a variety of films and other teaching aids to inform the American public about the nature of world hunger problems and the need for technical assistance and other aid programs. Works primarily with private organizations. Their "Walks for Development" have raised funds for such programs both at home and abroad.

American Friends Service Committee
160 North 15th Street, Philadelphia, Pa. 19102

For over fifty years the AFSC has expressed Quaker concerns for peace and world brotherhood through domestic and international programs of service, relief and education. Its domestic program of peace education and action seeks to apply pacifist belief to current war/peace issues and changes with the politics and understandings of those responsible for leadership in any given period.

American Peace Society
4000 Albermarle N.W., Room 304, Washington, D.C. 20016

The oldest American peace organization now has limited membership and staff. It promotes international arbitration as a means of resolving international disputes. Publishes *World Affairs* (quarterly).

American Veterans Committee
1333 Connecticut Avenue N.W., Washington, D.C. 20036

Composed of veterans and servicemen and women, the AVC is concerned with domestic policy and world affairs issues, particularly human rights, the United Nations and economic development.

Americans for Democratic Action
1424 16th Street N.W., Washington, D.C. 20036

An influential organization of American liberals concerned with national and international issues, especially human rights, economic development and current war/peace issues. Reflects dominant currents of thought in the mainstream of American liberalism.

Association for International Development
374 Grand Street, Paterson, New Jersey 07505

Provides technical and professional skills to the developing nations and conducts training programs in the U.S. Publishes *Dialogue* (bi-monthly).

Brookings Institution
1775 Massachusetts Avenue N.W., Washington, D.C. 20036

One of America's major research agencies; does research, education and publications work in the fields of economics, government and through its Foreign Policy Studies division initiates discussion on major issues.

CARE (Cooperative for American Relief Everywhere)
660 First Avenue, New York, N.Y. 10016

Distributes food, medical and technical assistance to people in other countries.

Carnegie Endowment for International Peace
345 East 46th Street, New York, N.Y. 10017

A programming foundation, the Endowment concentrates on research and educational activities in the area of international organization, diplomacy, and the role of military force in international politics. Publishes *International Conciliation*.

Catholic Peace Fellowship
339 Lafayette Street, New York, N.Y. 10012

Offers draft counselling and legal assistance to Catholic conscientious objectors and others concerned with conscription. Pacifist in philosophy and often engages in demonstration activity.

Center for the Study of Democratic Institutions
P.O. Box 4068, Santa Barbara, California 93103

An organization devoted to clarifying the basic questions of freedom and justice as they are raised in the twentieth century. Among other areas, study is focused on economic order, political process, law, communications, science and technology, war as an institution, and the American character. Sponsors publications, conferences, national and international convocations; encourages study-discussion programs.

Center for the Study of Teaching About Peace and War
Wayne State University, 784 Grosberg Religious Center, University Center, Detroit, Michigan 48202

Facilitates school programs for improving international understanding and seeks to improve teaching methods in the war/peace field. Includes a reference center of current resources, curriculum consultant services, workshops and seminars for public schools, private schools and colleges.

Center for War/Peace Studies
218 East 18th Street, New York, N.Y. 10003
"Aims to bring independent specialists with skill and knowledge on the problems of war and peace into a working relationship with the leadership of American nongovernmental organizations."

CCCO, An Agency for Military and Draft Counseling
2006 Walnut Street, Philadelphia, Pa. 19103
Provides counseling for potential conscientious objectors and others thinking through their position on participation in warfare. Publishes the *Handbook for Conscientious Objectors*.

Clergy and Laymen Concerned About Vietnam
475 Riverside Drive, New York, N.Y. 10027
Organizes opposition to U.S. policy in Vietnam. Works primarily among Protestant clergy and laymen.

Committee for World Development and World Disarmament
218 East 18th Street, New York, N.Y. 10003
Devoted to disseminating information on world development and disarmament.

Council on International Relations and United Nations Affairs
833 United Nations Plaza, New York, N.Y. 10017
Seeks to create knowledgeable and informed opinion concerning the United Nations on college campuses.

Council for a Livable World
1346 Connecticut Avenue N.W., Washington, D.C. 20036
Brings together the scientist and layman in a program which promotes comprehensive disarmament and the abolition of war. Contributes to the campaign funds of candidates who support policies which the Council feels will accomplish its aims.

Council on Foreign Relations
58 East 68th Street, New York, N.Y. 10021

An influential research and study organization of foreign policy specialists. Sponsors seminars, lectures and off-the-record meetings. Publishes *Foreign Affairs* as well as studies and reference works.

Council on Religion and International Affairs
170 East 64th Street, New York, N.Y. 10021

A national organization which brings together Catholic, Protestant and Jewish leadership in an effort to acquaint them with the moral and ethical considerations affecting foreign policy. It conducts seminars, publishes pamphlets and paperbacks on ethics and foreign policy and conducts Washington Consultations, which are three-way conversations among policymakers, academicians, and religious leaders. Publishes *Worldview*.

Data International
437 California Avenue, Palo Alto, California 94306

Information clearing house providing technical assistance to developing countries through correspondence.

Farmers and World Affairs
1201 Chestnut Street, Philadelphia, Pa. 19107

Promotes interest among farmers in international affairs. Sponsors the Farmer Exchange Program giving Americans the opportunity to visit the developing countries and brings farm leaders from these countries to the U.S. Holds institutes and conferences on international affairs for farm leaders.

Federation of American Scientists
2025 Eye Street N.W., Washington, D.C. 20006

A membership organization concerned with the impact of science on national and international affairs. Promotes public discussion, sponsors meetings and conferences, makes policy proposals. Publishes *FAS Newsletter*.

Fellowship of Reconciliation
Box 271, Nyack, N.Y. 10960

Founded as a Christian pacifist organization, the FOR

is now a non-denominational pacifist membership organization. Works through conferences, peace education, protest and nonviolent vigils and demonstrations; publishes *Fellowship* magazine. Heavy current emphasis on international work.

Foreign Policy Association
345 East 46th Street, New York, N.Y. 10017

This national nonpartisan organization is aimed at stimulating thoughtful public opinion on international relations through educational programs and conferences, fact sheets and publications, primarily the *Headline Series*. Provides a yearly discussion program, *Great Decisions*, for which it produces a guide and coordinated TV presentations of current issues.

Freedom House
20 West 40th Street, New York, N.Y. 10018

A research, and education organization which publishes studies of particular issues. Concerned especially with distributing books throughout the world and with defending democratic government.

Friends Committee on National Legislation
245 2nd Street N.E., Washington, D.C. 20002

Rooted in the Religious Society of Friends, its goal is to translate religious concerns into political and social action. It takes stands on political issues, actively lobbies in Washington, and publishes an excellent monthly report, *FCNL Washington Newsletter*, on current legislative activity affecting disarmament, the U.N., world development, military expenditures and crisis issues relating to war and peace.

Fund for Peace
1865 Broadway, New York, N.Y. 10033

Seeks to secure support for eleven peace education and research organizations. Sponsors conferences to help increase public understanding of the need for strengthened international institutions.

Institute for International Order
11 West 42nd Street, New York, N.Y. 10036
Seeks to increase "support of the U.N. and a wider knowledge of the need and means of securing peace."

Institute for Policy Studies
1520 New Hampshire Avenue N.W., Washington, D.C. 20036
Studies public policy issues and publishes research reports in the foreign policy area. Special interest in ways to wage international conflict without violence, with the study of revolution and U.S. relations with revolutionary governments or movements.

International League for the Rights of Man
156 Fifth Avenue, New York, N.Y. 10010
Works through the United Nations and public education to implement the Universal Declaration of Human Rights.

International Voluntary Service
1555 Connecticut Avenue N.W., Washington, D.C. 20036
Trains young people from the U.S. to go to other countries to work in community service projects.

League of Women Voters of the United States
1200 17th Street N.W., Washington, D.C. 20036
Promotes informed participation in public decision making processes. Has published pamphlets on issues such as China, foreign aid and development and the United Nations.

Lutheran Church in America, Board of Social Ministry
231 Madison Avenue, New York, N.Y. 10016
Sponsors studies of Lutheran teachings and their relationship to social issues such as world peace. Publishes a newsletter of new materials for over eight thousand Lutheran ministers.

National Committee on United States–China Relations
777 United Nations Plaza, 9B, New York, N.Y. 10017

Seeks to engage public figures in a dialogue on U.S.–China policy, most of it directed toward increasing communication with, not isolation of, China.

National Council of the Churches of Christ in the U.S.A.
475 Riverside Drive, New York, N.Y. 10027

The central organization of most Protestant denominations—a division of international affairs, adult education, religious school department and overseas ministries all deal with war/peace problems.

National Council for the Social Studies
1201 Sixteenth Street N.W., Washington, D.C. 20036

Works for the "advancement of the professional interest and competence of social studies teachers at all levels"; particularly concerned with international affairs education.

National Council of Catholic Men (or Women)
1312 Massachusetts Avenue N.W., Washington, D.C. 20005

These two organizations offer a vehicle through which lay Catholic concern about war/peace issues may be expressed. They encourage studies of world affairs problems and the relevance of Christian ethics to them.

Negotiation Now!—National Committee for a Political Settlement in Vietnam
156 Fifth Avenue, Room 516, New York, N.Y. 10010

An organization of national leaders in a wide variety of organizations seeking to bring about an end to the war in Vietnam by addressing proposals for doing so to political decision makers and the general public.

National Interreligious Service Board for Conscientious Objectors
550 Washington Building, 15th and New York Avenue N.W., Washington, D.C. 20005

A service organization of more than forty religious bodies which provides counseling for religious objectors to war.

Conducts occasional nonviolent protest against the arms race and militarism. Publishes a newsletter featuring articles on nonviolent revolution.

New England Committee for Nonviolent Action
RFD1, Box 197B Voluntown, Conn. 06384
People-to-People
P.O. Box 1201, Kansas City, Missouri 64141
Seeks to promote international understanding by stimulating letters, sporting events and other forms of communication across national boundaries.

SANE
381 Park Avenue South, New York, N.Y. 10016
A peace action organization concerned with next steps to be taken in foreign policy. Current emphasis on changed national priorities (domestic needs over military expenditures).

Society for Citizen Education in World Affairs
139 Social Science Building, University of Minnesota, Minneapolis, Minn. 55455
Professional organization for the field.

Society for Social Responsibility in Science
Rockhill Road, Bala Cynwyd, Pa. 19004
An international society of scientists that refuse to work on military programs.

Union of American Hebrew Congregations
838 Fifth Avenue, New York, N.Y. 10021
Its commission on social justice has in recent years given a special emphasis to peace work. Developed programs for youth on problems of conscience and war.

United Auto Workers, International Affairs Department
1126 16th Street N.W., Washington, D.C. 20036
Undertakes international relations educational programs, exchanges and economic aid projects in many countries. Political education programs and publications often focus on war/peace issues.

United Nations Association of the United States of America
345 East 46th St., New York, N.Y. 10017

Urges better understanding of and support for effective U.S. participation in the U.N. A membership organization, it has over two hundred chapters throughout the U.S.; at the national level the U.N.A. of the U.S.A. works with over one hundred cooperating voluntary organizations. Publishes *Vista*.

United States Committee for UNICEF
331 East 38th Street, New York, N.Y. 10016

Supports the work of the U.N. Children's Fund through such programs as the sale of Greeting Cards and the Halloween Trick or Treat Program. Resources include program material, speaker services, filmstrips and displays.

World Federalists of U.S.A.
1346 Connecticut Avenue N.W., Washington, D.C. 20036

A national membership organization affiliated with the international World Federalists. Its goal is world peace through world federal government. The emphasis is on long-range, orderly, constitutional means of changing the U.N. into a world federal structure. It builds support for its points of view through lobbying in Washington, organizing local chapters, conducting study groups and promoting speakers and literature on world law. Publishes *The Federalist*.

Volunteers for International Technical Assistance
230 State Street, Schenectady, N.Y. 12305

An association of scientists, engineers and businessmen who offer their free time and skills in providing technical know-how in response to requests from developing countries.

War Resisters League
339 Lafayette Street, New York, N.Y. 10012

A national pacifist organization based on ethical and

humanist values and opposed to armaments, conscription and war everywhere in the world. Stresses individual responsibility and conscientious objection to war. Works through education, protest and political action.

Women Strike for Peace
2140 P Street N.W., Washington D.C. 20036

Women's political action committee directed against "war and destruction." Sponsors peace walks, vigils, demonstrations and public meetings. Most activities and resources point out the dangers of U.S. military policies.

Women's International League for Peace and Freedom
2006 Walnut Street, Philadelphia, Pa. 19103

An organization pledged to nonviolent means of establishing the political, economic, social and psychological conditions in the world which can assure peace, freedom and justice. Particular political views advanced have changed as leadership has changed in recent years.

World Law Fund
11 West 42nd Street, New York, N.Y. 10036

An educational organization which seeks to promote an understanding of the role of law in the construction of a peaceful world order. Works principally with schools, colleges and universities and sponsors teacher-training programs, seminars, curriculum conferences and contests.

World Without War Council of the United States
Office of the President, 1730 Grove Street, Berkeley, California 94709

Links leaders of a variety of organizations in a planning, catalytic and communication center for work for a world without war. Regional Councils in the Midwest, the Pacific Northwest and California. Conducts peace interne, leadership training, publication, organizational consulting, war/peace issues and conscience and war programs.

World Affairs Council of Northern California
406 Sutter Street, San Francisco, California 94108

An example of a number of regional nonpartisan, educational membership organizations whose major goals are to promote an "informed public opinion . . . and international understanding in the cause of world peace."

EVALUATING A PARTICULAR
ORGANIZATION:
A QUESTIONNAIRE

It is sometimes difficult to obtain an accurate understanding of a particular peace organization's ideas, programs and goals. The following questions are designed to help. Explicit answers to these questions are difficult to obtain, because many organizations are themselves unclear about their answers. But every peace group demonstrates an answer to these questions. The answers may be found in the speakers it sponsors and those it doesn't, in the literature it emphasizes, in the priorities it assigns to different activities, in the political alliances it forms and those it shuns. Understanding these answers and choosing among them is excellent training for intelligent and effective work for a world without war. Select several current peace organizations and try to determine what answers they would give to each question, then ask for an interview with a key staff person to see if you are right.

I. Understandings

Answers to the questions below define the basic understandings the peace organization wants to forward. The answers will be evident in the ideas highlighted and the ideas omitted from the material explaining the organization, in the pattern of action and inaction and in the books given special promotion. From the sum total of the organization's behavior, you can learn:

a) *Causes:* What is the organization's view of the causes of war: a particular ideological, economic or political system, the absence of world government or law, the nature of man, conceptions of justice, military organization, the distribution of power? The behavior of each organization spells out its answer.

b) *Roots:* What motivates an organization's work against

war: Do the members share religious or ethical beliefs that require them to act? Is it confidence in a particular solution to the problem of war? Is it simply another vehicle for demonstrating a rejection of American society that is part of a commitment to another political arrangement or social theory. One must distinguish here between the shared public answer to this question and the private mysterium that puts a particular individual into motion.

c) *Politics:* You will frequently encounter peace groups that present themselves as "above politics." However earnest their intention, there is no way to say anything meaningful about war/peace problems without affecting politics. It is therefore useful to try to understand the political stance an organization is taking. Questions in this area are considered in the section on *Politics* below.

d) *Issues:* Does the organization take a stand on specific war/peace issues before the President, Congress, the U.N. or the American public. Every year fifty or more war/peace issues are embodied in specific legislation, Presidential directives or U.N. resolutions. On which of these issues did the organization act? What position did it take?

e) *Change:* What does the organization see as the prime levers of social change: the development of new ideas, their widespread distribution, work with specific elites? Does change come when economic or political power is organized? What theoretical assumption is the group acting on as it considers the relation between grass roots activity and leadership decisions? What specific groups in the population are seen as of special importance in producing changed attitudes and changed governmental policy?

II. Politics

Action on war/peace problems is life and death action on the central problems of politics: who will rule and to what ends? It is therefore important to know an organization's politics. Calm, careful discussion of the questions below is essential if you are to understand whether the enormous emotion poured into a peace cause group makes sense.

Where does the organization stand in relation to the contending power centers? What is its view of American society and of various Communist and other power centers in the world? Does the organization, while in fact taking political positions, refuse to clarify its politics on the grounds that political distinctions heighten international tensions and add fuel to the cold war? Do they argue that they can only affect their own government and therefore never citicize other governments, thus building a half truth orientation into their work? Does their work reflect a single villain orientation: America or the Communists? Do they present themselves as opposed to an arms race but in fact never challenge America's program of military deterrence? Do they portray Communist-led revolutions as progressive and deserving of support, as none of our business, as bad solutions to real problems, or as a threat to be crushed?

What political policy emphasis do they have toward contemporary conflict? American withdrawal, an emphasis on international intervention to keep the peace, American initiatives toward a disarmed world under law, emphasis on a military deterrent while attempting to remove the threat of war through negotiations, increased use of American military power? Does their work reflect a primary concern for building a strong sense of world community through the U.N. action to aid needed change in the developing nations? Do they emphasize rejection of reliance on mass violence? Do they recommend a totally hostile approach to all Communist nations? Do they resist American opposition to any element of Communist power or purpose?

What is their program for achieving power? Are they building a party which seeks decision-making power by the ballot, by disruption and building discontent so that present procedures can no longer function? Or is their goal to permeate society with new understandings and values so that no matter who rules, decisions will reflect them? Is their aim polarization and the strengthening of their pole or do they seek a new consensus for their ideas? Do they see protest in itself as a virtue or, while recognizing that temporary social disruption can produce new insights, do they see that systematic attempts to encourage alienation can undermine the sense of community on which progress depends?

What is their view of the good society? Politics consists of more than power; it is also the alternate conception of how men should live together. What is the organization's view? Are they seeking an end to all conflict or to war? Do they believe men should fight for their conception of justice? If so, and without mass violence, then how? How do they define freedom, law, equality, justice, peace, community? Which are most important?

What is their relation to other groups acting on war/ peace problems? Do they undertake cooperative action? With groups holding what political goals, in pursuit of what political ends?

III. Profile: Facts About The Group

Range: Does it operate locally, regionally, nationally or internationally? What is its relationship to other groups?

Membership: Sources, character, requirements? Size: of core group, active participants, supporters, mailing lists?

Control: Who makes the key decisions?

Staff: How many? What are they responsible for? How paid? Do they initiate activities or carry out the directives of a policy board? Are they trained? Are they aware of other groups in the field? In what other public affairs activities do they play leadership roles?

Legal and Financial Status: Are they incorporated? Tax exempt? How large a budget? A few large contributions or many small ones?

History:

Origin: How old is the group? Who organized it? What

were the circumstances? A charismatic leader, a new body of thought, a political issue, outgrowth of a pre-existing tradition (e.g., socialist, pacifist, religious)?

Later developments: What are the notable events in its history? What ideas or policy changes were important milestones in the organization's history? Who were the key personalities?

IV. Activity

Assessing the work an organization actually does is the best way to discern its primary purposes.

Audience: Who is the organization trying to reach: women, businessmen, national decision makers, mass audiences, the disadvantaged, the alienated, the powerful, intellectuals, youth, political leaders, columnists? The answers to these questions will provide major evidence of how the organization sees social change taking place.

Materials and Channels: What tools does it use: literature, films, mass media, newsletters, demonstrations, study groups, public meetings, lobbying? Does it work through established institutions such as libraries, schools, political parties and television? Does it organize committed cadres?

Programs: What continuing activity does it carry out? Is it primarily focused on getting members to do work themselves? Does it service other organizations? Has it a program on: research, legislation, publication, training, children?

Criteria for judging success: Is it measured by: membership, budget, quality of ideas, size of participating group at its events, legislation passed, number of people working, public attention, response from decision makers?

V. Character

How is the organization seen by the community? How does it see itself? A group's character or style is often the determining factor in whether a person supports it. Which of the following best describes the kinds of people associated with the organization: achievement oriented or witness orientated, radical or conventional, religious or secular, old or young? Who is attracted to it: women, political activists, community leaders, beards, high heels, dashikis? Does the group aim at strengthening a small, committed nucleus or does it seek wide participation? Is it focused on crisis issues or on a long-range perspective? Is it well-financed or does it operate on a shoestring? Do its offices feel clean, ordered, expensive, earnest, intense or sacrificial?

AN OVERVIEW

Analyzing a Peace Organization

UNDERSTANDINGS

Goals: How defined?

Issues: Specific stands on war/peace issues?

Roots: Why is it working?

Causes of War: What causes (this) war?

Change: How it thinks national policies and individual attitudes change?

Politics: Its view of the contending powers, the good society, other groups in the field, how to get power?

PROFILE

Structure:

Range: Where does it work?

Staff: How large and how well trained?

Control: Who runs it?

Membership: Size, character, requirements, sources?

Legal and Financial Status: Incorporated, tax exempt, budget, fund sources?

History:

Origin: When and who?

Later Developments: Events? Ideas? Personalities?

WORK

Audience: Who does it try to reach?
Programs: What activities does it conduct?
Criteria: How does it judge success?
Materials/Channels: What tools does it use?

CHARACTER OR STYLE

Small committed nucleus/Wide participation
Radical/Conventional
Religious/Secular
Old/Young
Achievement oriented/Witness oriented
Special clientele: Women, youth, beards, political, community leaders? Clean, ordered, expensive, earnest, intense, sacrificial?

KEEPING INFORMED:
A READING MAN'S
FILTER

THE READING MAN'S FILTER
*The World Without War Council's selected listing
of War/Peace Periodicals*

Every reading man needs a filter. In fact, every reading man has one, often one that is primarily shaped by advertising and promotional techniques. Why not consciously shape your own? Choose periodicals that offer a level of intelligence, point of view, or degree of sophistication that must be reached for deliberately. The following list of periodicals will help you choose periodicals worth the effort. They span the full range from political opinion weeklies to scholarly journals and include some of the best newspapers and specialized publications that regularly cover foreign policy issues and topics related to achieving a world without war. Some are organizational house organs that regularly present a single point of view. Others focus on a particular problem area presenting many points of view on that topic.

Addresses given are for subscriptions; for editorial offices, consult a recent issue of the periodical.

ANNALS (Bi-monthly)
The American Academy of Political and Social Science
3937 Chestnut Street, Philadelphia, Pa. 19104
A scholarly journal that also carries articles of unusual value for non-specialists. Each issue is devoted to a single topic and contains a number of articles by different authors; also an extensive book review section.

ARMS CONTROL AND DISARMAMENT: A *Quarterly Bibliography with Abstracts and Annotations*
U.S. Arms Control and Disarmament Agency

U.S. Government Printing Office, Washington, D.C. 20402

A comprehensive and annotated digest of domestic and foreign books and articles on arms control and disarmament.

ASIAN SURVEY (Monthly)

The Institute of International Studies, University of California

2234 Piedmont Avenue, Berkeley, California 94720—Edited by Robert Scalapino

Devoted exclusively to contemporary problems and developments in Asia, emphasizing comparative and international research in the social sciences. Excellent survey articles for the layman.

ATLAS: *The Magazine of the World Press* (Monthly)

368 West Center Street, Marion, Ohio 43302

Published in English, *Atlas* presents articles, cartoons and photos from leading foreign newspapers and magazines. Notes on the political orientation of the source are given as an aid to interpretation. A most helpful way to sample opinion in other countries.

BULLETIN OF ATOMIC SCIENTISTS (Monthly—10 times)

Educational Foundation for Nuclear Science

935 East 60th Street, Chicago, Illinois 60637

A journal of science and public affairs that grew out of physicists' World War II encounter with the Bomb. Concerned with the social responsibility of scientists, it covers a variety of political, cultural and scientific subjects. Its analysis of technical developments as they affect international relations and world affairs is especially useful.

CHINA QUARTERLY

Published by: Information Bulletin Ltd.

133 Oxford Street, London W 1, England

on behalf of: The Congress for Cultural Freedom

Excellent specialist journal on contemporary China,

edited by Roderick MacFarquhar. Contributors include the foremost scholars in the field.

CHRISTIAN CENTURY (Weekly)

Christian Century Foundation
407 South Dearborn Street, Chicago, Illinois 60605
"An ecumenical weekly" with contributed articles on matters of religious, political and social concerns, as well as news of the Christian world. Part of the spectrum of liberal publications.

CHRISTIAN SCIENCE MONITOR (Daily except Sundays and Holidays)

The Christian Science Publishing Company
1 Norway Street, Boston, Mass. 02115
An international daily published in Boston, Los Angeles and London, this newspaper gives substantial coverage to national, foreign and international affairs in carefully written and thoughtful news stories and news analyses. Its background to the news articles is especially useful.

CHRISTIANITY AND CRISIS (Bi-weekly)

Christianity and Crisis, Inc.
537 West 121st Street, New York, N.Y. 10027
A protestant magazine devoted to the role of the Christian in today's world. Features opinion articles by leading clergymen, educators and statesmen. Aimed at intellectual leaders. Originating from Reinhold Neibuhr and John Bennett's opposition to the pacifism of the thirties, it now offers a spectrum of liberal and radical thought.

COMMENTARY (Monthly)

The American Jewish Committee
165 East 56th Street, New York, N.Y. 10022
Consistently carries provocative, thoughtful and substantial articles on public policy issues and the arts. Excellent editing successfully offers material to the intelligent lay reader which is usually restricted to specialist journals. War/Peace and related topics are a major concern. Reprint service for their most significant articles.

COMMONWEAL (Weekly)
  Commonweal Publishing Co.
  232 Madison Avenue, New York, N.Y. 10016
  Liberal and radical Catholic thought on public affairs, literature and the arts.

CURRENT (Monthly)
  Plainfield, Vermont 05667
  Contains selections from a wide range of periodicals, newspapers, books, and speeches relative to contemporary problems of democratic society: "the significant new material from all sources on the frontier problems of today." Often counterposes well selected statements of opposing views.

CURRENT HISTORY (Monthly)
  1822 Ludlow Street, Philadelphia, Pa. 19103
  A monthly magazine written primarily for students, each issue is devoted to a specific country, area, or topic of foreign policy or international relations. Regular features include a chronology of world affairs and a "Current Documents" section.

CURRENT THOUGHT ON PEACE AND WAR
  (Bi-yearly)
  Wisconsin State University, Oshkosh, Wisconsin 54901
  Provides very brief authoritative descriptions of recent books, articles, government and U.N. documents and research in progress on international issues. Covers current research on war/peace topics in all of the disciplines. Primarily a tool for scholars.

DIALOGUE (Monthly)
  Foreign Policy Legislation Clearing House Newsletter, Published by:
  The World Affairs Council of Philadelphia, Pa.
  The John Wanamaker Store, Third Floor Gallery
  13th and Market Streets, Philadelphia, Pa. 19107
  Concise information on Congressional debates and Ad-

ministrative action on important U.S. foreign policy legislative issues.

DISSENT (Bi-monthly)
   Dissent Publishing Corporation
   509 Fifth Avenue, New York, N.Y. 10017
   Debate and analysis of significant contemporary issues and events, primarily from a Democratic Socialist (antitotalitarian) point of view. Aimed at intellectuals.

EAST EUROPE (Monthly)
   Free Europe Inc.
   2 Park Avenue, New York, N.Y. 10016
   Has ceased publication. A journal of information and analysis of political, social, economic and intellectual trends in Eastern Europe. Edited from a sophisticated anti-Communist point of view.

THE ECONOMIST (Weekly)
   Subscription Department, New Mercury House
   81 Farringdon Street, London, E C 4, England
   Detailed coverage of contemporary political, international and economic affairs from an intelligent, conservative point of view. One of the most influential world periodicals.

ENCOUNTER (Monthly)
   Subscription Department
   25 Haymarket, London SW, England
   Primarily devoted to literature and the arts, but also contains excellent articles on political and social affairs. Thoughtfully critical of totalitarian politics.

FAR EASTERN ECONOMIC REVIEW (Weekly)
   P.O. Box 160, Hong Kong
   U.S. Subscription Agent: Stechert-Hafner Inc.
   31 East 10th Street, New York, N.Y. 10003
   Topical news articles, country-by-country reports, analyses of developments throughout Asia. Much more political and social coverage than its title would indicate.

FCNL WASHINGTON NEWSLETTER (Monthly)
   Friends Committee on National Legislation

245 Second Street N.E., Washington, D.C. 20002

Concise and extremely useful coverage on war/peace issues before Congress and the President from a liberal, anti-military, internationalist point of view.

FELLOWSHIP (Monthly)

Fellowship of Reconciliation

Box 271, Nyack, N.Y. 10960

Well established pacifist journal, including articles, reviews, poetry, theology, social analysis and current issues; includes a special Peace Information Bulletin issued every two months.

FOREIGN AFFAIRS (Quarterly)

Council on Foreign Relations, Inc.

58 East 68th Street, New York, N.Y. 10021

Influential articles on U.S. foreign policy and world affairs. Contributors often include present and past world statesmen. *The* prestige journal for serious "establishment" thinking about world affairs.

THE GUARDIAN (Weekly)

197 East 4th Street, New York, N.Y. 10009

A radical weekly newspaper presenting a variety of new and old left views. Committed to confrontation politics, uncritical of, if not sympathetic to the Communist world, and sharply critical of American society, these articles offer a point of view which needs to be seriously considered.

I.F. STONE'S WEEKLY (Bi-weekly)

4420 29th Street N.W., Washington, D.C. 20008

Personal newsletter specializing in Washington affairs; highly critical of U.S. policy. Often a source of news items not available in other publications. Sometimes crudely unbalanced in presentation, but a rare radical voice that occasionally criticizes Soviet and Chinese policies as well as the West.

INTERCOM (Bi-monthly)

Center for War/Peace Studies

218 East 18th Street, New York, N.Y. 10018

Highly useful *resource* publication listing new books, pamphlets, documents, audio-visual aids, conference and special events, governmental and voluntary agencies concerned with foreign policy and international affairs.

INTERNATIONAL ORGANIZATION (Quarterly)
World Peace Foundation
40 Mt. Vernon Street, Boston, Mass. 02108
Scholarly journal concerned with inter-governmental agencies. Articles by authorities in the field and annotated summaries of activities of international organizations.

INTERPLAY: *The Magazine of International Affairs*
(Monthly—10 times)
200 West 57th Street, New York, N.Y. 10019
Devoted to democratic values, *Interplay* presents insightful articles critical of the State Department's moral rhetoric and the revisionist, moralistic critique of that rhetoric. Reflects a sophisticated, internationalist point of view. A new publication.

THE JOURNAL OF CONFLICT RESOLUTION
(Quarterly)
University of Michigan, Ann Arbor, Michigan 48104
Subtitled a "Quarterly for Research Related to War and Peace," this journal presents scholarly articles from a variety of disciplines. Focus is on the applications of the behavioral sciences to international relations and to nonviolent forms of conflict resolution.

JOURNAL OF PEACE RESEARCH (Quarterly)
Gydas vei 8, P.O. Box 5052, Oslo 3, Norway
A scholarly journal, printed in English, presenting articles on technical aspects of disarmament, peace keeping, conflict theory, race relations and nonviolence.

MANAS (Weekly)
P.O. Box 32112, El Sereno Station,
Los Angeles, California 90032
Concerned with the principles which move world society on its present course, and with the search for con-

trasting principles. A curious, serious and sometimes insightful mixture of anarchist, pacifist, theosophist and modern psychiatric thought brought to bear on problems ranging from the education of children to the ending of war.

MANCHESTER GUARDIAN (Weekly)
Manchester Guardian Weekly
3 Cross Street, Manchester 2, England
Contains the best from a British liberal daily newspaper. Marked by thoughtful reporting and influential editorials. Reading it is an unusually useful experience for those who have never seen U.S. policy from abroad.

THE NATION (Weekly)
333 Sixth Avenue, New York, N.Y. 10014
News items and interpretations often sharply critical of U.S. policy. A left liberal perspective that has played an influential role in the liberal community.

THE NATIONAL OBSERVER
11501 Columbia Pike, Silver Springs, Maryland 20904
One of America's few national newspapers. Consistently presents well-conceived and concise backgrounds to the news focusing especially on points where domestic personalities and politics impinge on war/peace decisions.

THE NATIONAL REVIEW (Bi-weekly)
150 East 35th St., New York, N.Y. 10016
A journal of opinion from a ferociously conservative viewpoint, edited and published by William F. Buckley, Jr. Foreign affairs coverage consistent with support for military regimes and military solutions to combat the spread of Communism. Lively and sometimes deft in puncturing liberal and New Left assumptions and values. Give it to a Ramparts reader.

NEW AMERICA (Twice-Monthly)
1182 Broadway, Room 402, New York, N.Y. 10001
Democratic Socialist newspaper that analyzes the news and reports on democratic movements for social change in the U.S. and the world.

THE NEW LEADER (Bi-weekly)
American Labor Conference on International Affairs
212 Fifth Avenue, New York, N.Y. 10010
A sophisticated, small-circulation opinion journal known for initiating lively controversies with the liberal community. Perspective is Democratic Socialist and anti-Communist.

THE NEW REPUBLIC (Weekly)
Subscription Department
381 West Center Street, Marion, Ohio 43302
The largest circulation liberal weekly. Opinion on the current political scene—usually from positions roughly similar to those espoused by Americans for Democratic Action but with contemporary New Left currents occasionally intermixed.

NEW STATESMAN (Weekly)
Great Turnstile, London, WC 1, England
A review of contemporary Birtish and world affairs, usually presenting views from the Labor Party left on out. Also lively cultural commentaries.

THE NEW YORK REVIEW OF BOOKS (Bi-weekly)
The New York Review, Subscription Service Department
P.O. Box 79, Des Moines, Iowa 50301
Review essays of contemporary books and political and cultural events provide the framework for a tendentious political publication that perfectly reflects and sometimes initiates current left, literary, radical fashions. Widely influential in recent years. Its often brilliant and sometimes thoughtful articles are aimed at the campus left.

THE NEW YORK TIMES (Daily)
229 West 43rd Street, New York, N.Y. 10036
On occasion less objective than a great newspaper ought to be, but still the most complete and reliable source available. Its "News of the Week in Review" section, contained in the Sunday edition, is a news magazine in itself.

ORBIS: *A Quarterly Journal of World Affairs*
Foreign Policy Research Institute, University of Pennsylvania
3508 Market St., Suite 350, Philadelphia, Pa. 19104
A quarterly review edited by Robert Strausz-Hupe, concerned with "American foreign policy, Communist strategy and free world security." A scholarly bulwark of the hard line, anti-Communist camp.

PEACE NEWS (Weekly)
5 Caledonia Road, Kings Cross, London, England
U.S. Subscriptions: Peace News c/o American Friends Service Committee
160 North 15th Street, Philadelphia, Pa. 19102
International pacifist newspaper "for nonviolence and unilateral disarmament." Tends to adopt the politics of current street demonstrations, but sometimes drops anti-establishmentarianism for provocative attempts to advance the frontiers of pacifist thought.

PEACE PRESS (Bi-Monthly)
International Confederation for Disarmament and Peace
3 Hendon Avenue, London N3, England
News of peace organizations around the world, emphasizing ICDP affiliated groups. An amalgam of pacifist and left peace groups in the West formed on a neutralist basis as an alternative to the Moscow dominated World Peace Council, and including Yugoslav and Italian Communist affiliates.

PROBLEMS OF COMMUNISM (Bi-monthly)
Superintendent of Documents, U.S. Government Printing Office
Washington, D.C. 20402
A publication of the U.S. Information Agency providing analyses and significant background information on various aspects of Communism throughout the world.

THE PROGRESSIVE (Monthly)
The Progressive, Inc.

408 West Gorham Street, Madison, Wisconsin 53703

From the political perspective suggested by its name, this journal offers lively signed articles and comment. A liberal publication somewhat differentiated from *The Nation* and *New Republic* by its Midwest birthplace and a profound interest in work to end war.

RAMPARTS (Monthly)

1606 Union Street, San Francisco, California 94123

Devoted primarily to attacks on American liberals and to a "withdrawal from the American Empire." High bouncing muckraking and energetic attacks in every direction but left. Give it to a *National Review* reader.

SATURDAY REVIEW (Weekly)

Subscription Department

380 Madison Avenue, New York, N.Y. 10017

A review of important books and occasional peace articles. Note especially articles on world law and Norman Cousins's editorials.

SCIENTIFIC AMERICAN (Monthly)

415 Madison Ave., New York, N.Y. 10017

Although devoted primarily to articles in the sciences, virtually every issue contains an article on a public policy issue. *Scientific American* articles on disarmament and arms control have been widely influential.

SURVEY (Quarterly)

Published by: Information Bulletin Ltd.

133 Oxford Street, London W 1, England

on behalf of The Congress for Cultural Freedom

A valuable specialist journal reviewing developments in East European and Soviet affairs.

SURVIVAL (Monthly)

Published by: The Institute for Strategic Studies

Distributed by: Research Publications

18 Victoria Park Square, London E.2, England

A digest of significant articles and documents dealing with military topics, arms control and disarmament issues.

TRANS-ACTION (Monthly—10 times)
  Box A, Rutgers, The State University
  New Brunswick, New Jersey 08903
An interdisciplinary behavioral science publication, presenting articles on significant sociological discoveries and projects, written for non-experts.

UNITED NATIONS MONTHLY CHRONICLE
  United Nations Publications, Room 1059
  United Nations, New York, N.Y. 10017
The monthly record of debates and actions in the United Nations. Activities of the various organs and agencies are concisely reported.

THE WALL STREET JOURNAL (Daily, Monday–Friday
                              also regional editions)
  30 Broad Street, New York, N.Y. 10004
Although primarily concerned with news of business and finance, this newspaper provides well-written, well-researched, signed articles and features on national, foreign and international affairs. Often superior to the mass press.

WAR/PEACE REPORT (Monthly)
  218 East 18th Street, New York, N.Y. 10003
Stimulating, brief articles and reports of fact and opinion on progress toward a world of law and order, with special emphasis on arms control and disarmament, the United Nations, growth of world law and citizen activity on behalf of world peace.

WASHINGTON MONTHLY
  1150 Connecticut Ave. N.W., Washington, D.C. 20036
A magazine with a purpose: "to help you understand our system of politics and government, where it breaks down, why it breaks down and what can be done to make it work." Articles on a wide variety of public policy issues.

WORLD MARXIST REVIEW (Monthly)
  Distributed by: Progress Books
  487 Adelaide Street West, Toronto 133, Ontario, Canada
A serious review on international affairs from within

the Communist world, containing theoretical and informational articles by leading Communist writers.

WORLD POLITICS (Quarterly)
Princeton University Press
Princeton, New Jersey 08540
An outstanding university quarterly dealing with problems of international relations of a general and theoretical nature, emphasizing social change. Edited by Cyril E. Black and Richard A. Falk.

THE WORLD TODAY (Monthly)
Oxford University Press
Press Road, Neasden, London NW 10, England
Articles for the general reader on current world problems and their background issued by the Royal Institute of International Affairs.

WORLDVIEW (Monthly)
Council of Religion and International Affairs
170 East 64th Street, New York, N.Y. 10021
A wide range of thoughtful opinion and analysis on problems of religion and international affairs.

SPECIALIZING:
UNDERSTANDING A PART
OF THE FIELD

Much of the material in this book has been general. You should now have an overview of the field and have begun to develop special interests within it. If you are primarily interested in nonviolence, or world law, or disarmament, it is best to follow your interest and specialize in that field. What do you need to know to be able to bring specific, specialized knowledge to bear on a specific part of the war/peace field? We take the disarmament area as our example. You should know:

1) *The specialized periodicals covering problems of arms control and disarmament (e.g., Worldview, Orbis, Friends Committee on National Legislation Newsletter and Foreign Affairs).*

You probably already follow the disarmament issue in general circulation magazines or newspapers. It is important to familiarize yourself with the scholarly journals and occasionally to switch general circulation newspapers or magazines to better understand other political perspectives.

2) *The best introductory pamphlets, books and research center reports dealing with disarmament problems.*

Go back to the disarmament section (Chapter 2) of the bibliography and select the major books in the field. They will give you a start. Then turn to the specialized periodicals in the "Reading Man's Filter" (Resource G) and develop a more extensive reading list from *Current Thought on Peace and War* and the *Arms Control and Disarmament Quarterly.*

3) *The government agencies, congressional committees and staff in the Office of the President who are responsible for disarmament problems.*

Each President has different advisors who are particularly concerned about disarmament questions. You should know who on the President's personal staff is influential on disarmament questions. Who are the members of the National Security Council, the congressional committees, the Pentagon, State Department and CIA branches concerned with disarmament? Who is heading the U.S. Arms Control and Disarmament Agency? What access does he have to the President?

4) *The staff and particular sections of the United Nations that deal with disarmament problems and the specialized international agencies involved.*

Does the U.N. General Assembly have disarmament questions on the agenda for this year? What issue is being discussed? Is the Eighteen-Nation Disarmament Committee meeting? What is the Secretary General of the U.N. doing to promote disarmament negotiations and agreements? Who in the U.S. delegation is especially concerned with disarmament questions?

5) *What specific disarmament issues will confront the President, the United Nations and American public opinion this year.*

Are new technological developments shaping the arms race? What new weapons systems require congressional appropriation this year? What disarmament legislation is pending in Congress? What other issues will be discussed: nuclear proliferation, zonal disarmament, citizen responsibility, international supervision and inspection?

6) *The voluntary organizations that do educational and political work on disarmament issues; the positions they have taken on specific issues.*

Look over the section on organizations and pick out those that are particularly interested in disarmament questions. Write to them for a description of their activities. Many community organizations have taken positions on disarmament issues. Request a list of organizations and the positions they have taken.

7) *The individuals presenting the major distinctive approaches to the problem, their arguments and their responses to their critics' arguments.*

As a debate develops over an issue, it is important to

know the contending schools of thought. As you follow the debate in general circulation and scholarly journals, you will probably notice schools of thought within which most spokesmen defer to the arguments of a scholar or expert. It is important to know who these experts are.

8) *Educational materials in the field: bibliographies, films, tapes, reports, reprints, speakers in your area or nationally and program materials.*

There is a wealth of educational materials available but you need to know how good they are and where they may be obtained.

9) *Your own standards, context, values, goals and conception of what you are doing.*

This is a reminder that although you have specialized, you are only working on part of the problem. How does your work on disarmament relate to ideas on world law and on economic development? What goals are you pursuing in the disarmament field which might be better achieved by international agreements in other areas?

All of this sounds like too much; a minimal filing system, a tie-in to one of the good foreign policy or peace organizations in your area and a sustained intention to build your own understanding, will soon produce another genuinely knowledgeable person.

Passion and ignorance are too frequently combined in the peace movement. It is possible to do your homework on that part of the war/peace problem that interests you most. You'll be a valuable resource in your community or organization if you do.

The principle objectives of the Council are:

Establishing the goal of ending war as a guiding force in American life;

Clarifying realistic strategies and defining specific tasks essential to achieving that goal;

Engaging the leaders of private organizations and institutions in appropriate work through their own constituencies to translate these strategies into public policy;

Offering through national and regional intelligence and action centers the catalytic, training, publishing, programming and coordinating services needed:

Demonstrating models of continuing work in the climate-setting sectors of American life (e.g., mass media, education, labor, business, religion);

Providing a continuing overview of the American peace effort designed to counter the waste and futility of many past efforts by common attempts to develop standards for effective work.

Write for full information on current programs, publications and work opportunities.

World Without War Council Offices

National: Office of the President, 1730 Grove Street, Berkeley, Calif. 94709

Office of the Chairman of the Board, 838 Fifth Ave., New York, N.Y. 10003

Midwest: 116 S. Michigan Ave. (Room 1505), Chicago, Illinois 60603

Northwest: 4235 Roosevelt Way N.E., Seattle, Washington 98105

Eugene: 119 E. 10th Ave., Eugene, Oregon 97401

Portland: 215 S.E. 9th Ave., Portland, Ore. 97214

Pacific Central: 1730 Grove Street, Berkeley, California 94709

Author Index

Title Index